The Roots of
American Exceptionalism

The Roots of American Exceptionalism

HISTORY, INSTITUTIONS AND CULTURE

CHARLES LOCKHART

First published 2003 by
PALGRAVE MACMILLAN™
175 Fifth Avenue, New York, N.Y. 10010 and
Houndmills, Basingstoke, Hampshire, England RG21 6XS.
Companies and representatives throughout the world.

PALGRAVE MACMILLAN is the global academic imprint of the
Palgrave Macmillan division of St. Martin's Press, LLC and of Palgrave
Macmillan Ltd. Macmillan® is a registered trademark in the United
States, United Kingdom and other countries. Palgrave is a registered
trademark in the European Union and other countries.

ISBN 1–4039–6195–6 (cl.)
      1–4039–6196–4 (pb.)

Library of Congress Cataloging-in-Publication Data
Lockhart, Charles, 1944-
The roots of American exceptionalism : history, institutions, and culture
/ Charles Lockhart.
     p.   cm.
Includes bibliographical references and index.
ISBN 1–4039–6195–6 (cl.)—ISBN 1–4039–6196–4 (pb.)
   1 Political planning—United States.   2. United States—Politics and
government.   3. Comparative government.   I. Title.

JK468.P64L63   2003
320'.6'0973—dc21

                                                          2003041025

A catalogue record for this book is available from the British Library.

Design by Letra Libre, Inc.

First edition: September 2003
10 9 8 7 6 5 4 3 2 1

Printed in the United States of America

To Jean, for all her guidance

CONTENTS

Preface

As someone who studies politics in several different societies, I am frequently surprised by how sketchy the understandings of intelligent, well-educated Americans are of the most fundamental differences between politics in the United States and in societies relatively well-known to Americans such as the United Kingdom or Canada. Superb students and competent professionals, even those who are well informed about American politics and policy, often appear confused when the conversation shifts to British parliamentary democracy or the Canadian national health insurance program.

Particularly for young persons, among whom the years spent acquiring an undergraduate education frequently amount to their densest period of personal learning and identity formation, I think it is especially unfortunate that their attitudes toward American political institutions and policies are formed so frequently in the absence of any cross-societal comparisons. Without knowledge about cross-societal policy differences and, particularly, the variations in experiences, beliefs and values that underlie those differences, American students have little basis for critically evaluating policy alternatives and forming their own policy preferences. It is only, as John Stuart Mill contends, by explicitly weighing the contending beliefs and values which underlie alternative courses of action and reaching our own conclusions as to what is appropriate that we become true individuals, rather than simply pawns in a game driven by someone else's initiatives. I think that most students and other citizens would benefit from examining why United States policies in a variety of areas are frequently quite different from those adopted by other advanced industrial societies.

To this end, I develop a schema for analyzing cross-societal policy differences that draws on historical, institutional and cultural variables. I use this schema to examine and explain why United States policy in the areas of taxation, financing of medical care, abortion, immigration/citizenship differ from those adopted by Sweden, Canada,

France and Japan, respectively. I show how a portion of this schema is generally sufficient for predicting these differences. Additionally, I draw on the schema to explain the processes by which the United States might adopt policies more similar to those of these other societies and the nature of the circumstances under which we might expect these processes to develop. I hope that my efforts will foster both better knowledge about how American political institutions and policies differ from those of other advanced industrial societies and, particularly, more extensive thought as to whether these differences will and should persist.

I want to thank Princeton University Press for permission to reprint the material appearing in figure 1.2. Thanks as well to Gunnar Grendstad and Kluwer Academic Publishers for permission to reprint the material appearing in table 2.1. My description of Douglas-Wildavsky "grid-group" theory, pp. 14–19, is similar to that which has appeared in a number of other articles and books. There are as well a few other short descriptive passages that are similar to sections of previous publications. Portions of chapter 2 parallel my "American and Swedish Tax Regimes: Cultural and Structural Roots," *Comparative Politics* 35:4 (July 2003). I gratefully acknowledge permission from the City University of New York to reprint this material.

In the course of putting this study together, I have benefited—as usual—from a number of kindnesses from a range of colleagues. Alan Wolfe transformed my early vision for a comparative public policy volume into a project focused on contrasting United States' policy in various areas with the policies of other societies. Gary Freeman listened patiently while I developed the structure of the book. He was also kind enough to give me detailed criticism on the immigration and citizenship policy chapter. John Ambler helped me locate resources with respect to French abortion policy. Don Jackson generously read the abortion policy chapter and corrected me on a number of aspects of American abortion policy. Sven Steinmo has listened to me argue with him on a number of professional panels. He has always been generous and good natured about our disagreements. I would like to think that his persistent advocacy of institutional explanations for policy differences between the United States and other advanced industrial societies has expanded my own capacity for explaining these differences. Sven's excellent work was also helpful to me in constructing the tax regime contrasts between Sweden and the United States in chapter 2. Richard M. Coughlin helped to raise my familiarity with Swedish politics generally. Peter Hall has continued to provide crucial moral support. Debbie Baldwin provided valuable technical assistance with respect to tables and figures. Rick Delaney did a fine job of copyediting. As a scholar approaching the upper reaches of his sixth decade, I have had to learn that increasingly brief periods of time bring, not only intellectual growth and wonderful experiences, but also loss. I am sorry to say that my long-term friend and colleague, Gary Bonham, succumbed to a lengthy bout with brain cancer during the course of this project. I miss him.

Jim Riddlesperger has been an extremely supportive department chairperson and has greatly facilitated my work on this and other projects. My dean (and also a political scientist), Mary Volcansek, has improved the friendliness of my institutional environment to comparative analysis. TCU awarded me a research leave in the spring of 2001, which enabled me to develop a draft of the manuscript. I am grateful for the institution's support of my work. David Pervin at Palgrave acquired a pair of extraordinarily helpful reviews for this manuscript, and these reviews have provided the basis for subsequent revisions. I owe a debt to both David for eliciting the reviews and to the anonymous reviewers for their comments. Additionally, David made a number of helpful comments on earlier drafts.

Above all I am thankful for two persons whose lives have been intertwined with my own. A day never goes by when I fail to think of what Aaron Wildavsky might offer for advice in my moments of indecision. I remain grateful for his influence and hope that he would think that it has made me a better student of comparative politics than I was before we met. My wife Jean—to whom this book is dedicated—has provided me with a wonderful model for handing the many crucial aspects of life apart from studying politics comparatively.

I remain concerned that a book which, to at least some degree, compares four policies across five societies is bound to contain some mistakes. Naturally, responsibility for these mistakes is mine, and I want to absolve all of the aforementioned persons, without whom this book would not have been possible at all, from any responsibility in this regard.

CHAPTER I

Introduction

From its inception, many analysts have argued that the United States is an exceptional society. While different commentators have focused on various aspects of American society (e.g., Wilson 1998; Kingdon 1999), they have collectively portrayed the United States as pervasively distinctive. So American exceptionalism manifests itself in a variety of ways. In terms of public policy, for instance, Sweden's well-financed state supports ambitious public income maintenance programs which help persons deal with various vicissitudes of life. In contrast, the much less well financially endowed American government musters a less extensive range of these programs, leaving persons more reliant on their private resources. While few societies do as well as Sweden in providing their public sectors with revenue, among the advanced industrial societies of Western Europe, North America and the Pacific rim, most provide considerably more than does the United States.

Additionally, poor Canadian families have far better access to medical care than do poor American working families. Again, among advanced industrial societies Canada's national medical-care insurance program is representative of a pattern. The United States is the only advanced industrial society which lacks a public program assuring financial access to a broad range of medical care for the vast majority of its citizens. Moreover, abortion policy has stirred less extensive volatile passions in France than in the United States. Indeed, the passions to which abortion questions have given rise in the United States appear stronger than those associated with this issue in other advanced industrial societies. Further, while the Japanese treat citizenship as an exclusive status, Americans are much more inclusively inclined with respect to membership in society. A number of societies are more favorably disposed toward immigration than Japan. But Japanese restrictiveness with respect to granting citizenship finds sympathetic echoes in many societies. The openness of the United States to transforming migrants from other societies into citizens is relatively unusual. So, across a broad range of public policies, United States practices are repeatedly distinctive by the standards of other advanced industrial societies, the most obvious external reference point for expectations.

EXPLAINING AMERICAN EXCEPTIONALISM

How are these and related policy differences between the United States and other advanced industrial societies to be explained? Analysts have relied on a number of factors. Most of their considerations can be organized under three broad categories: history, institutions and culture.

HISTORY

By "history" I refer to the varying experiences that have confronted different societies. One factor which helps to explain cross-societal policy variations of the sort introduced in the previous paragraphs is varying experience with sharp sudden social dislocation. That is, how frequently and severely have experiences such as wars or economic depressions disrupted the lives of a society's members? For instance, for nearly a century—from the mid-1800s through the mid-1900s—Germany was "encircled" by adversaries harboring irredentist designs on portions of its territory.[1] A society in this situation may—as did the Germans—experience repeated rounds of warfare on its own territory or at least the nearly perpetual threat of such activity. In response to such severe contingencies, the society may develop public institutions (e.g., a large standing army) and policies (e.g., public programs providing benefits to injured veterans and war widows) that differ in kind or at least degree from the public sector activities of societies that face more benign external conditions.

While some military conflicts are purposely planned by particular societies, for many of the societies drawn into these struggles, the events are appropriately categorized as accidents or "contingencies," meaning that their occurrence lies beyond the capacity of public officials to control. Similarly, while economic depressions may result from policies which are later determined to have been ill-advised, they are not apt to be brought on purposefully. Events which develop sharp and severe social dislocation are frequently experiences which happen to societies rather than activities which they choose.[2] However, variations in the specific historical contingencies which particular societies confront are apt to shape their public institutions and policies in distinct ways.

For instance, until the 1950s the United States was unusually well insulated from the threats of foreign attack and many international economic problems. While the British razed portions of Washington, D.C, during the War of 1812, broad oceans to the east and west hampered European and Asian states in projecting their military power onto North America, and the United States homeland was routinely free from external attacks and even the threat of such attacks. Further, across time the societies on the United States' northern and southern frontiers became increasingly weak militarily in comparison to the United States and offered progressively less in the way of security threats.[3] So in comparison to Germany the United States enjoyed a relative absence of external security threats. This relative advantage reduced the need for the United States to have a large permanent military, and it maintained no standing military of consequence prior to the mid-1950s. The major American military conflict prior to the Second World War was domestic rather than externally imposed: the Civil War. While a significant standing military did not remain in the aftermath of this war, the conflict did produce an extensive program of veterans' benefits which lingered into the early twentieth century (Skocpol 1992). Further, American geographic isolation from Europe and Asia, in conjunction with a rapidly growing internal market, has meant that, in comparison to the circumstances of many other societies, domestic economic activity has been vastly more important to the health of the American economy than international trade. As a consequence, while the American economy has experienced its own periodic internal difficulties, it was—at least until the 1930s—relatively shielded from economic shocks originating in Europe and Asia.

So some American public institutions and policies likely differ from those of other societies in part because the United States' historical experience has been exceptionally free from attacks on its homeland by foreign powers and relatively insulated from deleterious economic developments in other societies. Yet sharp sudden social dislocations are not the only sorts of historical contingencies that may help to shape public policies. A second factor, the slowly cumulating effects of gradual changes in the circumstances of everyday life, may also foster innovations in political institutions and policies. While some of these changes may be anticipated, even desired, the full range of their social consequences may not be foreseen or salutary. Thus they too may often be considered historical contingencies. For instance, the industrialization process that occurred in the United States and a number of other societies across the

nineteenth century fostered increasing urbanization, the progressive replacement of extended families by nuclear households, and the growth of
wage dependency.

In the United States, in particular, large proportions of the population
gradually shifted from living in extended families which worked their
own property (e.g., farms or other small businesses) and that often produced at least a portion of the goods the family consumed, to living in
nuclear households in urban environments and supporting themselves by
selling their labor to employers. These new circumstances increased the
relevance of programs—initially mostly private but increasingly over
time public—designed to help households cope with certain social hazards such as illness, injury and aging as well as the work disability which
all three could cause. For instance, on a family farm a grandfather could
shift from heavy to lighter tasks, even inactivity, and still be supported by
two younger generations of family workers. Yet in an urban environment,
an increasingly decrepit grandfather with a long record of self-support
might be unable to obtain room, board and other assistance from the
struggling independent households of his adult children. Supporting an
elderly person poses more severe problems for an independent couple
working outside the home with a small apartment and a wage-deter-
mined budget. Accordingly, as greater proportions of a society's population confront these conditions, popular appreciation of public pensions
which help the elderly to live independently in retirement is apt to grow.

Inglehart (1997) has postulated a more recent political "revolution"
stemming from gradual changes in everyday life. He argues that, as advanced industrial societies have become more affluent and public social
programs more extensive, the tradeoffs between more material acquisi-
tion and improved intangible, quality-of-life benefits have begun to shift.
Across Scandinavian societies in particular, persons have become more
interested in leisure, environmental protection and participation in
workplace and political decisions. Further, they are increasingly willing to
pay for these benefits in terms of reduced earnings and/or higher prices
or taxes. These shifting preferences have in turn fostered the development of new political institutions (e.g., Green political parties) and public policies (e.g., more extensive environmental protection legislation).

To the degree that societies experience similar gradual changes in the
character of everyday life, there are apt to be some communalities to the
political institutions and policies which they develop to cope with the
problems these changes pose. Thus as Wilson (1998) and others point
out, advanced industrial societies have followed elements of what could
in broad outline be called a common trajectory across most of the last

century. In all these societies tax rates have increased substantially across time. Accordingly, the size (as a percentage of GDP) and activity levels of their public sectors have grown sharply as well. While the last century includes periods of public sector consolidation or retrenchment as well as growth (Heclo 1981), the governments of all advanced industrial societies currently carry a broader range of responsibilities than governments have historically shouldered. This is particularly the case in the area of social policy: i.e., public social services such as education and medical care as well as income maintenance for social hazards such as disability, unemployment and aging. Contemporary advanced industrial societies provide public social insurance against a broader array of the vicissitudes of life than citizens have ever previously enjoyed.

If advanced industrial societies are following a truly common policy trajectory, we should expect to find convergence among their policies rather than exceptional societies with systematically unusual public institutions or policies among their number. Yet in spite of common trends of both circumstance and policy among the advanced industrial societies, these societies are in some respects more different today than they were in the mid-nineteenth century. For instance, when no society had public revenues amounting to more than a tiny fraction of its GDP, no society differed from another in this regard by 25 percentage points, as Sweden and the United States do now. When there was little that medical-care professionals could do to cure the sick or repair the injured, no society made a systematic public effort to assure medical care to its citizens. Now most do, but the United States does not. The abortion practices of most societies have differed across time, but public regulation of abortion—and thus cross-societal regulatory differences—are likely more pronounced today than they were in the mid-nineteenth century. When only a tiny fraction of persons ever traveled far from the locale of their birth, immigration and citizenship issues were modest and migrants were virtually unregulated. Various societies now practice sharply different regulation of these matters. So while advanced industrial societies undoubtedly share aspects of a common trajectory, this common experience does not eliminate, and may even expand, their institutional and policy differences. Technological and economic development have gradually increased societies' capacities for providing medical care or regulating geographic mobility, and various societies choose to use these new capacities differently.

So as Inglehart (1997) suggests, societies' historical experiences are not deterministic. Repeated warfare does not automatically produce greater military preparedness or more extensive veterans' benefits. Rather, historical contingencies' consequences for public policies occur through their effects on the preferences of persons who experience disruptive effects of new contingencies and who also have some capacity for shaping policy. In contemporary liberal and social democracies this includes the citizens who elect public officials. But public officials and other political elites are particularly important in tailoring new public policies to emerging social problems or opportunities (Almond and Verba 1963). We shall return to this process in the "Culture" section below.

INSTITUTIONS

Another category of factors which contributes to exceptional American public policies involves the nature of the United States' broad political institutions. These institutions influence the direction of policy innovation in at least two general ways. First, many members of succeeding generations of citizens are socialized to accept the existing character of their institutions and the policies designs to which they contribute. These persons include both the adults who actually work in the institutions (March and Olsen 1989, 159-66) and others such as ordinary citizens who grow up among the institutions, use them and become accustomed to them (Rohrschneider 1994).

Acceptance is often affective rather than critical. For instance, while there are exceptions, citizens' reasons for accepting existing American political institutions frequently have less to do with a deliberative weighing of the relative advantages and drawbacks of the responsibility and accountability associated with parliamentary democracy (Wilson 1885) vis-à-vis checking the potentially rash actions of bare majorities through the separation of powers, and more to do with the comfort of familiar American institutions, whatever their drawbacks, in comparison to relative unknown alternatives. As Edmund Burke argued, many persons derive their preferences unthinkingly from acceptance of the familiar, especially when dealing with aspects of life with which they have little firsthand experience, rather than from rational calculation of the relative merits of various alternatives.

Socialization stemming from long familiarity with particular institutions tends to build acceptance of these institutions vis-à-vis alternatives even among persons who dislike specific institutional features. For instance, Americans are fond of complaining about the inefficiency of their public institutions. James Madison and others purposely built some of this inefficiency into American public institutions in order to block popular majorities from tyrannizing the interests of various minority factions. Yet few contemporary complainers appear prepared to trade the American separation of powers for more efficient parliamentary institutions. For many citizens, socialization produces preferences for familiar institutions regardless of their specific drawbacks. The affective institutional acceptance that socialization produces hampers dramatic shifts in policies. In practice, then, innovations tend to involve incremental shifts from existing policy design.

A second way in which existing institutions influence the direction of policy innovation is that the character of these institutions may make some new policy directions more feasible than others. For example, when the Clinton administration attempted to introduce national health insurance in the early 1990s, it proposed a program that worked through the existing system of multiple insurers. As we shall see in chapter 3, Canada has a national health insurance program which is much admired among many American reform advocates. Canada's program is a "single-payer" plan in which all patients in particular provinces (in a looser sense the entire society) have the same insurance provider. The Canadian program offers greater simplicity and in some respects efficiency than did the Clinton plan. But Clinton tried to reduce opposition to his proposal by minimizing the plan's disruptiveness to the existing pattern of relations among patients, medical-care providers and insurers.

In contemporary political science terminology, the explanatory factor at issue here is known as "path dependency." That is, once a society starts building particular public institutions (e.g., a presidential as opposed to parliamentary democracy) or policies (e.g., the financing of medical care), it becomes increasingly difficult across time to effect institutional or policy change which breaks free of the initial path's confining influence. So if a society's public sector has traditionally focused on a narrow range of purposes (e.g., securing social order against external and internal threats), it may gradually pick up new specific activities (e.g., pensions for the elderly or the occasional support of a foundering but crucial industry). But this society will not easily adapt to the same range of public purposes as another society, which, perhaps as a result of threats to its security, sets out early on to develop an active extensive public sector.

Thus path dependency also exerts a restraining influence, restricting the adoption of public policies which represent significant departures from current practice. Yet path dependency relies on sources of restraint which transcend the affective preferences for the familiar that we encountered in our discussion of socialization above. Sharp changes of policy direction are generally precluded, advocates of this perspective argue, because the existing structure of societal institutions makes certain changes extremely difficult. For instance, over time a government built on a separation-of-powers foundation will, following this initial path, develop progressively greater fragmentation by assigning specific responsibilities to different institutions. So, for instance, in the United States Congress, the revenue raising process is separated from the process for approving substantive legislation initiatives. Steinmo (1995) argues that this separation makes improving the funding for public social programs such as Medicaid much more difficult than in other societies in which less fragmented institutional structures foster greater coordination of these two processes. In the United States the battle for augmenting public social program benefits has to be waged multiple times before different audiences (e.g., multiple committees in each house of Congress). If opponents of particular proposals are victorious in just one of several venues, they can effectively block program expansion.[4]

Other analysts who draw on the influence of social structure in explaining American exceptionalism look beyond formal governmental institutions. Hartz (1955; see also Lipset 1990) contends that the absence of feudalism in the United States has hampered the development of more modern collective (e.g., social democratic) approaches to solving social problems. Further, some analysts (e.g., Katznelson 1986) maintain that the ethnic heterogeneity of the American population has hindered the capacity of American workers to organize for mutual benefit, creating an American working class that is weaker than the working classes of many European societies.

What institutional analysts (institutionalists) such as Steinmo (1994, 1995; Steinmo and Watts 1995) who focus on the influence of broad political institutions in shaping policies do not generally attempt to explain, however, is how the United States got started on a particular path of institutional development in the first place. Institutionalists who focus on broader aspects of American social structure offer more help with respect to this question. Hartz (1955), Lipset (1977) and others point out that the English and other Europeans who migrated in the seventeenth and eighteenth centuries to the portions of North America that eventually became the United States were disproportionately seeking different forms of social organization than those then prevailing in Europe.

In New England religious dissenters were particularly common among seventeenth-century migrants. While various sects quarreled among themselves, they shared a preference for more egalitarian, congregational forms of worship and social life than the relatively hierarchical forms practiced by the Church of England or Roman Catholicism. Persons seeking greater social mobility and economic opportunity than then available in Europe were particularly common among the early-eighteenth-century migrants who settled in what later became the Middle Atlantic states. They exhibited more individualistic entrepreneurial spirit than the European peasants and workers who stayed behind. Early migration to what became the American South was more characteristic of the hierarchical patterns that then prevailed in Europe. But even here, there tended to be some disaffection with European practices. Second and subsequent sons of landed English families, who chose to create their own estates in America rather than live on the fringes of English society as military officers or ministers, were unusually common among émigrés to this region. While the Europeans who constructed early political institutions in North America in the seventeenth and eighteenth centuries borrowed much of what they built from European ideas, many of them were predisposed to institutional designs which represented innovations from the political practices that prevailed across Europe in this era (e.g., the enfranchisement of a relatively high proportion of adult males on local issues).

Wood (1992) contends that an opportunity for firmly securing the path of these innovations appeared when the proportions of the population least enthralled with British practices mounted a successful revolution in 1776. The Revolution had the effect of driving many American Tories to Canada or back to England, leaving a population that was even less predisposed toward European practices and reinforcing the views of the members of the American population who remained. The subsequent Constitution of 1787, while attracting the opposition of many persons in the American population who were most ill-disposed toward prevailing European political institutions, nonetheless provided a solid basis for some of the distinctive political principles of a population which held views not then widely accepted outside the United States.

So these works suggest that the distinctive path of American institutional development originated in the historical accident of an unusual population whose members selected themselves for migration to the colonies that eventually became the United States on the basis of shared aspects of disaffection with the patterns of political thought and practice prevailing in Europe in the seventeenth and eighteenth centuries. The predispositions of this population were reinforced by the exodus of persons loyal to English practices before, during and after the Revolution as well as by the construction a decade later of a Constitution which, imperfectly, formalized central principles of shared aspects of their political orientations.[5] So paths of institutional development do not appear magically. As I suggested at the end of the preceding "History" section, varying institutional designs represent the contrasting preferences of persons who construct them as ways of realizing distinctive purposes which arise from their differing life experiences. Accordingly, it is time to turn our attention to these rival purposes.

CULTURE

Culture interacts with both societies' history and their paths of institutional development, the topics of the preceding two sections, in shaping societal policies. I begin this discussion with a specification of what I mean by culture. In part, I use the term to denote shared fundamental beliefs and value priorities. The two categories of beliefs most central to political aspects of culture involve conceptions of human nature and views as to how humans relate to their social environments. In part as well, I use culture to denote predispositions to construct and maintain distinctive social institutions and policies which fit with persons' fundamental beliefs and embody their high-priority values.

For instance, many members of the informal or "natural" (Burke, *Reflections on the Revolution in France*) aristocracy which governed England in the eighteenth century were inclined to view humans as sharply unequal in their practical capacities and morality. Further, British political elites' challenging experiences with civil war, revolutions both bloody and "glorious" (not bloody), holding dominant powers on the continent of Europe at bay, and managing a growing colonial empire persuaded them that most persons' capacities were insufficient to support their active involvement in political life. Beliefs in unequal human capacities as well as the extremely challenging nature of humans' social environments and corresponding commitments to the values of political inequality and achieving social order through an elite's expertise predisposed eighteenth-century British political elites to particular political institutions. Accordingly, only a tiny percentage of English adults could vote, and for practical purposes English public policy was determined by leading members of a couple hundred families. Colonists in America, while generally considered English subjects, played no formal role in determining English public policy, including policy toward its North American colonies. Rather, the colonies were viewed as appropriately deferring to the superior political judgments of metropole elites in London as to what policies served the collective welfare of England and its empire.

While persons in the American colonies were not culturally united, relatively high-handed British taxation and regulation of colonial life in the aftermath of the French and Indian War strengthened the political position of persons who evinced different views of humans and their social environments than those described in the previous paragraph. Following John Locke (*Second Treatise*), many of these persons perceived humans (members of the colonial and English political elites in particular) as being more equal than the English political elite imagined. In particular, these persons thought that the colonists' views on what policies were appropriate for them should be heard and generally honored. Further, while life in North American colonies was arduous, social conditions of relative open opportunity fostered widespread belief that ordinary persons could master their own fates through conscientious application of their relatively equal broad talents (e.g., rationality). These beliefs engendered support among colonists for values of relative human equality and liberty. Accordingly, many colonists sought greater autonomy from English control. While until the final period prior to the Revolution formal independence was not a widely held objective, extensive support existed for a looser association (i.e., as dominions in an empire) which would allow colonial autonomy on local or domestic dominion issues.

These brief examples of cultural orientations are sufficient to allow us to examine how history, institutions and culture interact in the explanation of the peculiarities of specific societies' public policies. First, persons' fundamental beliefs and value priorities come from their experiences with the world.[6] As we notice from differences among siblings reared in the same household, the experiences of all persons contain some unique aspects. So even when citizens of a particular society share experiences with societal catastrophes, their processes of selectively attending to and interpreting social life are bound to differ in some respects. Yet across large numbers of persons broad similarities of experience are apt to produce important commonalities with respect to fundamental beliefs and value priorities. So, to return to an earlier example, it seems unlikely that Germans born in the early years of the twentieth century and who struggled through the First World War, lengthy and deep economic depression, the Second World War and the national disintegration that followed could reasonably be expected to have the same degree of faith that many Americans have in the belief that most persons are capable of mastering their own fates. Even among Americans, the generally milder experiences with these two wars and the Great Depression of the 1930s produced a decline in this belief. In each society, but particularly in Germany where duress was greater, harsh experiences helped to produce beliefs that human social environments could overwhelm many persons. Accordingly, predispositions that public programs aimed at assisting persons overcome by the social catastrophes which they faced were desirable, even necessary, were common among citizens.

So persons' experience with life molds their fundamental beliefs, value priorities and policy predispositions: in short, their cultures. Among persons with a capacity for shaping public institutions, these predispositions are apt to prompt efforts to construct or maintain particular patterns of institutional and policy designs. When a society is starting virtually from scratch, as were the early colonists in America, they are likely to construct a path of institutional development consistent with their beliefs and values. For most societies much of the time existing institutions provide significant constraints on feasible policy innovations. Existing institutions may represent embodiments of one cultural orientation which has been predominant in a society or, more likely, some compromise among rival orientations which compete for political influence. Most innovative measures are not apt to deviate sharply from the path of development which has emerged across lengthy periods of societal history.

Thus efforts on the part of adherents of cultures with modest influence in a society to introduce policies at odds with the dominant path are not likely to succeed. Even eloquent pleas by high-profile reformers (e.g., Bok 1997; 2001; Kuttner 1997; Sunstein 1997; Glendon 1987) that the United States adopt policies that are popular and constructive in other societies (e.g., more adequate public sector revenues, a national health insurance program, an abortion policy of compromise and greater restraint with regard to immigration and citizenship) rarely produce the policy innovations which they advocate. In an important yet somewhat myopic sense an institutionalist explanation is correct: a fragmented institutional structure easily blocks policy proposals with broad societal consequences but relatively modest constituencies from being adopted. Somewhere along a convoluted legislative process, these proposals are apt to be derailed.

But this explanation begs questions as to how and why the American legislative process became so convoluted and remains so or why certain initiatives have such limited constituencies in the United States when they are broadly accepted in other advanced industrial societies. In order to address these questions adequately, we need to consider explanatory contributions from the history and culture categories. That is, explanations for the particular character of societal policies grow more thorough as multiple factors from all three explanatory categories—history, institutions and culture—are included. Across this study I will employ a causal model or sequence in which, generally, historical experience contributes to forming the developmental path of a society's broad political institutions. This path then helps to shape the society's political culture, particularly that of its political elite. Members of this elite then construct specific policy designs which realize their culture's distinctive beliefs and value priorities. However, as I demonstrate at numerous points in the course of this study, this sequence—while common—does not hold a monopoly on the causal and purposive processes leading to the construction of particular public policies.

Before introducing a conception of culture which works particularly well in conjunction with historical and institutional explanatory factors, I want to specify what I see as culture's most significant niche with respect to explaining particular policy designs. Generally, the success of policy innovations hinges on their compatibility with long-standing paths of policy development that are consistent with the dominant cultural orientation among a society's political elite. Persons do not shift their adherence among cultures frequently. Consequently, the relative proportions of a society's population and political elites which adhere to rival cultures tend to remain relatively stable. So cultivating the support necessary to adopt significant policy innovations at odds with a society's prevailing path of policy development is a demanding task that is only rarely successful.

However, historical contingencies which create sudden and significant social dislocation open possibilities for what I call a "dual-process" pattern of policy change. First, significant changes in circumstance may alter the cultural orientations held by the general citizenry. Further, adherents of what has been a minority cultural orientation in a particular society may become emboldened by serious social dislocation. Accordingly, the new circumstances may foster the formation of an electoral coalition between the more numerous and invigorated adherents of a previously minority culture and the adherents of another, formerly antagonistic culture. Second, previously marginalized elites, drawing on this electoral coalition, may enter the ranks of governing officials. As these persons—who have been socialized to a culture distinct from the one responsible for the existing path of policy development—enter the political elite, they are apt to replace some policies reflecting that existing path with innovations drawing on their contrasting beliefs and value priorities (Cox 2001). While this dual process pattern of sharp policy change is initiated by disruptive historical forces, the character of the policy changes it produces draws on the beliefs and value priorities of a culture distinct from the one which has been responsible for the previous path of policy development.

As we shall see in more detail in chapter 2, changes similar to those described in the previous paragraph occurred in the United States in reaction to the Great Depression of the 1930s and the subsequent Second

World War. Throughout most of its previous history, adherents of a cultural orientation favoring limited government had been highly influential in the United States (Lockhart 2001a). But the social dislocation of the Depression changed some persons' cultural orientations and emboldened others who had favored a larger, more active government all along. These changes helped to bring to office a political elite which supported more active public measures to deal with domestic economic problems and subsequently foreign security threats. In the course of a decade, the size and activity levels of the American national government grew substantially. While considerable retrenchment occurred among these new programs in the aftermath of the two precipitating crises, some of the innovations endured. After the Korean War in the mid-1950s, a substantial standing military remained minimally through the cold war. Further, social security, adopted in 1935, has become the largest line item in the American federal budget. Yet across the last three decades, in the absence of historical contingencies posing similarly severe social dislocation, the size and activity levels of the American national government have gradually drifted back toward the historical baseline of a relatively modest state. The social dislocation associated with the 2001 attack on the World Trade Center has certainly prompted a sharp increase in public sector activity in the areas of intelligence, policing and defense which will likely persist into the future. However, the increase in public social policy activity prompted by this event appears to have been both narrowly focused and short-term.

INTRODUCING GRID-GROUP THEORY

Culture is sometimes used as a sort of "magic bullet." That is, it is employed in a loose sense to explain virtually everything about a society (Limerick 1997). I introduce here a specific theory of culture and apply it—in conjunction with other explanatory variables—throughout this study. Grid-group theory is an approach to cultural explanation that can help us understand why public policies with effects that are appreciated in some societies are not acceptable in others. The theory was conceived in sociology (Durkheim 1951), refined in cultural anthropology (Evans-Pritchard 1940; Douglas 1992, 1986, 1982a, 1982b, 1978) and has been recently advanced and applied more generally in political science (Thompson, Ellis and Wildavsky 1990; Ellis 1993; Coyle and Ellis 1994; Lockhart 2001b). It explains how persons derive a limited range of answers to basic social questions such as how the world works and what humans are really like (Wildavsky 1994). Grid-group theorists argue that persons' answers to these questions produce orientations toward two basic social dimensions: grid and group. The grid dimension distinguishes the degree to which persons accept that there are other superior humans whose judgments are valid for and binding on them. So in practice, the grid scale registers the relative acceptance of human inequality. The group dimension measures the significance of group boundaries. In practice, the group scale registers differences in levels of cooperation among group members as opposed to between them and outsiders. The theory thus helps to fill a notorious void in the social sciences (Becker 1976, 133). It explains how distinctive social relations preferences are formed as a consequence of various grid and group positions (Schwarz and Thompson 1990: 49). The range of actual social practice is constrained, since only four general ways—each admitting variations—of responding to these issues are socially viable.[7] Preferences for various patterns of social relations prompt supporting justifications or cultural biases and vice versa. Together, the preferences and justifications create distinctive ways of life or cultures. (See figure 1.1.)

For instance, where low tolerance for external prescription is reinforced by weak feelings of group membership, we find an individualistic

Figure 1.1   Grid-Group Theory's Dimensions and Cultures

way of life organized by self-regulation among voluntary, shifting, contract-based networks of persons. Promoting such a way of life among persons perceived as self-interested, with roughly equal broad competencies such as rationality, is one purpose of Smith's *Wealth of Nations*. Increasingly strong feelings of group affiliation together with weak prescription entail a way of life that grid-group theorists call egalitarian. From this perspective broadly equal humans, unmarred by natural flaws destructive of social harmony, ideally prefer to organize into small societies that reach collective decisions through discussion-facilitated consensus. This process is reminiscent of Rousseau's descriptions of the social ideal in *The Social Contract*. High feelings of group affiliation in conjunction with perceptions legitimizing strong external prescription create a realm of hierarchy. In this view, the activities of unequal humans—with various social shortcomings that require monitoring and control—are appropriately guided by experts at the helm of vertically arrayed institutions. The ideal polis portrayed by Plato in *The Republic* illustrates this way of life. In the upper-left-hand region of figure 1.1, weak feelings of group affiliation intersect with perceptions of external direction. Grid-group theorists call this way of life fatalism. The unhappy combination of recognizing constraint by others but not feeling part of any broader social collective predisposes fatalists to social avoidance rather than varying forms of social interaction. One manifestation of avoidance is that fatalists rarely construct works of political theory; their views have, however, been well portrayed by others (Banfield 1958; Turnbull 1972).[8]

Grid-group theory's conception of culture is distinctive in two ways which facilitate the theory's use in conjunction with variables from the history and institutional categories. First, in contrast to a convention by which cultures (sometimes allowing for multiple subcultures) are thought of as roughly coincident with nationalities or societies (i.e., French or Chinese culture), grid-group theorists argue that all four of their theory's global ways of life are present in varying proportions in all large-scale societies (Grendstad 1999). Similarly to the interaction of different amino acids in biological systems, each way of life provides services for the others that they cannot create for themselves. Societies are thus typically "multicultural" in this sense. This means that some relatively egalitarian Americans (e.g., Derek Bok 1997, 2001) are apt to be more sympathetic to selective aspects of Swedish public policy than some individualistic Swedes. These individualistic Swedes are also apt to be more sympathetic to particular aspects of prevailing American policies than Derek Bok and other similarly minded Americans (Nordlund and

Coughlin 1998). Further, it is often possible to identify the organized factions involved in important episodes of a society's history (e.g., major political struggles) as the adherents of rival cultures. The relative influence of rival cultural factions on these struggles wax and wane as various historical contingencies produce conditions favoring one faction and then another. For example, the Great Depression and the Second World Wars raised fears for economic and physical security and for a time strengthened the advocates of an active extensive state (i.e., hierarchists) vis-à-vis the advocates of a small inactive national government (i.e., individualists) who have generally been more influential in the United States.

Additionally, grid-group theorists conceive of culture, in part, as beliefs about humans' natural and social environments that rest ultimately on experience. Distinctive conceptions of human nature follow from varying beliefs about the way the world works. Together, these beliefs about humans and their world locate persons with respect to the grid and group dimensions, support characteristic value priorities and spawn preferences for specific social institutions. Accordingly, a second distinctive feature of grid-group analysis is that the theory illuminates tighter, more constrained relations between particular sets of beliefs and value priorities (i.e., cultural biases) and the distinctive institutions that embody them than do many other theories of culture (Ross 1997).

For instance, individualists perceive bountiful and resilient natural (Locke, *Second Treatise,* ch. 5) and social (Nozick 1974) environments. They also view humans as self-interested and equal in broad capacities. These humans are thus properly motivated and sufficiently capable to master their own fates in a cornucopian world. Accordingly, individualists prefer to rely primarily on self-regulation among persons. For individualists, a network of contractual (voluntary) relations that shifts over time as interests do is the preferred social institution. For them, government—with its inherent coercion—is frequently destructive of their preeminent value, a particular ("negative"—Berlin 1969) conception of liberty, and should be limited in its domain and activity.

Egalitarians, in contrast, see a fragile environment. Not only is the natural environment subject to depredation, but social contexts—the inner city—are easily perverted as well. Egalitarians believe that humans are naturally benign in their motives and broadly equal in both basic capacities and needs (Gewirth 1978), thus complementing this delicate context. Yet humans are easy prey for social stratification, which damages central egalitarian values of relatively equal interpersonal respect and material condition. Egalitarians believe that by undoing natural human equality, stratification creates arrogance in the dominant and resentment in the subordinated, perverting in the process the natural goodness of all. Accordingly, egalitarians ideally prefer social relations among relatively small societies, which can manage without much stratification and which distribute a limited material bounty fairly equally—exemplified by the aphorism "live simply so that others may simply live" or as Schumacher had it, "small is beautiful" (1973). These societies strive to reach collective decisions through open discussion resulting in consensus (Downey 1986; Zisk 1992). In large-scale societies egalitarians frequently form coalitions with hierarchy in order to gain specific benefits and to project their way of life into society at large. Thus in the twentieth century egalitarians frequently coalesced with hierarchists to support varying forms of social democracy, through which they accept more coercion (i.e., a large active state) in order to acquire greater equality (e.g., various public social programs).

Hierarchists believe in a more complex, tolerant/perverse context. Both natural and social environments are sufficiently robust to support some exploitation, but if humans press too hard, disaster is apt to follow. Figuratively, humans live on mesas, not needing to worry about minor variations in the table-top terrain, but having to stay clear of the encircling cliffs. This view of the human environment elicits a conception of humans that, in contrast to those of the low-grid cultures (i.e., individualism and egalitarianism), attributes great importance to disparities of specific talents. Experts in various matters are required to discern crucial natural and social boundaries not equally evident to everyone as well as for ascertaining how humans should adjust their behavior in conformity with these limits. For hierarchists, many of the same obvious interpersonal differences that individualists and egalitarians believe to be inconsequential take on moral and social significance. Accordingly, hierarchists prefer to organize society into vertically arrayed institutions which honor their preeminent values of social order and harmony realized through expert leadership. Experts guide these institutions, attempting to fill persons' lives with sanctioned activities. In this way, hierarchists believe, the lives of less capable and more seriously flawed persons are improved and the collective objectives of society are better advanced.[9]

So persons use the different cultures to which they adhere, not only to interpret their environments, but for guidance in shaping them as well, striving to form and sustain the distinctive institutions and policies that embody their rival sets of beliefs and value priorities. This is particularly clear during infrequent moments of sharp political change. For instance, across slightly more than a decade between the mid-1770s and the late 1780s, Madison discarded both the hierarchical British empire in which he had grown up and the egalitarian Articles of Confederation that developed out of the revolutionary movement of the 1770s. Through a new constitution, he chose instead to construct a unique set of institutions admirably tailored to the culture of individualism that he had encountered in the course of his education through the works of Locke, Montesquieu and others.

THE STRUCTURE OF THIS VOLUME

SOCIETIES INCLUDED

I employ the historical, institutional and cultural variables introduced above in this study to explain why prominent United States' policies are so different from those of other societies. Specifically, I contrast the United States with four other societies: Sweden, Canada, France and Japan. While this sample has its limitations, it represents considerable variation on important independent variables: experience with contrasting historical contingencies, distinctive paths of institutional development and variations in the relative influence of rival cultures.

For example, in the instance of culture, this sample includes the advanced industrial societies most obviously dominated by grid-group theory's three rival socially interactive cultures as well as an advanced industrial society that possesses an extensive population of fatalists. The United States is the contemporary large-scale society in which individualism is most dominant (Devine 1972; Lipset 1996; Verba et al. 1987; Huntington 1981; Wilson 1997). Additional egalitarian influence suggests the characterization of the United States as an antistatist (Huntington 1981) "low-grid" society. Egalitarianism is at least as prominent in Sweden as in any other contemporary large-scale society, and it is supported in some of its objectives by significant influence from the other high-group culture, hierarchy (Grendstad 1999). This combination constitutes one form of what grid-group theorists call a "high-group" society. Japan represents a society in which hierarchy is dominant although bolstered by egalitarianism, thus providing an example of the obverse form of high-group society (Ishida 1983). In contrast, France represents a "low-group" society in which the incidence of fatalists is particularly high. Fatalists' penchant for social avoidance fails to translate into societal influence in the sense of constructing particular forms of macrosocietal institutions. But the efforts of adherents of the three socially interactive cultures to organize French society to their differing preferences have been burdened by the breadth of public alienation attributable to large numbers of fatalists

(Grendstad 1999; Ehrmann 1983; Putnam with Leonardi and Nanetti 1993). Canada represents a middle ground among the relative extremes provided by the United States, Sweden, Japan and France. While Canada is more individualistic than Sweden or Japan, it is also more high-group than the United States (Lipset 1990), and fatalism is less common among the Canadians than among the French.

Inglehart (1997) provides an alternative cultural schema for distinguishing societies, and my sample also provides considerable variation in terms of his schema's dimensions. (See figure 1.2.) One of these dimensions is built on Weber's (1946, 295-301) distinction between traditional and secular-rational authority. In practice, this dimension distinguishes the relatively secular societies of Europe, North America and East Asia from the more traditional societies of Africa, South Asia and Latin America. Inglehart's second dimension is constructed from "survival" preferences for more material improvement that typically accompany industrialization in contrast to "well-being" preferences for upgrading the quality of life (e.g., leisure, environmental protection, participation) that are associated with the "postmaterialism" of advanced industrial societies. This dimension distinguishes the still-industrializing societies of Eastern Europe and, less extreme in this regard, those of East Asia from the more advanced industrial societies of Northwest Europe.

In Inglehart's terms, my sample covers slightly over half of the survival versus well-being dimension, ranging from relatively materialistic Japan to highly postmaterial Sweden. My sample covers slightly less than half of the traditional to secular-rational authority dimension. The United States lies on the traditional side of the midpoint between traditional and secular-rational authority, and Japan and Sweden are both well into the secular-rational authority zone. My sample thus misses both extremes of this dimension, most obviously the lower third occupied largely by African and Latin American societies, as well as much of the survival portion of the material-postmaterial dimension, occupied largely by industrializing societies. Yet a focus on secular, relatively advanced industrial societies is appropriate for this study inasmuch as these societies provide the vast majority of policies that capture the interest of American reformers as possibilities for adoption in the United States.

There are some similarities between Inglehart's (1997) positioning (in terms of sample mean scores) of the five societies on which I focus and the relations among these societies in terms of the relative influence of grid-group theory's rival cultures. The two relatively high-group (i.e., hierarchical and egalitarian) societies (e.g., Japan and Sweden) hold similar and relatively secular-rational positions on Inglehart's authority dimen-

Figure 1.2   Societies Arrayed on Inglehart's Dimensions

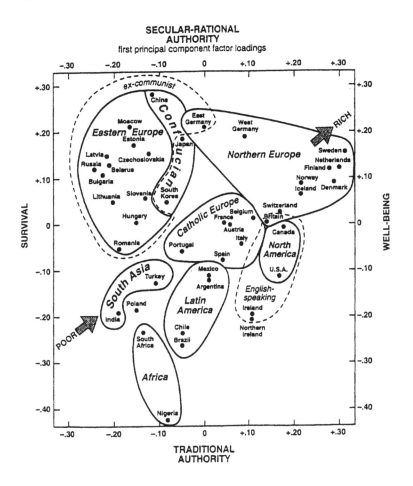

(Inglehart 1997, 93)

sion, but Japan lies on the material side of the materialism-postmaterial-
ism dimension; whereas Sweden occupies the most postmaterial position.
The low-grid United States and the low-group France both lie considerably more toward the traditional end of the authority dimension than
Japan and Sweden. The United States' position is both more traditional

and more well-being oriented than that of France. So the low-grid United States is more similar to Sweden on this latter dimension, while France is more similar to Japan. As before, Canada occupies a middle-ground position in the space bounded by the other four societies, but it is closer to the United States and France than to Sweden and Japan.

POLICIES EXAMINED

With respect to what we could call the dependent variable, I sample several distinct types of contemporary public policy, and the four societies whose practices I compare with those of the United States offer sharp variation in policy character. I attend first to prominent aspects of public material redistribution by examining the process of extracting revenue as well as a significant category of public expenditure. I focus on the revenue side in chapter 2 by contrasting the taxation practices of Sweden and the United States (Steinmo 1993; Witte 1985). The largest general category of public expenditure in all of the societies that I consider involves the various public social programs which form their differing welfare states. In chapter 3, I examine a significant aspect of these expenditures by contrasting Canadian and U.S. practices with regard to financing medical care through public programs (Lipset 1990). I also scrutinize two high-profile issues in which public policy acts more to bestow legitimacy than to redistribute material resources. In chapter 4, I contrast French and American approaches to legitimizing abortion. Additionally, among the most basic questions of political organization are those involving membership in society (Walzer 1983). I consider this issue in chapter 5 by contrasting Japanese and American approaches to immigration and particularly citizenship. I offer my conclusions with respect to cross-societal policy emulation in chapter 6.

Three of the societal policies which I contrast with American practices have been the direct focus of prospective emulation for various American reformers, and the fourth is a logical candidate for such attention. American activists adhering to both the high-group cultures (i.e., egalitarians and hierarchists) have, for instance, decried the relative paucity of American public coffers. Although Americans are taxed less than the citizens of nearly all other advanced industrial societies (OECD 1994), many of them complain about what they perceive as high taxes. Yet some Americans (Bok 1997) argue that current revenue levels are insufficient to adequately support crucial public activities. As numerous American reformers have pointed out, Sweden represents a sharp and salutary contrast in this regard. Additionally, a gap in the American social policy repertoire that has attracted extensive attention involves the reluctance to provide universal financial access to a broad range of medical care through public policy. Nearly all presidents since Franklin Delano Roosevelt have made some effort to close at least portions of this gap. Publicly supported medical care has expanded across this period, but the United States remains in Wilensky's (1975) terms a welfare "laggard" on this score. The Canadian national health insurance program has been suggested by many American reformers as a promising example for American emulation.

Further, few controversies have more convulsed American political life over the last three decades than the status of abortion. Selected aspects of French reproductive policy (e.g., RU-486) have been controversial in the United States. American use of RU-486, for instance, has been both advocated and castigated by Americans associated with "pro-choice" and "pro-life" factions, respectively. Overall, however, aspects of French reproductive policy are not well known among the American public, save for those persons exceptionally attentive to reproductive policy issues. Yet French policy with respect to abortion offers substantial differences from American practices and has not prompted the degree of controversy in France that abortion rights have in the United States. Thus American reformers have suggested aspects of French abortion policy as models for American emulation (Glendon 1987). Finally, across American history, the relative leniency of American immigration and particularly citizenship practices has periodically aroused the ire of various nativist groups. The contemporary period is only the most recent of these episodes. For nativists, much stricter standards such as those practiced by the Japanese represent an appealing alternative, even if nativists are not prone to suggest American emulation of other societies' practices.

CASE STUDY PROCEDURES

I draw on George and Smoke's (1974—see also George and McKeown 1985) concept of focused comparison in the four policy contrasts comprising chapters 2 through 5. In each of these cases I follow a similar process. First, for each new society involved in the policy contrast of a particular chapter I examine a variety of data which reveal distinctive historical experiences, disparate paths of institutional development, and contrasting attitudes of mass publics and particularly political elites that help to ascertain the relative prominence of grid-group theory's rival cultures. Second, I draw on the distinctive institutional preferences of the cultures that grid-group theory distinguishes to predict how public policy in the particular area in question differs between the two societies. I then contrast the designs of the actual policies, examining differences between them. Third, I show how societal differences in historical experiences, patterns of institutionalization and prevailing cultural preferences interact to produce these cross-societal policy differences and explain how they create obstacles for the United States adopting a policy similar to that of the other society in question as some American reformers urge us to do.

Consequently, the explanations that this study offers for the distinctiveness of United States public policies lie at the intersection of historical, institutional and cultural approaches to politics. This combination provides particularly powerful insights as to why U.S. public policies are so pervasively distinct from those of other advanced industrial societies. While culture may be no more important than the two other elements of these explanations, I think that its contributions are less widely appreciated among contemporary political scientists. Thus at particular junctures I emphasize its essential contributions to the overall explanatory pattern. Indeed, I think that culture makes essential contributions, not only to explaining the difficulties for American emulation of other societies' institutions, but for social theory more generally.

Particularly as conceptualized through grid-group theory, culture provides a means for complementing, not only historical and institutional analysis, but also rational-choice theory. Yet these prominent modes of analysis are generally perceived as rivals. Rational-choice theory provides a productive central assumption: persons attempt to realize stable preferences efficiently. In this sense, it represents a theory of preference implementation. But Etzioni (1988) and others (Sen 1977; Mansbridge 1990; Jencks 1990; Wolfe 1993) show that much of social life is driven by motivations—interpersonal commitments based on duty or love—distinct from the egoistic and hedonistic preferences that rational-choice theorists generally assume. Grid-group theory conceives of these distinctive motivations as socially embedded in the cultures of hierarchy, egalitarianism and individualism, respectively. In turn, these rival cultures, which rest on different experience with the world and bases for personal identity (Ross 1997), supplement the preference implementation focus of instrumental conceptions of rationality with a crucial concern for preference formation, helping to explain why various persons cling to the different objectives that they prefer.

Thus grid-group theory's version of political culture theory (Eckstein 1988) also offers a means for constructively augmenting rational choice theory so as to provide a more complete theory of preference formation and implementation than either of these two elements offers on its own. We return to this topic in chapter 6 to combine instrumental rationality and cultural biases into distinctive "rationalities," that is, inclinations to support distinctive objectives efficiently as well as to add institutional predispositions by formulating three contrasting "institutional/policy formation imperatives," one associated with each of grid-group theory's socially interactive cultures.

CHAPTER 2

Tax Regimes in the United States and Sweden

F ew alternative indices reveal societies' predominant political orientations more clearly than taxation policies or regimes. A society which practices modest tax extraction will inevitably produce public institutions less extensive than those of a society with a considerably higher level of extraction. Accordingly, the former will leave more responsibilities in private hands (those of individuals, families, charitable institutions, businesses and the markets through which they interact); whereas the latter is apt to realize a broader range of societal objectives through public programs.

In the sections below I engage in the following tasks. First, I briefly contrast salient historical experiences of the United States and Sweden as well as the divergent character of these societies' major public institutions and their political cultures. Second, I show how the contrasting institutional designs of the United States and Swedish tax regimes fit with these experiences, institutions and cultures. Third, I consider the interactive flows of causality among history, institutions and culture. This last task is undertaken in part with reference to a specific practical question that reflects an important concern of this study, namely: what other changes would be required (and how might they come about) for the United States to adopt a tax regime similar to Sweden's.

CONTRASTING SOCIETAL HISTORIES, INSTITUTIONS AND CULTURES

UNITED STATES

History.   As I suggested in chapter 1, in comparison to many other societies the United States has had a relatively mild historical experience with both economic disasters such as famines and depressions and attacks by foreign powers or groups (e.g., Al Qaeda). For instance, while the Great Depression of the 1930s caused much social dislocation in the United States, American economic trials were less severe and long lived than those endured by many other societies during this period. Similarly, the United States suffered many casualties in the Second World War, yet its continental base remained essentially unscathed, and it sustained far more modest proportional loses than any other major party to the conflict. The United States' most gripping conflicts have been domestic struggles with Native Americans and particularly the Civil War, both of which now lie far beyond the personal experience of current citizens. A different sort of historical accident holds importance for this study. The early migrants from Europe to the regions which subsequently formed the United States held various disaffections with European political practices that shared some common implications and prompted distinctive colonial political practices such as the broad dissemination of political voice on local issues.

Institutions.   Serious struggles erupted early in United States history about the appropriate developmental path for American political institutions. Both colonial agitation for greater autonomy from the British Empire during the 1760s and early 1770s and the subsequent successful Revolution engendered extensive support for limited and largely local government. But experience with the constraints on life under the Articles of Confederation prompted concerns among other Americans for more capable central public institutions which could, among other matters, better facilitate both foreign and domestic commerce. For a time a struggle between this latter faction (the Federalists) and their opponents who favored limited and local government (the anti-Federalists) followed a pendulum-like oscillation. The anti-Federalists dominated from the mid-1770s through the late 1780s; while the Federalists—the initiators of the 1787 Constitution—acquired the upper hand through the 1790s. A somewhat chastened anti-Federalist orientation regained influence in 1800. Across the balance of the nineteenth century the norm of a relatively small and inactive national government generally prevailed. Brief interludes of greater activity occurred, with the Civil War representing the most notable nineteenth-century expansion of public sector size and activity.

In the twentieth century the United States experienced three successive episodes of growth in public institutions and their activities. The first of these was the result of the Progressive movement prior to the First World War. In response to widespread fears about public safety (e.g., the purity of food products) in an economy increasingly dominated by powerful industrialists serving a national market, the Progressive movement strengthened the American national government's regulatory capacity by introducing a national civil service and a number of executive agencies designed to restrain selective excesses of various industries (Skowronek 1982). The second episode of public sector expansion occurred during the 1930s and early 1940s as the Roosevelt administration responded to the Great Depression with the public program innovations of the New Deal and to foreign threats with American involvement in the Second World War. In the course of a decade, the size and activity levels of the American national government expanded sharply in response to these two historical contingencies. A third episode of rapid growth in public sector responsibilities was initiated in response to the "rediscovery" of poverty (Harrington 1962) roughly simultaneously with the rise of the Civil Rights Movement in the early 1960s. President Lyndon B. Johnson subsequently mounted a "war on poverty" through the development of his Great Society programs.

Since the early 1970s, in the absence of historical contingencies posing social dislocations on the scale of the Great Depression, the size and activity levels of the American national government have gradually declined, particularly in the areas of social policy that the New Deal and Great Society periods had developed. Until the 2001 attack on the World Trade Center, the American national government was drifting in a direction reminiscent of the historical baseline suggested by the bulk of the nineteenth century involving a relatively small and inactive national government. Even this recent increase in public sector activity appears to be focused narrowly on defense related activities (e.g., intelligence, policing and military services).

This portrayal of American national government development in terms of a few short-lived flurries of activity (i.e., the Federalist decade of the 1790s, the Civil War, and the more sustained peak of activity initiated by the Great Depression), set against a general background of much lower activity, may convey an impression of societal agreement on a limited role for public institutions. Yet disagreement about the appropriate path of political development has always existed among Americans (Hirschman 1982; McClosky and Zaller 1984; Schlesinger 1986). For instance, both the Hoover administration's laissez faire response to the early days of the Great Depression and Roosevelt's subsequent more ambitious program of public sector activity were highly contentious. Socially disruptive historical contingencies tend to strengthen the political position of persons favoring greater activity. Nonetheless, against a history of social dislocation that is relatively mild, the United States has shown more reluctance to build a large active state than have many other societies.

In comparative perspective two general and enduring features of this developmental path of broad American political institutions stand out as exceptional. First, the United States has always had decentralized national political institutions. The 1787 Constitution reduced the truly remarkable structural fragmentation prevailing under the Articles, but the resulting institutional structure remains more decentralized than is common among other societies. Features supportive of this characterization include not only the multiple branches of government with their distinctive personnel, varying terms of office and counterpoised powers, but as well an unusually loosely structured executive branch and a meaningfully bicameral legislature with relatively independent committees and political parties affording weak interest-aggregating capacities. This relatively decentralized institutional structure systematically hinders initiatives in support of broad national objectives and reflects into the present Madison's priority for safeguarding the liberty of minority factions from actions taken in pursuit of majority interests. Other persons, whose preeminent values include a harmonious, expert-derived social order or a person-respecting community, favor alternative institutions. Dominant American political elites have been little interested in altering this institutional structure so as to facilitate the coordinated national action that these other persons prefer.[1]

Second, patterns of interaction across the multiple institutions of American national politics are fragmented and conflictual. Emphasis lies on defending the concerns of numerous specific interests. Less attention is paid toward fostering legislation that reflects broad public interest. Indeed, the concept of pubic interest is met with widespread skepticism. Compromise among specific interests is hindered by the pervasive adoption—across a range of issues from the regulation of firearms to the rules governing abortion—of the language of rights (Glendon 1987). Each specific faction focuses on protecting an autonomous sphere of activity from various regulatory intrusions of government that are proposed by other factions rather than on deploying broad public programs, built through mutual compromise, for mitigating various problems confronting large numbers of citizens. President Ronald Reagan encapsulated this view in repeated expressions to enthusiastic audiences in the early 1980s that an active government was the problem, not the solution.

Culture. Broad agreement exists among scholars that the United States is a highly individualistic society (Devine 1972; Lipset 1996; 1990; Verba et al. 1987; Huntington 1981; Wilson 1997). So, it seems likely that, were the appropriate grid-group data available,[2] they would confirm what nearly all who address the matter claim: namely, the United States is a relatively unusual—if not exceptional—society in that its dominant culture is individualism. Further, I follow other grid-group theorists (Wildavsky 1991) in arguing that egalitarians and hierarchists have progressively fewer adherents and that fatalists form the least influential political culture in American society.

Variations in the relative prominence of rival cultures among different societies' political elites are more relevant to explaining cross-societal policy differences than variations in the proportions of their general citizenries who adhere to disparate cultures. In many, likely the vast majority of, societies hierarchists form the preeminent elite culture. They may govern by themselves (e.g., the former Soviet Union) or more frequently through coalitions with egalitarians (H-E coalitions, e.g., social democracies such as Sweden) or in conjunction with individualists as junior partners (H-I coalitions, e.g., the coalitions of "sword and yen" in Meiji Restoration Japan or "blood and iron" in Imperial Germany). As Huntington (1981) suggests, the predominance of individualists among the American population and particularly its political elite creates both problems and political patterns not present in many other societies. For instance, individualists prefer constitutionally limited and—ideally—local government, and across the vast bulk of the United States' history their views have prevailed. Huntington argues that in the United States individualists follow an "American creed" of liberty, equality of opportunity, democracy and individualism. Yet, Huntington contends, the anti-statist nature of this creed poses problems for practical governing, especially when historical contingencies that create significant social dislocation arise. So in practice these crises lead to violating the creed's principles as, for instance, when a larger, more active American national government developed in response to the Great Depression and the Second World War.

Once these historical crises are over, Huntington (1981) argues, the United States experiences a rebirth of individualistic principle and public sector retrenchment in periods of what he calls "creedal passion" that occur at regular intervals. Huntington exaggerates both the regularity and the uniformity of these principled reactions (Lockhart 2001a), but he does alert us to the periodic shifts in the cultural composition of political elites—and the consequences of these shifts for public policy design—that are necessary in a society dominated by individualists. For instance, the shifts between alternative periods of government retrenchment (the 1770s–early 1780s and the first decades of the nineteenth century) and state-building (1790s) coincide with periods in which individualists shifted back and forth between egalitarians and hierarchists as coalition partners, forming sequentially the individualistic-egalitarian (I-E) Revolutionary, the individualistic-hierarchical (I-H) Federalist and I-E Jeffersonian coalitions.[3] Similarly, the three periods of twentieth-century state-building that we discussed above (i.e., the Progressive, New Deal and Great Society) all occurred as hierarchists, alarmed about threats to public order, became increasingly active in elite coalitions with individualists.

SWEDEN

History.   Overall, Sweden's history includes more disruptive events than the United States has experienced, but much of this disruption lies in the distant past (Elstob 1979). A thousand years ago, for instance, Swedish society was repeatedly torn as leading families vied for power in lengthy internecine struggles. From the fourteenth century to the end of the Napoleonic Wars, Sweden was frequently involved in conflicts with other Scandinavian states as well as European powers generally. During this period the Baltic region was more central to European power struggles than it has been recently. Sweden suffered repeated attacks on its own territory and routinely fought wars with other Baltic states, even conducting campaigns deep into Russia and southern Germany. While these experiences surely influenced the developmental path of the Swedish state, they now lie far beyond the memories of living Swedes. Over the last two centuries Sweden has become more disengaged from the struggles among powerful states to prevail on the European continent. Sweden did not become actively involved in the twentieth century's two world wars. During the Second World War, for instance, Sweden maintained a fragile neutrality, locked between Soviet-dominated Finland to its east and Nazi-occupied Denmark and Norway to its west.

In the economic realm, Sweden has long been more dependent on international trade than has the United States. Thus Sweden has been less able to shield itself from distressing economic currents affecting other regions of Europe. Across the latter half of the nineteenth century and prior to significant industrialization of its economy near that century's end, unemployment and poverty were common. As a result, approximately 20 percent of the Swedish population emigrated during this period, most to the United States and Canada. In the last couple of decades various aspects of globalization (e.g., the growing penetration by foreign competitors of markets in which Swedish products have traditionally done well and the increased mobility of capital) have posed more severe problems of social dislocation in Sweden than those experienced by the United States.

Institutions. Between the mid-fifteenth and the mid-nineteenth centuries relative power among Swedish political institutions was contested by the monarchy and a parliament (Riksdag) that originally represented four estates: nobility, clergy, townsmen and peasants.[4] While Swedish monarchs varied greatly in capacity and focus, several attended to building a skilled bureaucracy and developing administrative procedures (Elstob 1979). During this four-century period these improvements in state capacities were often focused particularly on supporting Sweden's regular involvement in warfare. Monarchs were frequently able to reduce the Riksdag's effectiveness in limiting their prerogatives by playing the noble and other members of parliament off against each other. So, in spite of a history of multiple constitutions and a breadth of representation that was generous by then extant European standards, Sweden experienced periods of arbitrary monarchical rule. Indeed, the principle that the head of the national government (i.e., a prime minister and cabinet) were collectively responsible to the majority of the Riksdag was not clearly established until the end of the First World War.

So the path of Swedish political development took shape slowly. It has culminated to date in a parliamentary democracy with certain distinctive national features. Prominent among these is an exceptionally able national bureaucracy which is particularly active in exhaustively studying various social issues, recommending legislative innovations designed to mitigate social problems and formulating many of the details of these parliamentary solutions (Anton 1980). Accordingly, these central Swedish political institutions interact quite differently than do their American counterparts that I discussed in the previous section. Sweden does not exhibit the decentralization and fragmentation for which the United States is so well known. First, the representation of interests in Swedish society has been much more thoroughly organized and centralized into peak associations than in the United States. For instance, Sweden has had exceptionally high rates of unionization among its blue- and white-collar workers, and for most of the postwar period a substantial proportion of these workers were represented by central national spokespersons through the LO, the major Swedish trade union congress. The interests of business, particularly big business, have also been centrally represented through the Swedish Employers Federation (SAF). At least until the 1970s this corporatism was a largely voluntary two-sided version (i.e., relatively free of government involvement) distinct from the three-sided (inclusive of government) form characteristic of West-central Europe (Olsen 1996).

Second, as Steinmo (1993) explains, until the early 1970s the institutions of Swedish politics fostered considerably more incentives for compromise and collaboration among the various political parties than the alternatives employed in the United States (see also Anton 1980, 146). For example, there is a long-standing tradition of the government appointing expert commissions to examine prominent social issues and the parliament transforming commission reports into legislation (Kelman 1981). While this process has surely been subject to dispute, it remains remarkable in contrast to individualistic American practices whereby the representatives of numerous and diverse specific interests rarely defer to expertise about the collective good in such a fashion, organizing instead more decentralized and adversarial conflict-resolution procedures. Further, until the early 1970s Sweden's system of elections and representation created powerful incentives for other political parties to cooperate with the Social Democratic Party (SAP), which has dominated Swedish politics since the early 1930s (Steinmo 1993, 81-85). Representatives were elected to both chambers of parliament through proportional representation. In the upper chamber, however, only one-eighth of the chamber stood for each election and their terms were eight years. Thus the chances that any given election would produce sharp changes in party representation were extremely low. Through its lengthy popularity, the SAP gradually acquired a majority in the upper chamber. While the SAP has routinely had the largest representation of any party in the lower chamber since the early 1930s, it has frequently not had a majority. Rather, it generally works out compromises with various other parties on specific matters. Because the SAP could easily reject the legislative products of coalitions or blocks among other parties in the upper chamber until that chamber's dissolution in 1970, other parties were better off compromising with the SAP in the lower chamber than trying to put together a coalition of their own.

Collectively, these two features of interaction among Swedish political institutions comprise a distinctive version of corporatist centralization. Through the 1970s various labor interests were aggregated at the national level through the LO, and a similar process occurred with respect to business interests via the SAF. Across roughly the same period government initiatives were also coordinated through the use of expert commissions and SAP-dominated party compromises in the lower chamber of the Riksdag. Swedish political officials have developed institutional interaction patterns that facilitate coordinated approaches to constructing political programs designed to serve broad social objectives.

The extraordinary—by American standards at least—centralization of powerful Swedish political institutions in a fashion designed to foster accommodation provides a clear index of a society in which the adherents of high-group cultures are numerous and influential. Individualists fear that such institutions will tyrannize minority interests by enacting majority preferences and prefer the decentralized and limited political institutions that predominate in the United States. In turn, relations among these institutions are more adversarial (Anton 1980, 141-46; Heclo and Madsen 1987; Kelman 1981).

A caveat should be appended to this portrayal of Swedish political institutions which emphasizes how they differ from their American counterparts. Since the 1970s the pattern of corporatist cooperation and compromise that I have described has experienced difficulties. The increasingly global character of capital markets has sharpened differences in the interests of various sectors of business, and SAF coordination has atrophied accordingly (Olsen 1996, 14; Stephens 1996). Likewise, aspects of economic globalization have caused disruption of labor markets, sharpening differences between the interests of blue- and white-collar workers. As a result, the LO's capacity to coordinate the strategies of various unions has declined. Additionally, the 1970 decision to phase out the upper chamber of the Riksdag, prompted by the Liberal Party as a means for making government more responsive to the citizenry, removed an important incentive for interparty cooperation. As a consequence the comparatively smooth and efficient operation, characteristic of Swedish parliamentary politics for the quarter century following the Second World War, has been replaced by greater interparty conflict and increasing difficulties in producing legislation.

Culture.   Grendstad (1999) provides data on how Sweden's society is distributed across grid-group theory' four cultures. (See table 2.1.) Among the general public, egalitarians hold a slight edge over hierarchists (39 to 37 percent) while individualists and fatalists linger far behind (12 percent each). As I discuss below, it seems likely that among Sweden's political elites, hierarchists and particularly individualists are currently more numerous than these data on the general population suggest, the former perhaps outnumbering egalitarians among political elites. But many who study Sweden concur that egalitarians (in the varying guises of communists, Greens, labor union supporters and social democrats) are, by the standards of most other societies, exceptionally numerous and influential (Furniss and Tilton 1977; Esping-Andersen 1990; Heclo and Madsen 1987; Kelman 1981; Stephens 1996; Heckscher 1984; Petersson 1994; Lane et al. 1993).

As I suggested in my earlier discussion of American political cultures, the relative prominence of rival cultures among organized political elites is usually a more influential factor in shaping societal institutions than the relative frequency of their adherents among the population generally, and objectives common to the high-group cultures are very much in evidence among Sweden's political elite (Anton 1980, 149). Social concerns shared by Christian and secular socialist egalitarians, for instance, have been instrumental in providing persistent support for the Swedish welfare state (Furniss and Tilton 1977; Einhorn and Logue 1989). Yet while Swedish political institutions clearly reflect strong high-group (i.e., egalitarian and hierarchical) influence among Swedish political elites, individualists are present as well.

Table 2.1 Proportions of the Citizens of Twelve European Societies Adhering to Grid-Group Theory's Rival Cultures (1990)

Society	Hierarchy	Egalitarianism	Individualism	Fatalism
Norway	23	45	17	15
Denmark	18	53	17	12
Sweden	37	39	12	12
Iceland	39	45	6	10
United Kingdom	23	21	18	38
Ireland	18	21	21	40
The Netherlands	28	47	11	14
Belgium	22	24	18	36
West Germany	15	34	29	22
France	12	15	27	46
Spain	8	9	29	54
Italy	8	19	36	37

Source: Grendstad 1999, 473

Introducing Sweden's system of political parties will help to clarify the relative influence of rival cultures among Sweden's political elite. In contrast to the United States, in which two broad "catch-all" parties (Kirchheimer 1966) generally dominate, Sweden has a system of multiple, narrower parties which represent specific sectors of society. In some instances these sectors are the contemporary counterparts of various fifteenth-century estates (e.g., the clergy and the peasants). The Social Democratic Party (SAP) initially represented the industrial working class, but after the Second World War it broadened its constituency to include portions of urban white-collar workers and professionals. It has historically held egalitarian objectives, although—as we shall see shortly—the cultural purity of the means by which it has pursued these objectives has varied between mobilizing rhetoric and governing practice. Throughout the postwar period Sweden has also had a small communist party (now the Left Party) whose primary importance has been augmenting SAP influence in the lower chamber of the Riksdag (parliament) at a few junctures. There is, as well, a small egalitarian party of Greens. The Liberal Party has represented the individualistic perspective in Swedish politics as have, more recently, segments of the New Democracy Party (Steinmo 1993, 190). The Liberals, in conjunction with the Centre Party (representing agricultural interests), the Christian Democrats and what was long known as the Conservative Party (now the Moderate Party) have frequently formed a "bourgeois bloc." Among particularly the Christian Democrats and the Moderate Party, however, hierarchy is a significantly more prominent orientation than individualism.

CONTRASTING TAX REGIMES

I focus on variation in four characteristics of societal tax regimes. First, I am interested in the overall level of extraction. Second, I examine different views about the appropriate nature of public purposes which underlie taxation and prompt distinctive approaches to taxes. Such purposes include securing social order against external and internal threats, stimulating aggregate demand, encouraging savings/penalizing consumption, directing investment productively and redistributing income (Steinmo 1993, 3). Third, I compare the relative progressivity of societal tax packages which effects various social strata differently. Progressive taxes increase their rates as income rises. So, for example, a progressive income tax may appropriate income between $15,000 and $30,000 at 15 percent and income over $30,000 at

30 percent. A regressive tax, in contrast, increases its effective rate as income declines. Thus a 5 percent sales tax on $100 of goods (a $5 tax) represents a higher proportion of income for a person with a $20,000 income than for a person with a $30,000 income. Advanced-industrial societies rely primarily on five revenue sources: taxing personal income, consumption, property and corporate profits as well as collecting payroll deductions for various social insurance programs. While direct taxes (i.e., most save for those on consumption) are not always applied progressively, there are few technical (as opposed to political) barriers to building progressivity into them. Indirect taxes on consumption, such as sales or value-added taxes, have a strong propensity toward regressivity, and value-added taxes are also partially hidden from public view. That is, value-added taxes are applied at each stage in a good's processing (e.g., an animal hide transformed into tanned leather and then fashioned into gloves) and incorporated in the price paid by each subsequent manufacturing stage. Taxes at all stages are passed along to the retail consumer who will likely be unaware as to how much of the price she pays represents the taxes applied at various stages of the manufacturing process. Fourth, I consider how tax effects vary across various economic sectors. Public sector decisions to facilitate certain avenues of private investment are likely to tax persons in similar social strata but distinct economic sectors differently.

TAX REGIME PREFERENCES OF RIVAL CULTURES

Suppose for the moment that we had no information about taxation practices in the United States and Sweden. What expectations might we be able to derive about the design of these societies' tax regimes, in terms of the four criteria I introduced above, from knowing that individualists are routinely highly influential in the former and that the latter has been, at least until very recently, a society in which high-group orientations have predominated and egalitarians have been exceptionally influential? By responding briefly to this question, I do not mean to set aside the important contributions of history and institutional structure to explaining policy design. I reincorporate these variables in my analysis in the subsequent sections of this chapter. But in this and the other policy chapters of this study I want to highlight the predictive capacities derived from using the relative influence of grid-group theory's rival cultures among a society's relevant organized political elites as a "proximate" independent variable for policy preferences. That is, these cultures form the last step on a path of causal variables that contribute to shaping persons' policy preferences. Including all three steps (history, institutions and culture) provides a more complete explanation of policy design, but we may be able to predict persons' policy preferences from the last step: their culture.[5] As Hirschman (1970) contends, social situations generally leave persons multiple options for action, such as exit, voice and loyalty. Sweden's difficulty in providing employment for its expanding population at the end of the nineteenth century, for instance, moved some (relatively egalitarian) workers to agitation for various public sector reforms (voice), prompted other (more individualistic) workers to seek their fortunes elsewhere through emigration (exit), and caused still other (more hierarchical) workers to draw more deeply on their faith in the wisdom of societal elites (loyalty). Persons choose to respond differently when confronted by similar situations, and knowing their culture helps us to predict what choices they will make. So what predictions can we make about the contrasting tax regime preferences of individualists and the adherents of the high-group cultures?

First, we should expect individualists to prefer relatively modest extraction of private resources to the public sector. This preference is so strong that only extraordinary societal crises are apt to deflect individualists from pressing for this objective. In this manner, individualistic cultures maximize the degree to which material resources are left where individualists think that they are most productively employed: in the hands of capable self-interested private individuals. Second, individualists are apt to seek a limited range of objectives or values through state activity. They focus primarily on securing social (particularly economic) order from selected external and internal threats and, secondarily, on limited and rather narrow commitments to macroeconomic management and social welfare (Esping-Anderson 1990).

Third, individualists routinely perceive humans' varying social circumstances as arising largely from different conscious purposes among persons with roughly equal capacities (i.e., some choosing to become investment bankers, others preferring to hew sculptures). Further, in light of this view of "authored" lives, they also characteristically hold that equal citizens draw equal benefits from the services of the limited governments which individualists sanction. Accordingly, they favor roughly equal (as a percentage of income) tax obligations across the income distribution. These views place individualists in sharp opposition to hierarchists and egalitarians who—for distinct reasons—are more predisposed toward progressive taxes. For egalitarians, progressive taxes are fair both to the wealthy, whose privileged circumstances are not truly earned (Rawls 1971),[6] as well as to those of limited income, who experience a far more modest tax bite and for whom the higher tax rates of the economically comfortable provide a funding source for various public income maintenance and social service programs.

For hierarchists, who perceive sharp inequalities among persons' practical capacities and moral virtues, progressive taxes are a form of noblesse oblige, funding the sorts of public programs that less capable members of society require for their welfare. In contrast to these two high-group cultures, individualists perceive no principled case for progressive taxation. Because individualists perceive human environments—both natural (Locke, *Second Treatise,* ch. 5) and social (Nozick 1974)—as filled with opportunities, and humans—at least against this background—as having roughly equal capacities and the proper orientation—self-interestedness—for meeting their needs, they see humans as better able to master their own fates in the absence of differentiating tax rates.

Fourth, individualists are particularly wary about taxing entrepreneurial success. For them, persons who create jobs have an exceptional status. If the returns on their investment of capital and know-how are taxed unreasonably, then they will be less inclined to contribute their exceptional resources to innovations that will allow society to prosper. Accordingly, among societies in which individualists are influential, we should expect to find various forms—individualized to meet varying circumstances—of preferential tax treatment for job-creation contributions.

High-group societies, particularly those in which egalitarian influence is exceptionally strong, should follow different tax policy preferences. First, both high-group cultures have, in practice, come to accept high levels of state activity and thus taxation as desirable.[7] Second, high-group societies, especially those with extensive egalitarian influence, are among the most enthusiastic supporters of active welfare states. They fund an ambitious range of social programs through exceptionally high rates of extraction of private resources to the public sector. This extraction allows democratic procedures to see to it that members of society have access to various benefits (e.g., social services such as education and medical care as well as transfer payments for aging, unemployment and disability) that help them to deal with the vicissitudes of life, rather than leaving such matters to the operation of impersonal markets or the vagaries of private charity. The high-group cultures disagree as to precisely why the welfare state is good. Hierarchists see it as necessary in light of sharp human inequalities in practical capacities and morality; while egalitarians see it as necessary for offsetting the remarkably different social environments that confront broadly equal humans. Because they cannot see social leveling as a good idea, hierarchists are less ambitious in their redistributive schemes than are egalitarians. Hierarchists have, as well, a more difficult time with democracy than egalitarians. But most contemporary democratic procedures (e.g., various levels of representation among elected officials and the growing influence of bureaucratic expertise) provide buffers between ordinary persons and the formulation of public policy.[8]

Third, in their redistributive ideals, and thus commonly in their rhetoric, egalitarians are routinely advocates of highly progressive taxation. In actual practice three factors tend to dampen this preference even in societies in which egalitarians are unusually influential. For one, the government activities which egalitarians also value highly require vast resources for their support, and, given the distribution of income among advanced-industrial societies, substantial taxation of the middle classes is necessary in order to raise sufficient revenue.[9] Another factor is that, among advanced-industrial societies, egalitarians are rarely in a position to realize their preferences entirely. They characteristically require support from hierarchical (social) conservatives or individualistic (i.e., "classical" Locke-Smith) liberals. Neither of these latter cultures, especially individualism, is inclined to push progressive taxation to the degrees that egalitarians prefer. A final, related factor is that, in societies in which private capital is an important economic resource, egalitarians have had to confront one of the ways in which the world works. If taxes reduce returns on capital investment in ways that capitalists oppose in principle or below capitalists' expectations of what they can get elsewhere, capital is apt to "strike" or, as a consequence of progressive economic globalization, increasingly to flee. In democracies at any rate, investment must be enticed, not coerced.

So, fourth, even high-group governing coalitions in which egalitarian influence is strong are apt to be cautious about taxing the returns on capital. In practice, such governments prefer to increase the breadth and depth (i.e., the revenue efficiency) of other taxes in order to support extensive public social program benefits than to sharply restrict capitalists in their returns on investment (Steinmo 1993, 156-60). As we shall see shortly, however, high-group societies are apt to protect capital through means distinct from those employed in societies in which individualists predominate. High-group societies are more apt to rely on revenue-efficient indirect taxes that are, in effect, shielded from public view and also to favor specific classes of capital that appear particularly promising from the standpoint of fostering national economic objectives.

The United States Tax Regime

Variables in all three of the explanatory categories that we consider in this study contribute to the United States closely fitting the tax regime profile just developed for a society with a high degree of individualistic influence. First, in spite of growth in government capacities and activities across the Progressive, New Deal/Second World War and Great Society episodes, the United States supports a government whose tax revenues, as a percentage of Gross Domestic Product (GDP), are often smaller than those of any other advanced-industrial society: generally, slightly less than 30 percent—from all levels of government—across the mid-1960s into the early 1990s (Witte 1985, 151; Congressional Budget Office 1987, 6; Pechman 1987, 31; OECD 1994).[10] The only close competitors for the United States in this regard are Japan and Australia. (See table 2.2.) Among the Scandinavian societies, in contrast, tax revenues have ranged from the upper 30s to the mid-50s in terms of percentage of GDP across this same period (Steinmo 1993, 132).[11] Even among the continental welfare states—Esping-Andersen's (1990) "corporatist" societies of Italy, France, Austria and Germany—public revenues have been 5 to 15 percent higher, as a proportion of GDP, than in

Table 2.2 Total Public Sector Revenues of Selected OECD Societies as a Percentage of GDP (1991)

Sweden (highest in the OECD)	60.0
Denmark	55.5
Norway	55.3
Netherlands	54.1
Finland	53.3
Belgium	50.2
Austria	47.2
France	46.1
Germany	45.3
Italy	43.3
Canada	43.1
Ireland	40.3
United Kingdom	38.8
Spain	38.6
Iceland	36.3
Japan	34.4
Australia	33.7
United States	32.2

Note: This table includes the societies in table 2.1 and, to support other comparisons made in this study, Australia, Austria, Canada, Finland, Japan, and the United States as well.
Source: OECD 1994, 40–41

the United States (OECD 1997, 1995, 1985). So while a few other advanced industrial societies have public sectors roughly as small in comparison to their economies as that of the United States, the United States is routinely near the bottom of the distribution in this regard. Further, none of the other advanced industrial societies which are close to the United States in terms of the size of their public sectors has been the leader of a worldwide set of military alliances. The United States runs on an unusually small public sector in spite of its exceptional international military obligations.

Second, the United States is well known for its fidelity to a Lockean conception of limited government. Complementary aspects of the cultural biases of its initial immigrants, a lengthy period of relative bounty with respect to real property as well as comparatively mild historical contingencies, and the early course (circa 1787) set for its institutional development path combine to support this outcome. United States hesitancy with respect to initiating and its subsequent incomplete realization of the expensive social programs associated with the modern welfare state are legendary, eliciting adjectives from "laggard" (Wilensky 1975) to "selective" (Skocpol 1987). While the contemporary American welfare state is not insubstantial, it pales in comparison to those of welfare state leaders in Western Europe, primarily due to the absence of a national health insurance program and the limited character of its support for families with children (OECD 1997). The United States has employed its limited public sector to support a narrower range of values and their associated practical political interests than have many other advanced industrial societies, particularly Sweden.

Third, the overall tax burden of American citizens is pretty flat across a broad range of incomes (Pechman 1985, 4). Witte finds that the limited progressivity which exists in some elements (e.g., the federal personal income tax) is largely attributable to revenue emergencies (i.e., meeting wartime expenses) rather than to preferences for progressivity (262). He characterizes the overall United States tax burden as proportional across the income distribution (4, 374). In particular, the American tax burden is noticeably flatter across the income distribution than its Swedish counterpart (Steinmo 1993, 2). The varying assumptions of different estimates lead to moderately different portrayals, but the American tax burden appears to rise very slowly and smoothly through a range from the lower 20s to the upper 20s (as a percent of income) across the income distribution. As we shall examine more closely shortly, for much of the postwar period the United States has had income tax rates that are more progressive than those of many other societies, yet the actual tax burden—as a percentage of income—has been nearly proportional. This seeming paradox occurs in spite of the fact that the United States continues to rely more heavily on taxes that have greater potential for progressivity than do some other societies.

In the United States, personal income taxes are the largest contributor to public sector revenue, with payroll taxes coming in a close second.[12] Income taxes are the classic example of progressive taxation. They were introduced across a range of societies early in the twentieth century as a means of increasing government revenues (generally to meet the expenses of war) and for taxing progressively (and thus in a way that adherents of the high-group cultures think is more fair). In practical application, American income taxes have been sharply progressive only during the period of the Second World War and have since become increasingly less progressive (Witte 1985, 262, 374). There are no significant technical obstacles to progressivity in payroll taxes, although the most prominent American payroll tax, that paid by individuals for social security, has capped the income subject to taxation and has thus been regressive at the upper end of the income distribution. In a technical sense, corporate profits taxes are also easily amenable to progressive application, although the United States has not relied heavily on such taxes nor employed them in a highly progressive mode. Many other advanced-industrial societies rely far more heavily on consumption taxes (e.g., sales and value-added taxes) than does the United States. Even if these taxes exempt many necessities such as food, they tend to be regressive because low-income persons generally spend higher proportions of their income than do persons with high incomes. Property taxes, again a modest contributor to the overall American tax burden, also tend to be regressive in application.

So the lack of progressivity to the actual tax burden in the United States appears in spite of relatively heavy American reliance on taxes that could easily be applied progressively. Indeed, for most of the postwar period, American income tax rates have been more progressive than those of many other advanced-industrial societies. "Tax expenditures" are responsible for this seeming inconsistency (Witte 1985). The American federal income tax code, in particular, is full of these expenditures, which allow persons to ignore certain types of income for tax purposes or to deduct particular expenses from their taxable income. Even the most widespread and thus expensive tax expenditures—deducting property taxes and mortgage interest on homes from income—have moderately regressive effects (276-87).[13]

So fourth, as Witte (1985, 377) and Steinmo (1993) both stress, a prominent aspect of what "tax reform" has meant in practice with respect to the federal income tax codes for both individuals and corporations has been the further extension of tax expenditures. Large numbers of specific riders to other legislation allow particular industries or, more commonly, corporations or persons more lenient rules than those applied generally. This is routinely accomplished through informal logrolling without much explicit conscious consideration of the consequences these "favors" hold for macroeconomic criteria. That is, these tax expenditures are commonly granted "individualistically" to persons or corporations on the basis of idiosyncratic pleas rather than to broad classes of industry pursuant to criteria designed to serve some explicit collective purpose such as redirecting investment from "sunset" to "sunrise" industries. By the early 1980s, tax expenditures of this sort amounted to the equivalent of 75 percent of federal income tax receipts (Witte 1985, 292).

SWEDEN'S TAX REGIME

Sweden fits the profile that I outlined earlier for the tax regime of a society in which the high-group cultures, particularly egalitarianism, are highly influential. First, among advanced-industrial societies, Sweden is either at or near the top in terms of public revenues as a percentage of GDP (Pechman 1987, 31). (See table 2.2.) Between the mid-1960s and the early 1990s, Sweden's public revenues ranged from nearly 40 to over 50 percent of GDP (Andersson 1987, 62). Proportionally to GDP, then, the United States' public sector was only about 75 to 50 percent as large as Sweden's.

Second, Sweden's lengthy early experiences with warfare—waged at times on Swedish territory—fostered the development of the high-grid cultures as opposed to individualism. Under these circumstances the idea that individual humans are capable of mastering their own fates was simply not credible to many Swedes. These circumstances cultivated as well reliance on a capable central government, particularly its executive. So Sweden's historical experiences produced both the presence and acceptance of active government.

As Sweden's challenges have shifted from national defense and territorial aggrandizement to coping with the social dislocation associated with industrialization and managing prosperity in an era of globalization, Swedish adherents of the high-group cultures have—for different reasons detailed earlier—become enthusiastic supporters of an active welfare state. Administrative reforms begun in Sweden long before the United States existed have produced a predisposition toward solving these new problems with a range of coordinated programs—education, medical care, child care, income maintenance and job placement—that enable an exceptionally broad range of persons to acquire full membership (Walzer 1983) in society. During the late 1980s and early 1990s, many Swedes (mostly individualists—see Nordlund and Coughlin 1998; Lane et al. 1993) contended that social programs had gone too far, and a "bourgeois bloc" which governed during 1991–1994 trimmed social programs (Olsen 1996; Stephens 1996; Lindbeck 1997). Yet Swedish society now appears to have reached a broadly acceptable compromise at a level of public social program support sharply above anything conceivable in the United States. The Swedes have reduced the generosity of some social programs, yet they remain clearly more interested in raising the revenue required for an extremely active welfare state than they are in further reducing their levels of taxation.[14]

Third, individual Swedish tax-payer burdens, while varying in a pattern distinct from that of the United States, do not fit all aspects of the profile that we might imagine for a high-group society in which egalitarians form the most numerous and influential political culture. The incidence of personal tax burdens rises more steeply from low to upper-middle incomes than in the United States, and the highest overall burdens experienced by individuals are much heavier (peaking at over 65 percent). But the burden declines somewhat for relatively high-income persons (Steinmo 1993, 2). Swedish corporate tax rates are now lower than those in the United States, but the effectiveness of this tax as a revenue producer is diminished in any case by a series of generally broad investment-stimulating tax expenditures (Olsen 1996, 6). As Steinmo (1993, 117) explains, the origins of these anomalies between social democratic preferences for taxing the wealthy heavily and Swedish public practices of limiting the tax burdens of the wealthy lie in practical necessity. Even in Sweden, where social democrats have arguably been more numerous and influential than in any other advanced industrial society, they have not dominated political institutions. The SAP has routinely needed the support of one or more of the "bourgeois" parties for major legislative initiatives, and the relatively smooth-flowing corporatism that I described in the section on Swedish political cultures, relying on expert commissions and interparty cooperation among other institutions, required compromises. Governing SAP leaders came early on to the conclusion that taxing capital gently was necessary for securing a degree of bourgeois acquiescence for the SAP's social agenda (117, 88-91, 156–60).

Sweden nonetheless follows different taxation practices than those employed in the United States. Sweden relies heavily—even more heavily than the United States—on personal income taxes to support its public sector. But Sweden makes less of an effort to augment personal income taxes with either corporate profits taxes or property taxes. Instead, the vast bulk of public revenues beyond those attributable to income taxes are raised in roughly equal amounts through payroll taxes and a stiff value-added tax (Pechman 1987, 31). It is Sweden's reliance on these taxes, particularly the latter, which is regressive in the upper stretches of the income distribution, rather than any extensive program of personal tax expenditures, that largely accounts for the reduced burden of taxation among high income persons (Andersson 1987, 67). Thus in contrast to American practices, the Swedish approach treats broader categories of persons similarly and raises extensive revenues more efficiently.

Fourth, tax expenditures have typically been employed in Sweden in a more disciplined fashion than in the United States. In Sweden, they are more obviously instruments of the government's macroeconomic objectives and designed to achieve collective societal benefits. Accordingly, these expenditures tend to favor specific classes of capital that appear promising from the standpoint of fostering national economic objectives. During the years 1991–94, when the "bourgeois bloc" governed, Swedish tax structure changed mostly so as to realize egalitarian values less fully and individualistic values more clearly. Personal income tax rates for high-income citizens were reduced, and regressive value-added taxes were increased. But tax expenditures were also further systemized and modestly reduced. The SAP has reversed some of these "bourgeois bloc" changes since returning to the government in 1994 (Olsen 1996, 8, 10).

HISTORY, INSTITUTIONS, CULTURE AND CAUSALITY

Virtually all analysts attribute—at least implicitly—some influence to varying societal historical experiences in explaining cross-societal policy differences. Yet most contemporary analysts emphasize aspects of institutional structure in their explanations of political outcomes, such as the tax regime features on which I have focused. These institutionalists vary in the degree to which they admit culture as an explanatory variable. March and Olsen (1989) are relatively open to what others (Kreps 1990; Legro 1996) call institutional cultures, but even institutionalists in this vein are hesitant about recognizing any explanatory capacity for cultural sources exogenous to the institutional environments of adult political actors. Another group of institutionalists, who have adopted a perspective they call historical institutionalism, are even more skeptical about culture as an explanatory variable (Steinmo, Thelen and Longstreth 1992). Among historical institutionalists,

Steinmo has focused the greatest attention on explaining tax regimes, arguing, for instance, that the "fragmented, decentralized system of 'committee government'" (1995, 324) explains the character of the American tax regime. For him, the "basic institutional features of American politics have shaped the incentives of tax policy-makers" (327) so that "Madison's institutional fragmentation protects small factions against large ones" (328). For institutionalists in this vein, culture does not shape institutions, but rather the reverse: "Not only have the fragmented political institutions shaped specific public policies in America; they have also, over time, shaped our national values and political culture" (328).

This last sentence offers an exceptionally clear statement of what, among institutionalists, is a sometimes implicit historical-experience, developmental-path-of-broad-political-institutions, culture, design-of-specific-policies causal sequence. This sequence has explanatory value, but it misses some significant, if often intermittent, causal and purposive processes. Paths of institutional development do help to form and support cultures. The beliefs and values that they embody shape some views of many persons who work within various institutions (March and Olsen 1989) and contribute to the early socialization of successive generations (Rohrschneider 1994). These paths also influence the fortunes of various cultures by facilitating some courses of action and hindering others. Significant policy innovation is, for instance, generally easier for centralized and relatively coordinated national governments than it is in the decentralized and fragmented United States.

Yet these claims for institutional influence have their limits. The design of broader institutions (e.g., constitutional fragmentation) certainly contributes to the character of specific policies (e.g., tax policy). But the form of these broader institutions cannot explain their own design. Rather, this explanation must be exogenous, and the distinctive institutional and policy designs favored by the adherents of rival cultures whose relative social influence develops from varying societal experiences offer promising sources for this explanation.[15] Institutionalists sometimes ignore half of the symbiotic loop involving culture and institutions and thus overlook evidence revealing that cultures help to shape and sustain institutions. In particular, they neglect the "multicultural" character of societies and the preferences which the adherents of rival cultures hold for distinctive institutional designs. These conflicting preferences fuel a social process whereby the adherents of rival cultures compete in striving to build disparate institutions because the respective institutions' contrasting features realize the different sets of constrained beliefs and values distinctive to each culture.

For instance, when the Liberal Party mounted a campaign against the upper chamber of the Swedish Riksdag in the late 1960s, it did so partly for the instrumental reason of wanting to increase its capacity for transforming its legislative proposals into policy. The upper chamber had long been dominated by the SAP and was unreceptive of Liberal legislation. But the Liberal campaign was also based on fundamental Liberal (individualistic) beliefs and values: e.g., that representative bodies ought to proportionately reflect the varying current views of roughly equal citizens. So there was as well a principled element to the Liberal initiative; removing the upper chamber was designed to make and actually made parliament more representative in this sense than it had been previously.[16] In contrast, at an earlier juncture the hierarchical Conservative Party had insisted on an upper chamber, designed to resist popular passing fashions, because of its skepticism that ordinary persons or their representatives had the capacity to guide the social collective in a constructive fashion. Similarly, when the "bourgeois bloc" governed in the early 1990s, the Swedish tax regime changed in ways reflecting individualistic beliefs and values more fully than their egalitarian counterparts.

So relations between culture and institutions are symbiotic: each influences the other. For instance, Inglehart (1997) shows that gradual trends of increased macroeconomic prosperity (i.e., historical contingencies prompting changes in various economic institutions) produced intergenerational cultural change that has, in turn, contributed importantly to transformations in political institutions (e.g., party systems and public policies). Culture and institutions thus work in tandem, and causality flows both ways. Yet for some inquiries one side of this symbiotic loop may be more relevant than the other, and this suggestion returns us to a question posed in the introduction to this chapter: What other changes would be required (and how might they come about) for the United States to adopt a tax regime similar to Sweden's?

How, If at All, Might the United States Emulate Sweden's Tax Regime?

In what, if any, contingencies can those American adherents of the high-group cultures, who want their society to emulate the aspects of the Swedish tax regime that we have examined, anticipate success? Few seem likely, but let us examine why. A starting point is provided by the structural argument that the fragmentation of existing American political institutions makes such a policy shift extremely difficult. Further, these existing institutions are unlikely to socialize Americans to new patterns of cultural allegiance (e.g., more hierarchy or egalitarianism and less individualism). In this sense institutions are the guardians of stability and inertia; they represent "crystallizations" of cultural preferences dominant in the past. As Inglehart (1997) suggests, instances of substantial political change are explained by cultural shifts that are characteristically prompted by significant historical contingencies which confront persons with new problems or opportunities that their existing institutions are ill-suited for overcoming or realizing.

For instance, even Americans occasionally favor more active public institutions and thus raise greater public revenue. The events that prompted United States involvement in the Second World War were perceived as threatening by many Americans who wanted a larger, more active state for security purposes. In other words, in reaction to this historical contingency some Americans moved "up-group" and "up-grid," becoming more hierarchical (i.e., favoring a more active state with greater coercive capacities) in response to foreign military threats. Wartime public revenues did represent a sharp break from previous experience, but it was spending that really shot up during the war. Even at the height of the war, federal revenues barely accounted for 25 percent of GNP; while federal expenditures approached 45 percent (Witte 1985, 151). The war was paid for by budget surpluses through the 1950s, during which federal spending fell far more sharply from war levels than federal revenues which have declined slowly as a percentage of GDP since the late 1940s. This experience suggests that even contingencies requiring serious resource mobilization for collective purposes may not prompt Americans to raise public revenues to levels rivaling Sweden's.

So cultural variables also offer a basis for skepticism about the United States emulating Sweden's tax regime, in that large proportions of American political elites and ordinary citizens do not want public sector revenues anywhere near as large as those which are routinely collected in Sweden. The most immediate explanation for this is that the populations (mass and elite) of these two societies are composed of sharply different cultural mixtures. For the large proportion of Swedes aptly characterized as high-group (i.e., egalitarians and hierarchists), public funding levels sufficient for a large active state are consistent with their differing, but nonetheless welfare-state-supportive beliefs about human environments, human nature and the values that their political institutions should serve. High-group Americans have similar preferences, but they form a much smaller proportion of their society's general population and political elite and are thus less influential in shaping public policy. Each of the high-group cultures in America appears outnumbered by individualists. The adherents of this latter culture hold views about human environments, human nature and the values that their political institutions should serve which lead them to prefer a modestly funded, relatively inactive state. It is reasonable, then, to imagine that we could not sharply upgrade the degree to which we extract resources from the private to the public sector in the United States without changing persons' cultures so that hierarchists and egalitarians became more numerous and individualists less frequent. And if their cultures changed in these ways, Americans would not only be amenable to higher public revenues, they would likely find appealing as well other high-group social structures, such as the more centralized, compromise-oriented political institutions found in Sweden, that would facilitate achieving their revised objectives.

We can improve on this cultural explanation of American tax regime preferences by considering why Americans have distinctive cultural predispositions. Americans are proportionately more individualistic than the citizens of Sweden and most other advanced industrial societies as a result of aspects of their society's history and their own personal experiences. The combination of factors such as relative economic bounty, ethnic diversity and few severe historical contingencies has fostered among Americans beliefs that persons can—may even need to—be the masters of their own fates, support for liberty which allows persons to achieve this objective and preferences for limited, relatively inactive government which facilitates these beliefs and values. Even Americans whose lives offer little support for these core beliefs and value priorities may nonetheless subscribe to them as a result of accepting the repeated exhortations of various socialization agents including the familiar structure of their existing political institutions.

We can also improve on the institutional explanation with which we started four paragraphs above by going behind the tax regime implications of institutional fragmentation and asking how the American political process came to be so fragmented and why it has remained so. This characteristic has its roots in the migration, to regions of North America that subsequently formed the United States, of persons who were more likely to disagree with prominent seventeenth- and eighteenth-century European political beliefs and practices than those who remained behind or who migrated to some other colonies (Lipset 1990). While these persons represented multiple cultural perspectives, their views had sufficient complementary aspects so that related political institutions that shared characteristics setting them apart from their European counterparts began to develop. The distinctiveness of these institutions was reinforced by the American Revolution, which drove many colonial Tories to Canada or England, as well as by the Constitution of 1787, which delineated a path for the development of political institutions that embodied selective aspects of this distinctive United States character.

In comparison to most other advanced industrial societies, even the more active central government that Madison and others created in 1787 is notable for its relative modesty and counterpoised (Lovejoy 1961) or fragmented decentralization. While the framers of this Constitution shared a desire for more capable government than the Articles offered, many of them also insisted on avoiding the sort of unbridled central authority through which England had smothered autonomy and freedom in the American colonies during the 1760s. The 1787 Constitution offers a clear example of the sorts of constraints on political institutions that individualists prefer. The skepticism—inherent to individualism—which this document evinces about powerful, coordinated public institutions, has not only been passed from generation to generation among individualists, but has also found sympathy among some American adherents of the high-group cultures seeking to protect themselves from the legislative excesses of the frequently dominant American individualists. Only dramatic historical contingencies have been able to prompt the development of an American public sector even roughly similar in size or activity level to those widely accepted across other advanced industrial societies. In the recent absence of such contingencies, the United States has shifted toward a tax regime and associated political institutions (e.g., more meager public social programs) with the features that I have argued individualists favor, a shift cultivated by the growing influence of individualists among American political elites in the past few decades.

Yet in spite of the breadth and depth of this explanation for the difficulty of the United States emulating the Swedish tax regime—which now draws on multiple historical, institutional and cultural elements—changes in societal experiences may alter citizens' cultural orientations. Shifts in influence among a society's cultures follow two general patterns. Likely the most common of these patterns involves the gradual (i.e., intergenerational), broad (i.e., mass and elite) change in cultural perspectives in response to long-term societal trends (e.g., industrialization or democratization) that Inglehart (1997) and Baker, Dalton and Hildebrandt (1981) chronicle. My example of the American reaction to the Second World War above offers an instance of another, contrasting, dual-process pattern. First, when persons' environments are transformed suddenly and significantly, their perceptions of how the world works and their beliefs and value priorities may change quickly. Persons effectively adopt another culture and shift their views about appropriate policies accordingly. But in order for a process of sudden cultural shifts among mass publics to be accompanied by sympathetic changes in public policy, it has to be reinforced by a second process through which the societal effects of disruptive historical contingencies prompt rapid change in the cultural composition of a society's political elite. In this second process, leaders adhering to one culture replace the adherents of another culture or perhaps the two elite factions form a coalition. Thus citizen dissatisfaction with the policies preferred by existing leaders to deal with socially disruptive circumstances brings adherents of a rival culture to power. The elite adherents of the ascendant culture are apt to replace some of the policies favored by the adherents of their receding rival with alternatives that better embody the formers' beliefs and values and afford new opportunities for overcoming the problems posed by the historical contingencies in question.

In the United States, for instance, the Great Depression emboldened and mobilized adherents of the high-group cultures while fostering uncertainty and hesitancy among individualists. Some individualists moved "up-group" and possibly "up-grid" in reaction to the social dislocations of the 1930s, becoming egalitarians or hierarchists (Wills 1987). In combination, these tendencies facilitated Roosevelt's formation of a dominant, hierarchical-individualistic (H-I) coalition which replaced Hoover's individualistic government and constructed a larger, more active state in response to the depression's socially disruptive effects. The replacement of some political elites (mostly individualists) with others (primarily persons with "bifocal" cultural biases drawing on hierarchy and individualism—see Lockhart 2001b, ch. 2) and the ensuing formation of a new dominant political coalition with this latter cultural orientation were crucial to producing the larger and more active New Deal state. Cox (2001) shows that related transformations occur in other societies.

Since the prevailing path of U.S. political development draws heavily on a Lockean preference for limited government, exceptional circumstances—historical contingencies posing sudden and severe social dislocation—are a necessary prerequisite for sharply expanding the size, activity and revenues of the American national government. These episodes attract new recruits to the American adherents of the high-group cultures and embolden the members of these cultures to more strenuous efforts at constructing public policies which embody their core beliefs and value priorities. Changes in the proportions of Americans who adhere to various cultures as well as shifts in the culture or cultural coalitions dominant among American political elites have occurred at several points across American political history in response to significant historical contingencies (Lockhart 2001a). These shifts are routinely accompanied by the pursuit of different political objectives and sharp changes in policy design aimed at realizing these revised purposes (e.g., replacing Hoover's individualistic, laissez-faire policy with the Roosevelt H-I coalition's programs of stimulating aggregate demand through increased public spending). But the timing and direction of these shifts do not appear to be easily amenable to purposive manipulation. Rather, sudden shifts in the proportions of Americans adhering to various cultures and in the cultural predispositions of dominant political elites are typically the consequences of developing historical contingencies (e.g., the attack on the World Trade Center) which prompt abrupt changes in the social environment and confront Americans with unanticipated problems and/or possibilities. In short, current American levels of extraction from the private to the public sector are apt to approach the level of Swedish practice only in reaction to historical contingencies whose socially disruptive effects would need to be at least as extensive as those produced by the combination of the Great Depression and the Second World War, thus cultivating the growth and coalition potential of the high-group cultures. Such contingencies appear rare and likely difficult to predict far in advance.

It is not yet clear whether the United States' current conflict with Islamic terrorists will prompt such changes. I think that, in itself, the World Trade Center attack will be insufficient to do so. If subsequent attacks of similar proportions eventually follow, then cultural change would be more likely. If Americans were routinely worried about highly destructive attacks by external adversaries disrupting their everyday lives, then many of them would surely move "up-group" and "up-grid," replacing their former high priority individualistic concerns about personal liberty and self-reliance with more hierarchical values for public safety and routinized collective help for persons unable to cope effectively with disruptive conditions beyond their control. For the moment, we shall simply have to wait to see how this situation develops. I return to this question in subsequent chapters, particularly chapter 5, where I think that what has already happened, along with likely future events, may be sufficient to move Americans in a hierarchical direction on immigration and citizenship issues. But similar movement on high-profile and extraordinarily expensive taxing and social program spending issues is apt to require more social disruption than we have experienced to date.

CHAPTER 3

Financing Medical Care in the United States and Canada

A t least as it has developed in the West, medical care is a social good (or a set of goods) which poses exceptional financing difficulties. The rapidly growing capabilities of practitioners to overcome the sickness and injury of their patients, and thus their potential for lengthening and improving the quality of life, make medical care an exceptionally important good. Persons' capacities for returning—from sickness or injury—to productive life frequently hinge on access to medical treatment. Yet the extensive scientific and technological efforts underlying an increasing proportion of these treatments makes them extremely expensive, placing even fairly mundane varieties of care beyond the means of many persons in the absence of schemes that transcend the private resources of households by spreading costs more generally via some form of insurance.

Walzer (1983) suggests that social goods carry inherent signals about the appropriate basis for their distribution. In his view, for instance, medical care should be distributed to a person (i.e., is a good for that person) if, and only if, she or he needs it. Accordingly, I do not want an appendectomy because I do not have appendicitis. Right now, an appendectomy represents a "bad" (pain and risk) for me rather than a good. Further, Walzer contends that these signals often produce widespread agreement among the members of particular societies with respect to the principles for the just distribution of various goods. Yet members of various societies routinely disagree about the nature of these inherent signals (Lockhart 1994). This disagreement appears vividly on medical-care financing issues in the United States. Walzer's conception of a consensus-garnering principle of need for the distribution of medical care is challenged by many Americans who perceive medical care as a "commodity" in the sense of being appropriately distributed by the ability to pay.

These contrasting views represent outcroppings of the distinctive cultural orientations that I examine in this study. Once again, the United States, in which individualists are unusually influential, is exceptional among advanced industrial societies. The view that Walzer espouses is widely institutionalized among such societies—including Canada—in various forms of what might generically be called "national health insurance." While such systems vary considerably from one society to another, they share a common concern of "decommodifying" significant portions of the medical care which these societies deliver. In the process they make these treatments available on the basis of need (sometimes augmented by modest patient copayments) and perhaps ancillary criteria such as queing on the basis of relative urgency and/or ability to benefit.

During the 1960s the United States moved closer to the practices of other advanced industrial societies by adopting significant public financial support for (implicitly need-based provision of) medical care for two specific populations, the elderly (Medicare) and portions of the poor (Medicaid), who have traditionally had particularly extensive needs for medical care but exceptionally limited access to it so long as it was distributed as a commodity. Nonetheless, the United States continues to stand apart from all other advanced industrial societies by leaving the provision of medical care for the vast majority of the population to the widely varying private capacities of individuals.

However, the unique combination of being a good that is both crucial, yet extremely expensive, has engendered a common American practice of private group insurance that is generally acquired through employment. But in contrast to varying national health insurance schemes, providers of private, group, employment-related, medical-care insurance remain businesses in competitive markets. In order to survive, they must make a profit or minimally avoid perpetual loses. This necessity leads to a host of limitations on both the breadth and depth of coverage. Generally, access to such insurance programs is directly related to marketplace power. Membership in high-status occupations or well-organized labor unions helps individuals to acquire coverage. Workers lacking these advantages are apt to have less-extensive or perhaps no insurance. Additionally, these policies characteristically involve more extensive limitations (e.g., for preexisting conditions) and require more extensive patient cost-sharing than do public systems in other societies.

So even in the United States, most medical care is provided through collective schemes, although for most citizens these schemes are private and market-based. The fragmented and disparate character of these schemes translates as well into significant variations in citizen experience. Persons with extensive insurance support enjoy medical care of exceptional quality, arguably better than that afforded citizens in any other advanced industrial society. Yet many Americans experience difficulties, virtually unknown in these other societies, obtaining even ordinary forms of medical care. Canada provides an interesting contrast to the United States because of its geographic proximity and its sharply different policy orientation, which has intrigued many American reformers.

CANADIAN HISTORY, INSTITUTIONS AND CULTURE

HISTORY

In contrast to Sweden, which, among advanced industrial societies, might be termed "most dissimilar" when contrasted with the United States, Canada and the United States represent a "most similar" pairing (Kornberg and Clark 1992, 255). Beginning in the sixteenth century both societies were formed by European migrants, English-speaking groups being prominent in each instance. Both have enjoyed relative isolation from the great powers of Europe and Asia and thus for two centuries have been free from military attacks by foreign powers. Canada has historically been more reliant on foreign trade, particularly with the much more populous United States. The two societies share many broad characteristics: liberal democracy, federalism, competitive economies fueled by private capital, and roughly similar overall standards of living, among others.

Many of the most obvious differences between the United States and Canada derive from the contrasting character of their initial migrants. Lipset (1990) contends that those who migrated to the portions of North America which eventually became Canada were more comfortable with the ideas and institutions then prevailing in Europe than were their counterparts who migrated to the North American regions that subsequently became the United States. This character was strengthened during the American Revolution by the relocation of many Tory loyalists from the American colonies to Canada. According to Clark: "Whereas the American nation was the product of a revolutionary spirit, the Canadian nation grew mainly out of forces of a counter-revolutionary character" (1962, 190-91; quoted in Lipset 1990, 10). Canada has thus been more broadly accepting of its European and particularly British legacy than has the United States, never mounting a revolution against Britain.

INSTITUTIONS

A more pronounced Anglophile heritage than that of the United States is clearly visible in Canada's political and other major societal institutions. For example, Canada remains into the present a member of the British Commonwealth, recognizing the queen as its head of state. Moreover, until fairly recently (1982), Canada lacked an independent constitution. Instead it relied on an act of the British parliament (the British North America Act of 1867). This act provided for the unification of the Canadian provinces into the dominion of Canada and functioned as the dominion's constitution. Additionally, it organized the Canadian national government on the British parliamentary example. These features contrast sharply with the early American desires for independence and continued American antistatist resistance to hierarchical trappings such as royalty.

Further, Canadian religious observances occur largely within the framework of three well-recognized, established churches: the Anglican, Roman Catholic and the ecumenical (Protestant) United Church. This practice is sharply at odds, not only with American efforts to separate church and state (particularly to avoid established churches), but as well with the American penchant for religious schisms and the proliferation of sects, both hierarchical and congregational in character. Canadian religious practices remain largely within the purview of long-standing traditions, while Americans proliferate new forms of religious observances in multifarious abundance.

Moreover, Canadian public spaces are marked by an elegance of design and maintenance. While their American counterparts may share the design element, they tend quickly to devolve toward what Galbraith (1958) referred to as "public squalor." The two sides of Niagara Falls offer a striking example. The beautiful Canadian side is largely public and exquisitely designed and maintained. Unsurprisingly, the American side is almost exclusively devoted to private commerce. Even this situation fails, however, to avoid squalor, for there is little evidence of Galbraith's "private opulence." Instead, private sleaze confronts the gorgeous public space across the Niagara River.

Additionally, various segments of Canadian opinion have long been institutionalized in separate, viable, national political parties: the (socially conservative) Conservative Party, the (economically conservative) Liberal

Party and the (social-democratic) New Democratic Party (NDP). These national parties compete at the provincial level with a host of regional parties, and the national parties (particularly the Liberal) have internal factions.[1] Nonetheless, Canada has long supported distinct national political parties with clear socially conservative and social democratic collectivist predispositions. In contrast, the United States has two major parties, each with a substantial contingent of economic conservatives and a varying assortment of the adherents of social conservatives and "social democrats." The Democratic Party is more "democratic" in this sense than the Republican, and for much of the twentieth century it achieved majority status by bringing segments of American "social democracy," economic conservatism and social conservatism together. However, this situation frequently hampered the initiation of legislation important to some of the party's supporters (e.g., guarantees of civil rights) since these proposals were anathema to other supporters. The Republican Party has traditionally been more economically conservative than the Democratic. But it periodically attracts a contingent of American social conservatives as well. In the 1970s the Democratic Party lost many social conservatives and some economic conservatives to the Republican Party, leaving the latter with a better current claim to majority status. Yet holding the economically conservative (i.e., George Bush, Sr.) and the socially conservative (i.e., Pat Buchanan) factions together represents quite a challenge for the Republicans. Nonetheless, neither American "social democrats" nor social conservatives have had any national success fostering a political party in the absence of a coalition with economic conservatives, and few adherents of the former two political orientations imagine much success for an American political party labeled either socialist or Tory.

Finally, as a transition to culture, Turner (1962) famously argues that the frontier gave American political culture its individualistic orientation, although Wills (1987, 94) believes that Taylor misjudges that orientation. Lockhart (1991) contends that a prominent culture of individualism shaped the character of the American frontier. Other societies have frontiers, but the character of frontier life varies across societies with different predominant cultures. Canada represents a case in point. Canadian national authorities sent the Royal Canadian Mounted Police into frontier regions contemporaneously with the earliest settlers (Lipset 1990, 91). Thus, order on the Canadian frontier was shaped in accordance with the preferences of these authorities. Consequently, the American tradition of volunteer posses or even vigilantes assisting a struggling local sheriff in maintaining a semblance of order and the accompanying self-reliant character of social life was never established.

CULTURE

As was the case for the United States in the previous chapter, attitudinal surveys of Canadians designed to ascertain the degree to which mass and elite publics adhere to the disparate cultural biases of grid-group theory's four rival cultures are lacking. Nonetheless, experts on Canadian society agree on the mixture of Canadian political cultures and particularly on how it differs from the American cultural mixture. I support their portrayal with survey data that distinguish Canadians from Americans in terms of beliefs and values distinctive to grid-group theory's rival cultures.

In comparison to the United States, Canada is a society in which both of the high-group cultures (i.e., hierarchy and egalitarianism) flourish and individualism languishes. Lipset (1990, 90) comments that Canada is likely the only society which relies on the police, the Royal Canadian Mounted Police, as a national symbol.[2] Hierarchy is obviously prominent. Yet Canada also exhibits clear indices of egalitarianism. Lipset thinks that we should not be surprised to find this combination, arguing that: "social democratic movements are the other side of statist conservatism: Tories and socialists are likely to be found in the same polity, while a dominant Lockean liberal tradition inhibits the emergence of socialism" (Lipset 1990, 149). As chapter 2 revealed, for instance, collaboration between the high-group cultures (hierarchical statist conservatism and egalitarian socialism) forms the basis for contemporary social democracy and the welfare state that it fosters, although Canada does not support as extensive a welfare state as a number of Western European societies (OECD 1985).

Lipset's characterization of Canadian political cultures is echoed by Hockin, who argues that Canada is dissimilar from the United States in that: "socialist and tory sentiments are admissible and natural" (1975, 10; quoted in Kudrle and Marmor 1981, 89). Kudrle and Marmor concur by pointing out that contemporary Canada supports not only "a significant socialist party, but there is also a distinctly un-American strain of paternalist thought on the right" (1981, 89). In comparison to the United States, then, Canada exhibits a less influential individualistic culture and more extensive egalitarian (social-democratic) and hierarchical (Tory) cultures.

While both societies reveal considerable internal cultural diversity, when Americans and Canadians are asked to express priorities among various values, significant cross-societal variation appears. For instance, Sniderman et al. (1988) constructed a series of questions juxtaposing the values of societal order and liberty (freedom of speech). They found that Canadians were much more willing than were their American counterparts to sacrifice personal liberty to order. These results suggest that the high-group cultures and particularly hierarchists are more numerous among the general public in Canada than in the United States. This conclusion is, in turn, consistent with the frequent observations of scholars that Canadians are more supportive of state regulation of individual behavior (e.g., interdiction roadblocks searching for drivers under the influence of alcohol) than are Americans, and are frequently openly dismissive of "rugged individualism" (Lipset 1990, 90). Similarly, a survey sponsored by the Science Council of Canada (1972) found that Canadian respondents were prone to the hierarchical values of safety and security with respect to investment and employment opportunities, respectively. Their American counterparts, in contrast, favored maximizing return (on investment) and salary (employment), thus revealing individualistic optimism about opportunity and less risk aversion than the more high-group Canadian respondents.

Among Canadians, beliefs about appropriate relations between government and business resemble those prominent in Sweden. That is, many Canadians see business's job as maximizing profits and think that it should not have to suffer much public regulation, which will hinder its efforts to this end. But this view engenders the complementary belief that a relatively active welfare state is a necessary corollary to such an unfettered market in order to smooth the rough edges of capitalism. In contrast, Americans are more prone to think that government should be judged by standards similar to those of business (e.g., economic efficiency), but they are more likely to favor regulating business in an effort to reduce or avoid disturbing outcomes (Lipset 1990, 132-33). Thus Canadians manifest more robust support for various public social programs (Lipset 1990, 139-40); whereas, Americans evince increasing hostility toward an active state and the increased taxes that it requires (Aaron 1996). These views are characteristic of the high-group cultures and individualists, respectively.

Additionally, in response to similar vignettes which force respondents to choose between the hierarchical value of social differentiation and the egalitarian goal of equality or, alternatively, between the individualistic objective of liberty and equality, more citizens in both societies favor social differentiation or liberty as opposed to equality. But among Canadians the proportions opting for equality in each case are substantially larger than among American respondents (Lipset 1990, 155-58). Similarly in actual life Canadians exhibit greater propensity for class consciousness and solidarity (e.g., labor union membership) than Americans, who are more oriented toward competitive individualism (Lipset 1990, 167-70).

CONTRASTING THE UNITED STATES AND CANADA

With one exception, Canada's experience with historical contingencies is not sufficiently different from the United States' to offer much help in explaining the sharp contemporary differences between these two societies in financing medical care. That exception is the political perspective dominant among its original immigrants, who set the development of Canadian political institutions on a path (e.g., retaining the crown and parliamentary form) evincing less concern for constraining state activity. By examining what some prominent Canadians say about the beliefs and values on which their system of medical-care delivery rests, we can get a better sense for the nature of cultural variations between the United States and Canada and their importance for differences in public policy.

Evans (1993) argues that a strong commitment to a mixture of hierarchical and egalitarian beliefs and values underlies the design of the Canadian system for delivering and financing medical care. For him: "At the most basic level, the public funding system embodies a view of the relationship between the individual and the environment." This view entails that: "When the patient recognizes a problem, she takes it to a professional, who diagnoses it and determines what treatment is medically necessary." This treatment generally carries no charge "because to charge the patient is to tax the sick" (10-11). This view of the patient needing help is characteristic of the high-group cultures. As Evans points out, "an alternative view might say that the natural environment provides ample opportunity to look out for oneself" (10). The belief that persons are capable of mastering their own fates is, as Evans suggests, among the most basic beliefs of individualists, and it lies at the foundation of most arguments between individualists and the adherents of the high-group cultures about the appropriateness of public social programs (Lockhart 2001b, ch. 9).

Yet hierarchists and egalitarians disagree as to why persons need external help and what sort of help they need. Hierarchists' rationale rests on beliefs in human inequality, the less capable (patient) needing the advice and support of the more capable (expert professional). For egalitarians, the problem lies in the varying degrees of difficulty that a heterogeneous environment poses for equal persons. A central city resident's health may be endangered by a variety of threats that impinge less severely on the life of a suburban resident. While professional consultation may be recognized as a necessity in the egalitarian perspective as well, the primary focus will be on the collective action of equal persons: creating a collective system of health care provision that, to paraphrase Marx, responds to individual needs and draws (through taxes) on individual abilities.

Evans (1993) portrays the Canadian national health insurance system as drawing as well on egalitarian values. He is dismissive, for instance, of the United Kingdom's (UK) willingness to allow those who can to buy medical care, superior in some respects to that offered through the UK's public National Health Service, in the private market. "Canada," he contends, "has a deep-rooted suspicion of class-based systems of any kind" (13). He concludes that, "while Canadian health care shares with European systems the underlying judgment that illness is an unavoidable misfortune, to be remedied by seeking and following professional advice with funding provided entirely or almost entirely through collective mechanisms, it differs in its powerful commitment to the principle that the provision of care and the pattern of funding should be the same for everyone" (14–15).

This last sentiment is echoed by Canadian Perrin Beatty, a Tory and former Minister of National Defense as well as Minister of National Health. He expresses dismay at an article in the *Chicago Tribune* critical of the Canadian national health insurance system because it, in effect, prohibits persons from buying a better quality of service or of accessing care more quickly by paying more. "The irony to me," Beatty avers, "was that, having grown up in our system, it never struck me that anybody would feel it was appropriate to buy better service or that someone could jump the line as a result of having money" (1993, 31).

Overall, Evans (1992) argues that: "The financing of health care thus serves as a mirror or a lens in which those dominant cultural values can be viewed and compared from one society to another" (159). He concludes that values prominent in the Canadian political culture differ from their U.S. counterparts in that: "the Canadian health care system reflects a strong commitment to egalitarianism combined with a strong respect for, and substantial confidence in, duly constituted authority" (165). Similarly, Lipset (1990) concludes that the United States remains predominantly Whig (Lockean individualism) while Canada retains both a more prominent Tory influence as well as what Lipset regards as the "flip-side" of hierarchical statism, a socialist influence.

CONTRASTING SYSTEMS OF MEDICAL-CARE FINANCING

MEDICAL-CARE FINANCING PREFERENCES OF RIVAL CULTURES

As in chapter 2, suppose we had no information about the organization of medical-care financing in the United States and Canada. What expectations might we be able to derive about the design of these societies' medical-care financing systems from knowing that individualists are more dominant in the former and that both of the high-group cultures are more prominent in the latter?

I want to structure a response to this question by drawing on three general medical-care delivery objectives (all carrying implications for medical-care financing) that numerous analysts recognize as compelling among advanced industrial societies: (1) achieving inclusiveness or the degree to which medical-care delivery approximates a goal of universal financial accessibility; (2) controlling expenses in terms of limiting total medical-care delivery costs as a percentage of GDP; and (3) assuring high-quality care, an objective which includes numerous criteria such as choice of providers, but focuses increasingly on the comprehensiveness of care, particularly access to cutting-edge treatments. Some analysts argue that it is possible for a society to do well on all three of these general objectives (Pollock 1993, 152-54). I think that these objectives require prioritizing and form what Fishkin (1983) calls a "trilemma." That is, doing well with respect to any two of these objectives, requires substantial sacrifices with respect to the third.

Each of grid-group theory's three socially interactive cultures is predisposed to sacrifice a different aspect of this trilemma. Individualists prefer to relax efforts aimed at achieving universal access in order to improve the quality of care for those who remain, while striving to deliver medical care in an economically efficient fashion. Hierarchists, or at least those hierarchists who must operate within the political ground rules of democratic, advanced industrial societies, are prone to sacrifice cost control in order to assure universal access and a relatively high quality of care. Egalitarians, in contrast, prefer to sacrifice the speed at which cutting-edge treatments—and perhaps other aspects of quality of care as well— are made generally available in order to assure universal access to a broad range of services and a manageable level of total expense. Let us examine how these preferences emerge from the cultural biases of these respective ways of life.

Individualists perceive human environments as beneficent and persons— against this encouraging background—as equally capable with respect to broad talents and as self-interested. They believe that persons are capable of mastering their own fates under these favorable conditions. Further, for individualists, medical care represents a commodity similar to other appropriately marketed goods ranging from coffee to yachts. Individualists think that each person ought ideally to be as self-reliant with respect to her medical-care needs or wants as she is with respect to these other goods. Individualists believe that creating public social programs to help some—or even all—persons obtain various goods, however well-intentioned, is an enterprise fraught with significant dangers. First, it invariably taxes some in order to help others. This sacrifices the liberty of the former (i.e., reducing their discretionary income) to the alleged welfare of the latter. But individualists interpret the welfare gains that others see in these efforts as a "mirage" (Hayek 1976a). They fear that providing such largesse holds destructive consequences for the recipients' incentives for self-reliance (Murray 1984). They are skeptical that self-interested persons will work to support themselves if public programs stand ready to provide benefits at the expense of others. Public social programs that distribute services such as medical care are even more pernicious than income-transfer programs since they entail regulating the professional activities of care providers. This practice again sacrifices liberty (individualists' normative lodestar) to—what are for individualists—dubious welfare claims. It is in this manner, Hayek believes, that the proverbial "road to hell" is paved with good intentions.

Accordingly, individualists prefer to leave the provision of medical care to private market interactions. Ideally, for them, medical care should not be addressed by public policy, and they are quick to label virtually all such efforts—regardless of their specific character—as "socialized medicine," a label that carries connotations of thorough regimentation including standardized services offering little sensitivity to individual needs. The traditional individualist ideal with respect to medical care is similar to the operation of other small businesses and entails individual practitioners plying fee-for-service medical care to patients who choose them as providers on the basis of the quality of their services. The growth in both the capacities and costs of medical-care services over the last few decades has, however, prompted adjustments in this model to allow both for layering and collective expertise (i.e., general practitioners backed up by specialists and group practices, respectively) to facilitate efficiency and private—generally group- and employment-based—insurance to manage the extraordinary costs. Individualists' preferred response to the medical-care needs of the indigent generally focuses on private charity applied preferably at the medical emergency stage. In the individualist's calculus the seeming heartlessness of such an approach is necessary in order to provide capable persons with the maximum incentives for mastering their own fates. Individualistic preferences for relying on markets as opposed to public programs foster a social environment which affords strong market incentives for scientific and technological medical-care innovation. Market competition also offers the hope of constraining price inflation and thus restraint with respect to overall medical-care costs. However, assuring financial access is not a priority. In this conception medical care is a commodity which is appropriately distributed largely by effective demand.

Among advanced-industrial societies, hierarchists—following the tradition of Bismarck[3]—have been predisposed toward increasingly inclusive public systems of assuring financial access to medical care. Moreover, hierarchists have been reluctant to curb growth in such programs in response to their increasing expense (in terms of percentage of GDP). These preferences are the result of fundamental beliefs quite different from those described for individualists in the previous paragraphs. Most basically, hierarchists perceive more difficult human environments. Both natural and social contexts involve sharp discontinuities between safe and dangerous activities, and the points at which danger arises are often unclear to ordinary persons. Moreover, hierarchists believe that humans have markedly different capacities for recognizing these discontinuities and for ascertaining how to act appropriately in light of them. For hierarchists, ordinary persons need the help and guidance of experts in various matters to perceive these dangers and to cope with the damage that they frequently inflict. For Bismarck, for instance, laborers confronting the threatening work environment of the early industrial age needed guidance with respect to avoiding a variety of dangers on the shop floor and help (i.e., medical care and modest living allowances during recuperation) with the consequences of the statistically inevitable mishaps that would arise.

In contrast to individualists, hierarchists are quite comfortable with augmenting what Machiavelli called the "majesty" of the state by expanding both public budgets and activities. So as the franchise expanded in various European societies which had predominant hierarchical cultures, there was a concomitant tendency to expand as well the sorts of social insurance programs (including medical-care insurance) which Bismarck had pioneered. For reasons that I relate shortly, hierarchists have frequently had egalitarian allies in the expansion of these programs, and their combined influence has made public endeavors that are conventionally, yet not entirely appropriately, called "national health insurance programs"[4] universal or virtually so among advanced industrial societies apart from the United States. Since these expansions provide medical care to many persons who would not otherwise have financial access to it, they tend to increase the proportion of GDP that medical care consumes. Further, hierarchists are willing to provide—or minimally, to allow for the provision of—exceptional and thus particularly expensive medical care for various societal elites. This can be done within public programs by, for instance, granting high-ranking public officials exceptionally thorough medical-care insurance. It may also be achieved by allowing wealthy persons to purchase superior private medical insurance and care. The provision of these more thorough layers of medical-care coverage also increases the proportion of GDP that medical care consumes. Consequently, societies in which hierarchists are preeminent tend to do well with respect to assuring citizens access to medical care and are also generally capable of providing cutting-edge medical treatments, although the latter may not be equally available to all. Yet these societies do not perform especially well with respect to limiting the portion of GDP that medical care consumes.

Egalitarians' beliefs and values differ from those of both individualists and hierarchists, so they are prone to set still different priorities with regard to the three general societal medical-care delivery objectives that I am using to organize the discussion of this section. In contrast to hierarchists, egalitarians believe that humans are equal with regard to broad capacities as well as needs. And in contrast to individualists, egalitarians perceive environments that are generally threatening, although the difficulties faced by some persons in this regard are much worse than those which others confront. The generally threatening character of human social contexts encourages egalitarians to rely on collective efforts to ward off various threats. That is, in contrast to individualists, they believe that the vast majority of humans face circumstances that would overwhelm individual efforts at mastering one's fate. Accordingly, societal-wide, public efforts to provide equal persons with financial access to medical care fit easily with the egalitarian worldview. A child's access to medical care should not, by egalitarian standards, be contingent on either the pocketbook or the social status of her parents. A child growing up in Watts has just as good a moral claim to medical-care resources as a child growing up in Scarsdale (Rawls 1971), but against the stratification of both markets and hierarchies, inclusive public programs are necessary in order to realize the former child's claim.

Yet egalitarians' perceptions of humans' relations with their environments leave them more hesitant than either individualists or hierarchists to expend extensive resources in meeting these claims. Egalitarians view human environments as fragile and likely to collapse if too much strain is placed on them. Accordingly, for egalitarians the term "environmental exploitation" carries pejorative connotations rather than being merely descriptive as it is for individualists, and they are more mindful than either of the stratifying cultures (i.e., individualism and hierarchy) of striving to limit the overall demands societies place on environmental resources. Thus egalitarians earn high marks with respect to the inclusiveness of the public medical-care programs that they prefer and with respect to the relatively modest proportions of GDP that these programs consume. But as a consequence of these virtues, egalitarian programs have great difficulty making quickly available to citizens the frequent and expensive innovations that contemporary medical science and technology produce.

MEDICAL-CARE FINANCING IN THE UNITED STATES

Prior to the mid-1960s, medical care was treated as a commodity in the United States in all but a few exceptional instances. As Starr (1982) relates, special public provision efforts have long been made for persons who provide valuable services to the social collective and who also face exceptional dangers: merchant seapersons, members of the military services, and veterans with service-connected maladies. Otherwise, medical care was dispensed in a way that conformed closely to the individualistic ideal introduced in the previous section. Most physicians were solo practitioners, essentially small businesspersons who exchanged specific medical services for prescribed fees. The layering of general practitioners and specialists as well as group practices were more common in urban centers. Prior to the Second World War, patients generally paid for these services out of their personal funds. Particularly in less urban areas, it was fairly common for physicians to use an informal sliding scale so that the relatively well-to-do paid more and the poor less for specific services.

American skepticism about big government generally and active resistance from physicians defeated Franklin Delano Roosevelt's effort to add a version of national health insurance to social security. The increasingly Republican Congress of the late 1930s rejected his proposal and a related one offered by New York Senator Robert F. Wagner (Hirschfield 1970).[5] But legal constraints on salaries and wages during the Second World War helped to foster private, employment-based, group medical insurance as employers began to compete for workers via nonwage benefits. This private insurance was far more common among high-status and well-organized workers than among the population generally. Additionally, the conventions of the time normally required patients to pay medical-care providers and then to apply for insurance reimbursement. Reimbursement generally amounted to a percentage of providers' fees minus various deductible amounts. Shortly after the war, Health Maintenance Organizations (HMOs), which provided medical services to specific populations for a standard annual charge along with relatively modest user fees, developed in some regions of the United States, particularly

California. Additionally, President Truman undertook, immediately after the war, a third major unsuccessful attempt to produce national health insurance, among other medical-care policy reforms. His attempt met strenuous resistance from physicians' organizations.

Both the capacities of medical-care providers and the costs of their services increased across the postwar years, and these developments helped to foster a greater sense of urgency about revising the system of medical-care financing. Lyndon B. Johnson was predisposed toward national health insurance, but saw it as an unachievable goal. He opted instead for an incremental approach, seeking to secure public insurance for the medical expenses of two segments of the population which had unusually high needs for medical care as well as exceptional difficulties paying for it: the elderly and the poor. The elderly routinely exhibit above-average rates of health problems, and in the 1960s they still had disproportionately low incomes. They had also generally lost any access that they might previously have had to private, employment-based, group insurance. In 1965, Johnson was able to gain passage for Medicare, which addressed these problems. The mandatory portion of Medicare (i.e., for which social security payroll deductions are made) involved insurance for hospital expenses. It followed the convention of private group insurance in that patients were expected to pay for a portion of hospital costs. Medicare also included voluntary, but highly subscribed insurance for physicians' fees, which was financed in part through beneficiaries' premiums but was subsidized by general tax revenues. This portion of Medicare also required patient copayments. The private insurance industry quickly developed policies, characteristically for groups of retirees (e.g., American Association of Retired Persons— AARP—members) which would cover most of the patient copayments required with respect to both hospitals and physicians. The only post-1965 increments to Medicare of any significance involved two 1972 steps which extended the program to disabled social insurance beneficiaries regardless of age as well as to persons suffering from end-state renal failure and thus requiring regular kidney dialysis (Marmor 1973, 2000).

Prior to the 1960s there had been a scattered patchwork of state and local programs offering some help to the working-aged poor with respect to medical-care expenses. President Johnson's Medicaid program expanded these efforts so as to cover the medically indigent generally and also standardized minimum benefits in this joint federal/state–level program. While some physicians have refused to deal with Medicaid patients, persons with Medicaid coverage have access to whatever medical care services their physicians think they should have with virtually no patient copayments.

While the medical "establishment" (i.e., interest groups representing physicians, hospitals and insurance companies) had been skeptical at best with respect to Medicare, physicians and, to a lesser extent hospitals, were initially won over by the increased market it generated for their services and the greater security of payment it offered. Through these factors Medicare contributed to rapidly increasing medical costs across the late 1960s and early 1970s. The Nixon administration attempted to slow medical-care price inflation through regulatory means such as Professional Standards Review Organizations (PSROs), which analyzed hospital statistics for overuse, underuse and misuse and Health Systems Agencies (HSAs), which monitored medical-care capital investment decisions.[6] But by the time the Carter administration undertook the fourth major attempt to achieve national health insurance in 1979, the proportion of GDP devoted to medical care was continuing to grow at such a rapid pace as to raise serious interest in HMOs as a means of cost containment. Physicians had been so favorably affected by Medicare that, while they disagreed with the specifics of Carter's proposal, they offered a related plan of national health insurance. But the insurance industry in particular and perpetual American individualistic resistance to larger, more-active government in general defeated Carter's efforts. The Reagan administration attempted to control costs through a variety of measures including limiting the charges for which hospitals could be reimbursed within various diagnostically related groups (DRGs). And the George Bush, Sr., administration had related sad experiences with public medical-care financing reforms, including an attempt to provide Medicare patients with better insurance against various "catastrophic" medical-care costs (Moon 1993, ch. 5).

But as Starr (1982) suggests, while physicians and hospitals attended to the threats to their professional interests that they perceived in various public policy proposals, another adversary—big business—began to outflank them. Across the 1980s large insurers increasingly dominated the medical-care market by offering employers various preferred provider medical-care plans (including HMOs) for their employees. These plans appealed to employers because they promised—and often delivered—lower rates of cost inflation. Initially, the hospitals and physicians "preferred" by particular plans were intrigued as well by the prospect of increased "business." Yet across time hospitals, physicians and patients have all lost independence with respect to the power of insurers. Hospitals and physicians have, informally, become "employees" of the insurers who mandate practices and prices. Patients find that their medical-care decisions lie, not within the autonomy of their own physi-

cians, but must fit within the guidelines of insurance company bureaucrats with whom they rarely interact. Rates of medical-care price inflation did slow across the bulk of the 1990s, but this benefit came at a hefty
cost in terms of provider autonomy as well as patient peace of mind and
sometimes physical well-being. The Clinton administration based its
1993 attempt to achieve national health insurance, the fifth major unsuccessful effort, in large measure on the cost-saving capacities of these
plans, which, generically, have become known as "managed care" plans,
but the administration was defeated both by traditional adversaries—
powerful economic interests (particularly small-business associations
and the insurance industry), the high proportion of members of Congress who oppose expanding public social programs, and general public
skepticism about more active government and higher taxes—as well as by
flaws in its own policy process (Aaron 1996; White 1995).

If there is a silver lining to the dominance of giant insurance companies in the financing of medical care, it lies in the obviously commercial
character that this situation imparts to the medical-care industry. It is no
longer credible to argue that the government ought to stand aside from
regulating the private relations between a patient and her long-standing,
well-disposed and all-knowing physician. As the industrial character of
medical care has become more obvious, what was once its special status
with respect to avoiding public regulation has atrophied. Thus both
American political parties now propose "patients' bills of rights," although the economic power and political influence of the medical insurers makes adding teeth to this legislation a difficult task.

In the last decade the remarkable rate at which new prescription drugs
for various serious maladies have been introduced and the extremely high
prices for many of these drugs have added a new wrinkle to medical-care
financing. Whereas as recently as 1990 the combination of hospitalization
and physicians' fees amounted to the vast majority of Americans' medical
expenses, prescription drugs now constitute a rapidly growing proportion
of the total (Anderson et al. 2000, 152). For many patients, prescription
drug expenses constitute the largest portion of their medical-care bills. Patients within HMOs and related preferred-provider plans generally acquire some coverage (patient copayments required) of prescription drug
costs. Persons with more traditional forms of American insurance generally do not have such coverage. Among the elderly, for whom prescription
drug usage is particularly high, HMO coverage is limited, problematic and
not apt to expand greatly. Thus, in response to an outcry from the AARP
and other groups representing the elderly, both American political parties
have proposed legislation designed to add prescription drug coverage to

Medicare's provisions. Both proposals limit coverage (in varying degrees) and require significant patient copayments.

Situation at the Beginning of the Twenty-First Century.   While specific changes are numerous, in broad outline the character of medical-care financing in the United States has been fairly stable for over three decades. A significant (about 20 percent) and slowly growing proportion of the American population obtains financial access to medical care through public programs (primarily Medicare and also Medicaid).[7] This group is composed largely of elderly persons and poor mothers and their children. Medicare patients also frequently buy private group insurance designed to cover most of the copayments that Medicare requires.

Another, significantly larger group (about 50 percent) is fairly satisfactorily insured with respect to medical-care costs by private insurance, generally group-based and acquired through employment. I say "fairly satisfactorily insured" because contemporary policies routinely carry substantial deductible amounts, copayments and other sorts of limitations (e.g., for preexisting conditions) and increasingly as well may deny patients coverage for treatments that are approved by their physicians.[8]

Another roughly 30-35 percent of Americans are about equally divided between the seriously underinsured and the noninsured. The seriously underinsured include many self-employed persons without access to group plans, and workers in small firms which contract for limited coverage. Characteristically, these persons cannot get insurance coverage for the medical problems that they are most likely to confront. So, for instance, a self-employed person with glaucoma may not be able to insure herself against glaucoma-related expenses likely to arise from this preexisting condition. The uninsured are disproportionately persons whose small-scale employers either do not offer insurance or whose wages are too modest to make such insurance affordable (Kronenfeld 1993, 140).

Our current medical-care financing environment is especially pernicious with respect to this last group. Medical-care providers have progressively become more aware of preventive counsel and care, in contrast to their former myopic focus on therapeutic treatments, and they can now help with a broad range of illnesses and injuries, particularly if these maladies are caught early. Yet whereas physicians once charged the medically indigent less than well-to-do patients, they now routinely charge them more. Physicians are constrained by insurers with respect to their charges to insured patients and attempt to redress these limits on their incomes by charging the uninsured more, frequently several times as much (Kolata 2001). Since the uninsured often have low incomes, this practice makes accessing medical care early in the course of a particular malady extremely difficult for them. So whereas the relatively well-to-do once subsidized the poor with respect to medical care in the United States, we now have a bizarre and immoral situation of the poor subsidizing the well-to-do. The uninsured can receive care at public hospital emergency rooms without paying, but they tend to use these services only after maladies are well developed (Kronenfeld 1993, 146).[9]

U.S. Medical-Care Financing and the Three General Medical-Care Delivery Objectives. American medical-care financing practices fit the pattern of priorities that I suggested above for a society in which individualism is the preeminent political culture, particularly among political elites. First, the United States knows no equal in terms of extending the horizons of medical-care possibilities. Extraordinary new treatments for a variety of ailments (e.g., the deterioration of sight in the elderly, particular forms of cancer), innovative surgical techniques (e.g., using lasers and/or embedding radioactive seeds rather than or in addition to traditional surgery for brain tumors) and remarkable advances with respect to prescription drugs (especially for chronic conditions such as elevated blood pressure or blood cholesterol) have expanded the horizons of what is medically possible in the United States. The frequent choices of elites from other societies to come to the United States for various forms of sophisticated treatments or to have American providers come to them underscores that the United States can provide cutting-edge medical care and other aspects of medical-care quality to a degree often unrivaled in other societies.[10] Furthering those improvements in quality of care that rest on scientific and technological innovations may not have been an explicit national choice for the top American priority with respect to the medical-care objectives trilemma. Rather, it seems likely that these developments represent the "natural" product of a society which is dominated by individualists and, accordingly, relies heavily on markets. Certainly the thoroughly market-oriented American society is adept at this task, and it is a popular achievement among individualists, who are especially numerous in the United States.

Particularly since the introduction of Medicare in 1965, a second high priority of American medical-care delivery policy has been cost containment. From the late 1960s into the present this objective has clearly taken precedence over efforts to extend financial access to medical care more inclusively. For individualists, rapidly escalating medical-care expenses represent high opportunity costs in terms of realizing alternative goals in other areas of endeavor. This is particularly true with respect to Medicare, which expends a substantial proportion of its annual budget to add modest increments to the often highly constrained lives of elderly patients (Congressional Budget Office 1983; Lubitz and Prihoda 1984— but see also Lubitz 1990). These funds represent resources that are not available to foster investment in what some may regard as more encouraging avenues of activity. Accordingly, the United States has sought, through a variety of avenues, to constrain the rate of inflation in medical prices and growth in the proportion of GDP represented by medical-care goods and services. As we shall see below, persistent efforts to achieve these ends have been surprisingly unsuccessful, although the United States experienced some improvement in its results in the 1990s. (See table 3.2—p. 81.)

If a particular conception of quality of care and cost containment represent the top two priorities for the United States with respect to the three preeminent medical-care delivery objectives, then my view of these three objectives forming a trilemma entails that the United States experience difficulty—even if it were predisposed toward—doing well on the third objective, inclusiveness. American experience certainly bears out this prediction. The United States is the only advanced industrial society in which a substantial proportion of the citizenry is left to pay out-of-pocket (and without the benefit of insurance reimbursement) for much of the medical care it receives. The various systems of financing the delivery of medical care in the United States do not allow a substantial portion (roughly 30 to 35 percent) of Americans the sort of access to medical care that is widely available among the citizens of other advanced industrial societies. Further, the deductibles, exclusions and copayment provisions associated with both private group insurance and Medicare add a concern about paying medical bills to worries about income interruption as well as the physical and mental distress that are inherent to illness and injury. So even for many Americans with financial access to medical care, exercising that access is painful in ways that the public policies of other advanced industrial societies enable their citizens to avoid. Clearly, in the United States the inclusiveness of citizens' financial access to medical care has been the lowest-priority objective of the three which I have examined, and American priorities across these three objectives fit the profile which I developed above for a society dominated by individualists.

MEDICAL-CARE FINANCING IN CANADA

Prior to the late 1940s, medical-care delivery and financing in Canada were similar in broad outline to their counterparts in the United States. That is, the prevailing modes involved private physicians and hospitals (the latter generally nonprofit institutions) exchanging services for fees which were paid by patients, some of whom had private insurance to cover a portion of their medical-care expenses. As in the United States, an early attempt (in 1921) to produce a national health insurance program failed. But in contrast to the United States, the provincial governments were more actively involved in the delivery and financing of medical-care services than were the American states.[11] In the eastern maritime regions, the northern territories and particularly the prairie provinces, local public hospitals with salaried staff were more common than in the more populous, urban and industrially developed province of Ontario and adjacent areas.

A more dramatic contrast with the United States developed in 1947 when the Saskatchewan provincial government introduced a universal (i.e., province-wide) hospital insurance program. This program was subsequently (1962) augmented by another, covering physicians' fees. These developments drew on the province's earlier experience with municipal public hospitals, but also represented innovations. Both hospitals and physicians retained their independence from the provincial government. While referrals from general practitioners were necessary for access to specialists in some cases, patients generally saw whatever physician they chose. But patients were not billed for services. Rather, providers contracted fee schedules for various services with the provincial government and were paid out of public funds for services rendered. The province paid for hospital expenses and physicians' fees from general tax revenues.

Saskatchewan's innovations were the products of a social-democratic provincial government. The Cooperative Commonwealth Federation (CCF), a precursor of the contemporary social-democratic NDP, experienced some resistance, including a short-lived physicians strike, but resistance abated quickly. Indeed, the innovations became generally popular successes, and other provinces began to emulate Saskatchewan's example. By 1961—prior to the introduction of Medicare in the United States—public hospital insurance programs were universal across Canada. Through the Hospital and Diagnostic Services Act of 1956 the national government facilitated the development and coordination of these programs by agreeing to pay for half of their expenses. Provincial programs vary with respect to some specifics (e.g., fee schedules), but federal funding requires that provinces assure: public administration, comprehensiveness (of services), universality, portability (from province to province) and accessibility (Evans 1992, 166).[12] By 1971, all Canadian provinces had introduced similar insurance programs for physicians' fees as well. So in slightly over two decades Canada transformed its system of medical-care financing from a largely private structure resembling its U.S. counterpart to a nearly exclusively public system, similar to some in Europe but quite different from the United States. Across this same period, medical-care delivery remained largely in the hands of private physicians, hospitals and other providers.

While there are some modest provincial variations, the contemporary Canadian system works roughly as follows. Patients and physicians each have differing versions of "freedom of choice." That is, patients may seek care from any physician they choose, and physicians can decide whether they wish to provide this care or not. In general, patients are not charged for the services rendered by their physicians.[13] Physicians—who are almost all private practitioners—submit claims for reimbursement to their provincial governments. Unless the physician is doing something exceptionally unusual, she will not be second-guessed about tests or treatments and will be reimbursed for services rendered according to a schedule of fees negotiated between providers and various provincial governments on an annual basis. In contrast, hospitals—save for some outpatient services—are not reimbursed for specific services but negotiate overall budgets with provincial governments on an annual basis. At both the federal and provincial levels the vast majority of the funds that support the delivery of medical-care services are raised by general taxation.

So, most medical care is not paid for directly by patients but rather funded through appropriations from general taxes. Provinces receive annual block grants from the federal government according to complicated formulas (Evans 1993, 7). These formulas are not based on actual expenses but generally end up providing something around 25 percent of annual provincial medical-care expenses. If a province's expenses in a particular year are exceptionally high, then the proportion of these expenses paid by the province will be unusually high as well. So the provinces have an incentive to spend efficiently, and periodic federal legislation strives to maintain these incentives. For example, the Canadian Health Act of 1984, among other provisions, prohibited physicians from privately charging their patients an additional amount—above the reimbursement figure negotiated with the province—for various services. Unsurprisingly, however, medical care accounts for the largest single element in the annual budgets of all provinces. Physicians are paid the negotiated rates for services up to certain annual income limits. Thereafter, their rate of payment for additional services is progressively reduced. Provinces vary as to whether they allow physicians to work outside the national health insurance plan.[14] Physicians who choose to work outside the plan are virtually unregulated. But in contrast to Britain and some other societies, Canadian physicians may not work both in and outside of the national health insurance system.

Annual provincial allotments from the federal government are designed to help pay, not only for a significant portion of that year's medical-care services, but also to prepare for future medical-care needs by helping to fund research initiatives, build new facilities (e.g., hospitals), train the next generation of medical-care providers, incorporate new technologies into practice, etc. While some aspects of central provincial planning in these and related regards have gone well (Adams 1993, 135-36), arguably better than in the United States (e.g., the distribution and sophisticated use of high-technology equipment such as various sorts of soft-tissue scanners), the overall concern of providing for the future through the rapid introduction of new medical technologies remains one area of relative Canadian weakness in comparison to the United States (Anderson and Hussey 2000; Bryce and Cline 1998).[15]

Situation at the Beginning of the Twenty-First Century. As with any other scheme of medical-care delivery and financing, the Canadian system has its strengths and weaknesses. One clear strength is its popularity among an astounding proportion of the population. In a recent survey, 90 percent of Canadians agreed with the following statement: "One of the things that makes Canada the best country in the world in which to live is the quality and availability of our health care system" (McKinnon 1993, 61). Patients are free to choose providers, are generally provided with high-quality care, and only rarely pay even minor amounts out of pocket. In comparison to Americans, Canadians may also be pleased that their medical-care delivery system consumes only 9.2 percent of GDP. This is about three-quarters of what the United States spends (as a percentage of GDP). Physicians and hospital administrators are usually more aware of the system's limitations, but they still generally tend to be favorably disposed toward the principles on which the program rests and recognize that its practical limitations vis-à-vis alternative designs are offset by various advantages (Estill 1993).

A decade ago there was considerable fear of a "physician drain" from Canada to the United States, but the growing limitations on the autonomy of American physicians who find themselves increasingly in the grip of large corporate insurance providers has dampened, though not eliminated, this concern. Perhaps the foremost problem confronting the Canadian system today involves insufficient capacity, particularly in major urban areas such as Toronto and Montreal. The process of funding research, planning medical education, maintaining and improving physical plant (e.g., hospitals) and integrating innovative therapies into common practice has not been adequate to meet increases in demand arising from population growth (partly from immigration), population aging and particularly the increased capabilities of medical-care providers (Charles and Badgley 1999, 130-33; Crossette 2001; Savage, Hoelscher and Walker 1999, 13; Tuohy 1999, 213). Other, generally lesser problems exist as well. For example, while Canadians are better off in this regard than are Americans, prescription drug expenses represent a growing problem.

Canadian Medical-Care Financing and the Three General Medical-Care Delivery Objectives.   Canadian medical-care financing practices fit a pattern of priorities that we should expect for a society in which egalitarians and hierarchists have both been more influential than in the United States. Both of these cultures exert obvious influence on medical-care delivery and financing in Canada (Evans 1993; Beatty 1993). First, Canada does extremely well in terms of making medical-care universally accessible. This is true, not only in terms of the financial aspects of access on which I have focused, but also with regard to physical access. This latter concern is more significant in Canada, which has a slightly larger land area than the United States (nearly 10 million square kilometers as opposed to 9,372,000) but a population of only slightly more than one-tenth of the United States (30 million as opposed to nearly 270 million [OECD 1999, 6-7]). A substantial majority of the Canadian population lives fairly close to the U.S.-Canadian border, so vast areas of Canada have extremely low population density, and this raises severe problems of physical access to medical care for relatively isolated persons.

But I continue to focus here on financial access. The strength of Canadian egalitarianism is clearly revealed in Canada's performance with respect to this objective. For a time in the late 1970s and early 1980s Canada allowed hospitals and physicians to charge patients modest co-payments. The 1984 Canadian Health Act effectively ended this practice with respect to physicians and reduced it among hospitals. Currently, most patients who acquire treatments from the vast majority of Canadian physicians and hospitals pay nothing at all to these providers. Additionally, most provinces cover the costs of out-patient prescription drugs for the elderly and low-income persons out of public funds. Many other citizens have access to private insurance (often group, employment-related insurance as in the United States) that substantially reduces the cost of such drugs. Even the patient-borne costs of long-term care, particularly for low-income persons, are remarkably low (Kane 1993; Pallan 1993; Adams 1993). While there are variations from province to province, overall Canadians have done a remarkable job of making personal finances an irrelevant consideration with respect to access to medical-care and related (e.g., long-term care) services. Perhaps more important than this fact as an index of egalitarianism is the pride Canadians have with respect to this situation. Across the political and socioeconomic spectra strong statements, such as Beatty's (1993, 31) cited above—to the effect that this is precisely the way things ought to be, that personal financial situations should have no bearing on access to care, including the quality of care and the speed with which it is delivered—are common.

Second, in comparison to the United States, Canada has done well with respect to constraining the escalation of total medical-care costs as a proportion of GDP. Table 3.1 compares the United States and Canada in this regard from 1960 through the mid-1990s. (See table 3.1.) In 1960—prior to the enactment of Medicare in the United States and the development of public insurance for hospital and physician's fees in Canada—both the United States and Canada expended (by current standards) modest proportions of GDP for medical care. Canada's expenditures were slightly higher than the United States. Since then, the trend of expenditures has been up for both societies—and other OECD members as well. Several factors contribute prominently to the escalating proportion of GDP that medical care consumes: various forms of public insurance have facilitated access to medical care for a broader portion of the population; the aging populations of advanced industrial societies have

Table 3.1 Medical–Care Spending as a Proportion of GDP

Year	United States	Canada
1960	5.3	5.6
1965	6.0	6.2
1970	7.5	7.3
1975	8.6	7.5
1980	9.5	7.5
1985	10.6	8.6
1990	12.0	9.2
1996	13.6	9.2

Source: Data for 1960–90 are from Adams 1993, 125; data for 1996 are from OECD 1999, 8–9.

been drawing on medical-care services more heavily; and medical-care providers have had an ever-increasing array of therapeutic treatments. Nonetheless, some societies have experienced more rapid escalation of medical-care costs than others. As table 3.1 shows, while American expenditures started out slightly below Canada's as a percentage of GDP, they have risen more rapidly, and the United States—while falling far short of Canada on the objective of inclusiveness or universality of access—now spends a considerably larger proportion of GDP on medical care than does Canada. In fact, while spending only two-thirds of American expenditures (as a percentage of GDP) in 1996, Canada produced better health status indices. Its infant mortality rate was 0.6/1,000 live births, while the United States had a rate of 0.8/1000. Similarly, Canada's life expectancy was 81.5 years for women and 75.4 for men; whereas in the United States life expectancy was 79.4 for women and 72.7 for men (OECD 1999, 10-11). It is hard to avoid a conclusion that across the citizenry generally Canada has done a superior job of protecting persons' health while utilizing a smaller proportion of its GDP to accomplish this task.[16] Both of these achievements indicate that Canada takes a more high-group (and particularly) egalitarian approach to medical care than does the United States.

While table 3.2 does not contradict this statement, it places both the United States and Canada in a broader comparative perspective. (See table 3.2.) The United States appears in a remarkable position; while likely doing less well than any other society included in table 3.2 with respect to achieving universal access to medical care, it has also done the poorest job of constraining medical-care expenses (as a proportion of GDP). Indeed the U.S. health-status statistics (e.g., infant mortality and life expectancy) are less encouraging than those of any of the other advanced industrial members of the OECD (OECD 1999, 10-11). In a sense the United States, with its emphasis on quality of care for those who can afford it, has used the most resources to produce the least encouraging health results for the general population.

A more surprising aspect of table 3.2, however, is Canada's relatively high position among OECD members in terms of the proportion of GDP spent on medical care. Aside from the United States, only Germany, Switzerland and France rank ahead of Canada in this regard. This underscores a point I made at the outset of the "Canadian History, Institutions and Culture" section of this chapter: while the United States and Canada can be distinguished, they have much in common; they are "most similar" or at least fairly similar societies. Canada likely performs as well as any other society in terms of the egalitarian lodestar of making medical care universally available to its citizens, yet it clearly does not perform as well on the other egalitarian concern of limiting total costs as a number of Western European societies in which egalitarianism is also prominent (e.g., Sweden). This is likely due in part to the combined pressure of Canadian hierarchists and individualists to keep the quality of care relatively high. It is reasonable to imagine that most of the societies near the bottom of table 3.2 perform less well than Canada on the quality of care objective, particularly those aspects involving the relative speed of deployment for new medical technologies (e.g., the UK's explicit relative cost/benefit comparisons that lead to decisions not to deploy some technologies).

So far, Canada earns high marks in comparison to the United States on two of the three general medical-care delivery objectives: achieving universal access and constraining total costs. Again, my claim that the three objectives form a trilemma entails that this encouraging performance on

Table 3.2 Medical-Care Spending as a Proportion of GDP Among Selected OECD Members (1996)

United States (highest in the OECD)	13.6
Germany	10.5
Switzerland	10.2
France	9.8
Canada	9.2
Australia	8.6
Netherlands	8.6
Sweden	8.6
Iceland	8.2
Austria	8.0
Norway	7.9
Belgium	7.8
Italy	7.8
Denmark	7.6
Finland	7.4
Spain	7.4
Japan	7.2
Ireland	7.0
United Kingdom	6.9

Note: This table includes the societies in table 2.1 as well as Australia, Austria, Finland, Japan, Switzerland, and the United States.
Source: OECD 1999, 8–9

the first two objectives extract a price with respect to the third. This prediction has certainly been realized by recent Canadian experience. Again, Canada's federalism is sufficiently robust so that conditions vary across provinces, but particularly in the Canadian "heartland" (i.e., Ontario and Quebec) significant problems have emerged. Provincial public officials receive annual block grants from the federal government. They are expected to augment these funds from provincial coffers and to use the combined resources to defray the expenses of the current year's medical care as well as to lay the foundation for future medical care through medical-care education and the construction of new facilities or the renovation and expansion of existing facilities. The combined focus on doing well for all current patients and holding down total costs, characteristic of egalitarianism, has led to slighting preparations for the future and thus reducing in certain respects the quality of care that the Canadian system is able to provide currently and into the immediate future.

One example, in particular, illustrates this problem. From the late 1970s through the early 1990s, Canadian public medical-care executives, driven by the goal of cost containment, engaged in a persistent and increasingly systematic effort to reduce expensive hospital utilization among Canadian patients. This effort helped to control cost inflation, but it was so protracted that it has begun to create serious resource inadequacy problems for a growing and aging population (Crossette 2001; Fooks 1999; Savage, Hoelscher and Walker 1999; Touhy 1999). Both hospital facilities and personnel have become too limited to meet current and short-term future levels of demand. Waiting lists for sophisticated treatments have grown, so that lengthy delays in receiving treatment are common. Patients for whom immediate treatment is crucial are sent to American hospitals. Emergency rooms—and hospitals generally—have simply refused on various occasions to accept patients with acute conditions because they have lacked the capacity for dealing with them.

In the recent past the Canadian system's inclusiveness and cost control priorities have lead to discounting the future to such a degree that the capacity for doing well by a portion of current patients has been lost as demand has grown. When medical care is considered a commodity, as it is by many in the United States, it is in the self-interest of various entrepreneurs to assure that they have sufficient services available to meet future demand increases. So, a market-based system, whatever its other shortcomings, is likely more responsive to the sorts of difficulties that have recently afflicted the Canadian medical-care delivery system, than are systems of central public administration. Minimally, a decentralized market system is unlikely to fall completely under the sway of one particular conception of the future as appears to have occurred in Canada. This is not to say that market-based systems are without serious flaws in this regard. Some American cities have recently confronted problems similar to those described for Canada above (*New York Times* 2002). But markets are more predisposed to prepare for these contingencies and sometimes more flexible in responding rapidly to them when they arise than are systems directed by central public managers.

HISTORY, INSTITUTIONS, CULTURE AND CAUSALITY

Similarly to the situation that we encountered with respect to the Swedish tax regime in chapter 2, there appear to be few, if any, contingencies in which those American adherents of the high-group cultures, who want their society to emulate the aspects of Canadian medical-care financing that we have examined, can anticipate success. Yet the question about emulating Canadian medical-care financing also raises considerations that were not present in the instance of the Swedish tax regime. There have, after all, been several serious and protracted efforts to achieve an American system of medical-care financing that would be roughly comparable to the Canadian system in its consequences for citizens' access to medical care. In contrast, there has been no popular hue and cry for a tax regime similar to Sweden's. Even during the external duress provided by the Second World War, American taxes did not come close to emulating the contemporary Swedish tax regime.

Free and Cantril (1967) show that, when many Americans think about abstract political ideals, they frequently think in terms of the Lockean limited state. But when they think in terms of the practical problems of everyday life, they are often more favorably disposed toward a larger, more active state that offers assistance in negotiating life's vicissitudes. So in practice, Americans are hesitant to scuttle social security pensions for the elderly and disabled as their abstract Lockean ideals would suggest, but they have also been reluctant to accept the tax increases (Light 1995) required to continue the program's benefits. Even high-group Swedes are likely more favorably disposed toward public social program benefits than they are toward paying the taxes that support these programs.

Yet in spite of repeated efforts by half of the presidents since Franklin D. Roosevelt to enact some form of national health insurance as well as more modest yet still significant initiatives to upgrade public medical-care financing programs on the part of the majority of the remaining recent presidents, the United States still lacks a medical-care financing system that makes medical care accessible to the population generally. Analysts differ in explaining this result, which represents an anomaly among advanced industrial societies. Some use explanations based on ideas or culture, drawing on various aspects of the unusual breadth and depth of skepticism toward active government in the United States (Lipset 1990; Kudrle and Marmor 1981; Evans 1992). Others stress the fragmented structure of American political institutions (Steinmo and Watts 1995; Weissert and Weissert 1996). Still others draw on both of these explanatory devices (Aaron 1996; Marmor 2000).

This third option appears more sensible since it includes a broader range of the factors that a number of analysts consider relevant, but it still leaves unresolved the question as to what other changes would be required (and how they might come about) for the United States to adopt a medical-care financing system similar to Canada's in its effects on access to medical care. There is a tendency among analysts who include this broader range of factors to treat the cultural predispositions of Americans as residual. That is, they rely primarily on institutional fragmentation—a weak presidency, decentralized authority in Congress, and conflictual relations among these and other institutions—and then add resistance among both public officials and various attentive publics to this particular policy direction and among the broader population to the growth of government in general. My analysis so far suggests that a more even-handed approach is preferable.

My view is that the distinctive fragmented character of American political institutions and the resulting conflictual relations among them stem clearly from the preeminence of individualists among the architects of the American path of institutional development set by the Constitution of 1787. This founding influence has been perpetuated both by passing individualistic beliefs and value priorities from one generation to the next within families and other mentoring relationships as well as by the socializing influence of existing institutions on succeeding generations. The result is that large numbers of Americans, both among the political elite and the general public, are individualistic in the sense that they are skeptical about relinquishing progressively more power to what they perceive as self-interested humans through ever more extensive government. Like Madison, they seek to protect human liberty from the unsettling traits they perceive in human nature, by fragmenting political institutions and juxtaposing their limited powers.

Admittedly, Americans are more torn on the issue of financial access to medical care than they are on the question of tax regimes. Hence when presidents press hard for the adoption of a national health insurance initiative, the issue hangs in the balance for a time. But to date, none of these struggles has produced national health insurance, and few—if any—students of American social policy expect this situation to change in the foreseeable future. Support for national health insurance in a predominantly individualistic society is vulnerable to various symbols, some specious (lack of choice—which the Canadian system clearly preserves) and others real (growing reliance of previously self-reliant individuals on public institutions for crucial services), that well-organized groups with deeply held principles and substantial material interests use to combat these initiatives.

American institutional fragmentation provides crucial assistance for those opposing various national health insurance proposals. If powerful resisting groups can influence a single critical institution (say a particular House committee), they may prevail. Further, differences between the American and Canadian versions of federalism likely help to account for the Canadian success in initiating a public program for financing citizens' health care. More by contingency than formal assignment, health responsibilities in Canada have historically fallen to provincial governments. Moreover, Canadian provinces are generally much larger (as a proportion of society) than are American states, and they have historically been more in control of their own destinies as well. Interaction between this historical contingency and these structural features help to explain why a Canadian province initiated a regional health insurance program prior to any American state. But the rapid subsequent emulation of this program by other provinces, facilitated by the quick offer of financial help from the national government, would appear to transcend explanations based on institutional structure, drawing instead on cultural biases among Canadians that are far more favorably predisposed toward this form of public policy than the views of their American counterparts.

Institutional fragmentation (or other societal institutional peculiarities) represents but one aspect of a multifactor and permeable causal sequence that begins elsewhere. Steinmo (1995, 324-28) and other institutionalists suggest a causal sequence that begins (sometimes implicitly) with the effects of powerful and unique historical contingencies, which set individual societies on particular paths of institutional development. Experience with these paths then helps to socialize persons to rival cultures. Socialization to various cultures helps, in turn, to account for the character of specific societies' policies since the adherents of rival cultures strive to construct contrasting designs. However, this causal sequence does not hold a monopoly on the beliefs and value priorities (cultures) which shape paths of institutional development or the character of specific policies.[17] The sequence is permeable to exogenous influences, as when Madison rejected the adult socialization acquired from his experiences with the British Empire and the Articles of Confederation and redirected the United States' path of institutional development by constructing a new Constitution drawn from elements of Locke and Montesquieu included in his early education. So there is as well a second causal flow. Beliefs and value priorities exogenous to the socializing influence of a society's existing path of institutional development may enter the first sequence through its culture stage. They may then exert influence "forward" toward particular policies and also—as in Madison's case—in the "reverse" direction back toward the path of development for broader institutions.

As long as prevailing American conceptions of human environments and human nature continue to embody individualistic visions of bounty and capable self-interestedness, respectively, Americans will persist in perceiving less need for help from public programs and be more skeptical about relying on them for crucial services than are Canadian citizens. This is the link in causal sequences that would have to change for the United States to successfully adopt a medical-care financing system similar—in terms of its consequences for citizen access to medical care—to Canada's. Moreover, if my argument about the trilemma afflicting the three predominate medical-care delivery objectives is correct, Americans would not only have to become more concerned about achieving greater inclusiveness of financial access, but also have to reduce their interest in realizing either a particular conception of quality of care or in improving control of medical-care cost inflation.

So a crucial question is: What circumstances would foster a shift among American political elites and the general public in an "up-group" and possibly "up-grid" direction? If we examine this question with a lengthy time horizon in mind (e.g., a century or more), then a variety of slowly developing historical contingencies may gradually transform both culture and the public programs that stem from it (Inglehart 1997). For instance, the combined effects of gradually growing affluence, increasing life span and the expanding capacities of medical-care providers have cumulated in both cultural and policy change in the United States as in other societies. The United States does not have national health insurance, but it now finances substantial portions of the medical care received by roughly a fifth of the population through public programs. Gradually changing social conditions have produced different expectations, for instance, with regard to assuring the elderly access to medical care for acute maladies. In other societies the policy innovations resulting from these changes have been more extensive. But a common cross-societal policy trajectory can, nonetheless, be discerned (Wilson 1998). So while the United States might continue, as a result of its preeminent individualistic culture, to exhibit greater limitations on public medical-care programs into the distant future, continued, gradual but—over time—significant changes in social circumstances might attenuate the differences between its system of financing medical care and the public programs of other societies in which the influence of the high-group cultures was more pronounced.

If we consider a less extended time horizon, we are more dependent on rapid social transformations to produce policy change (i.e., adopting some form of national health insurance). It is possible for severe societal crises to produce movement of large numbers of persons "up-group" and "up-grid" in a relatively short span of time (e.g., a few years). Such developments are likely contingent on the arrival of extremely disruptive societal circumstances such as wars, depressions, extensive natural disasters, etc. But as I argued in chapter 2, what tends to be critical for producing institutional change in reaction to such circumstances are shifts in coalitions among political elites which foster new policy trajectories (Lockhart 2001b, ch. 9; see also Cox 2001). Thus it is imaginable that, in reaction to a currently unidentifiable societal crisis at some point in the relatively near future, an elite coalition representing the high-group cultures might displace the currently more individualistic elites of the George W. Bush administration or their successors. Further, under these altered social circumstances, this coalition might find popular support for public policy initiatives (including one improving citizen financial access to medical care) that would seem unimaginable today. So, as with my conclusion in chapter 2, I contend that American adoption in the next few decades of a system of national health insurance roughly comparable in its medical-care financing effects to the existing Canadian system is apt to occur only in reaction to historical contingencies whose socially disruptive effects would need to be similar to if not more extensive than those produced by the combination of the Great Depression and the Second World War. Only such dire circumstances would cultivate the required growth in and increased coalition potential of the high-group cultures whose adherents would, in turn, favor and strive to produce such a public program.

Such a shift, from basing public policy on one culturally constrained set of beliefs and value priorities to another, may be viewed the "rational choice" of the adherents of the ascendant culture, which is attempting to realize efficiently a different set of beliefs and value priorities which they consider to be more appropriately tailored to the new circumstances. The constrained sets of beliefs and value priorities that represent one aspect of culture are reactions to experience. If experience changes enough, it makes sense that beliefs and value priorities will change, too. If a bountiful social milieu is replaced by a threatening one, then faith in self-reliance may reasonably be displaced by beliefs in the appropriateness of collective security. And efforts to realize this latter goal will produce different public policies—also indices of culture—than support for self-reliance. Such a transformation is certainly facilitated by the ascension of political elites already predisposed to the new goals, and in practice the displacement of one set of elites by another is likely the critical step. But the underlying enabling factor is the presence and nurture in society of reservoirs of persons whose rival sets of beliefs and value priorities foster the construction of different social institutions designed to cope with the distinctive problems threatened by various historical contingencies.

CHAPTER 4

Abortion Policy
in the United States and France

In the previous two chapters we have studied aspects of the redistributive activities that are central to the political economies of advanced industrial societies. These societies tax their citizens in varying but historically substantial degrees and then redistribute a significant portion of this public revenue to citizens in the form of public social programs which provide varying forms of income maintenance and a range of social services. We have examined how different societies prefer to deal with the public revenue side of this process in chapter 2 and focused on societies' distinctive preferences with respect to an important aspect of public social program redistribution—financing medical care—in chapter 3.

In this chapter and the subsequent one we turn to a related but distinct type of public sector activity. According to Easton (1965), politics involves the "authoritative allocation of values." That is, societies' political processes culminate in decisions on what is merit-worthy or, alternatively, vile, that are binding on everyone in society. More briefly, the political decision process bestows legitimacy on certain activities and outcomes. Virtually without exception the decisions, activities and outcomes that societal political processes legitimate are contested. One reason for their controversial character is that persons adhering to rival political perspectives disagree about values and vices. For social conservatives, stratifying institutions that support natural human differences in prudence and morality are essential to an orderly and harmonious society. For social democrats, who perceive humans as naturally equal in broad capacities and needs, these same institutions are evil, for in the process of disrupting natural human equality, they pervert natural human goodness.

So the legitimacy of these "products" (i.e., decisions, activities and outcomes) of political processes often rest less on their specific character, with which some will inevitably disagree, than on the manner in which they are produced. In democracies, for instance, social democrats do not routinely take to the streets in pitched battle when economic conservatives succeed in cutting public social program budgets. Rather, they seek to use the next election to regain a parliamentary majority that will allow them to return these programs to what they view as their appropriate levels of activity. Through violent and bloody experience, many persons of different political persuasions have come to the conclusion that their often conflicting objectives are better served in the long run by mutually agreeing to restrict the means of their political conflict in this fashion, even if doing so periodically results in discouraging setbacks.

While as Easton (1965) suggests, all political issues involve disagreements about values, some political issues illustrate this character of politics more clearly than others. It is to such issues that we turn in this and the succeeding chapter. In this chapter we examine how the United States and France deal with abortion. In the next we study how the United States and Japan handle immigration and citizenship issues. While regulating abortion as well as immigration and citizenship requires public funds which must be raised through taxes, the financial burdens of public policies in these areas are relatively modest. This allows attention to focus more clearly on the morality of the activities, rather than on the difficulties of paying for them. Is it good or bad to legalize abortions, or is it good and bad under different circumstances, and if so, what are those circumstances? Immigration and naturalization raise similar questions. Rival political perspectives disagree on such matters, and examining these issues gives us even clearer insight as to why the United States does not emulate the policies of other societies than we obtained from our examination of public sector redistribution in chapters 2 and 3.

Efforts to regulate aspects of sexual activity, which are so basic to persons' lives, attract attention and controversy nearly everywhere. As McFarlane and Meier (2001, 7-8) suggest, the demand for abortion is relatively inelastic. That is, abortions are likely so important to a significant portion of those who want them that these people will pay nearly any price, including a high risk of death, in order to obtain them. So the regulation of abortions has stirred controversy in France as well as in the United States. But variations in the historical contingencies that these two societies have confronted and the resulting differences in their paths of institutional development and cultures have produced distinctive struggles over and policies toward abortion. To learn how this is the case, let us first have a look at the French situation.

FRENCH HISTORY, INSTITUTIONS AND CULTURE

HISTORY

While persons in many regions of Europe were still consumed by local rivalries, regional leaders in the area that we now know as France managed, primarily through conquest but with some compromise, to meld their domains into a larger unit that included most persons of various French languages and traditions. France thus became one of the earliest "nation-states" of Europe. As a consequence France was a "great power" from late in the fifteenth century until the mid-twentieth century. During this period France engaged in frequent military conflicts throughout Europe. Success in these engagements required, and across the first three centuries of this period France developed, what became the model for the European version of the Ancien Régime, an absolute monarch served by a fairly capable group of advisors.

Since the demise of the Ancien Régime in the Revolution of 1789, France has endured several sharp shifts in its type of government or "regime." That is, abrupt transformations similar to but generally milder than that between the extreme autocracy of the Ancien Régime and the dramatic leveling of the Revolution have occurred repeatedly. Analysts differ in their characterizations of these shifts. Ehrmann (1983) stresses the contrast between representative republican regimes (e.g., the Third and Fourth Republics) and what he calls more "plebiscitarian" regimes which attempt to realize conceptions of what Rousseau called the general will by involving citizens in plebiscites at particular junctures (e.g., the Revolution—1793 stage—and aspects of the Fifth Republic after 1962). Pye (1988) shows that these latter regimes can quickly transform into forms of authoritarian rule, but Ehrmann downplays the authoritarian aspects of post-Revolutionary French regimes. Derbyshire (1988) concentrates on the contrast between authoritarian regimes (e.g., Napoleon, Louis Napoleon and Vichy as well as aspects of the Fifth Republic) and the different forms of republican regimes on which Ehrmann focuses.

A consequence of French society shifting among various regime types, each representing the distinctive beliefs, values and interests, is that the followers of sequential regimes have little in common. Authoritarians support monarchy and other stratifying regimes (e.g., the Nazi-inspired Vichy government), but they are much less able to lend their support to the intervening republican regimes that are, in different ways, more tied to the adherents of Rousseau or Locke. Similarly, while supporters of contrasting types of republican regimes find some aspects worthy of their support in different republican institutions, they are alienated from the intervening periods of authoritarian rule. Consequently, different segments of French society are distinguished by unusually great social distances (Ehrmann 1983). That is, in contrast to the United States, where in most instances the marriage of a daughter from a Republican family to a son from a Democratic household would not, on the basis of this distinction alone, be the cause of much hand wringing, the daughter of a family adhering to the socially conservative Rally for the Republic (RPR) marrying the son of a Socialist family in France would often be cause for mutual alarm. Interparty social distance is reinforced by the organization—stronger at some times and on some issues than others—of many adherents of rival political perspectives into antagonistic social classes: a socialist working class, an economically conservative entrepreneurial class, and a socially conservative "social aristocracy" composed largely of professionals.

Charles de Gaulle lent the immense charisma and authority that he had enhanced and acquired—respectively—as the leader of the Free French forces during the Second World War, to the development of the French Fifth Republic in 1958. The Fourth Republic had been nearly torn asunder by a variety of political conflicts, none so volatile as what to do with regard to revolutionary movements in French Indo-China and particularly Algeria. The antagonistic stalemate that arose around these issues created a crisis in French politics. In conjunction with de Gaulle's leadership, this crisis produced previously rare compromises. A major example involved grafting an extremely powerful president onto the traditional French parliamentary system. So in the Fifth Republic, supporters of republicanism retained a parliament, while authoritarians found solace in the addition of a dominant executive which has on occasion employed plebiscites. This combination of a strong executive and a representative parliament, in conjunction with several other factors discussed below, has moderated French political instability and, particularly over the last several decades, produced a society less torn by internal conflicts (Gaffney 1991; Jenkins 2000, 120-21; Reynolds 2000).

INSTITUTIONS

Sharp regime transitions from authoritarian to republican and back at frequent junctures have hampered the modern French state in developing a coherent path of institutional development. This situation has been exacerbated by the high levels of instability characteristic of the governments of the Third and Fourth Republics, spanning most of the years between 1870 and 1958. Both of these republics supported a range of political parties. Several parties were sufficiently popular among voters so that no single party commanded a majority in parliament. This led to coalition governments which tried to hold diverse perspectives together. Leaders frequently failed to satisfy the disparate elements of their governing coalitions. Accordingly, these governments were unseated, often after having served for only a short time, by parliamentary votes of no confidence once a partner had defected from the coalition.

This party system was supported by the significant social-class distances separating different segments of French society, so this structure has contributed as well to France's problems in developing a coherent path of institutional development. Indeed, Lijphart (1977) calls France a "centrifugal" society. That is, for lengthy periods in French political life different segments of society have all pulled away from the center in varying directions, and sometimes, at any rate, there has been little left to hold society together. For instance, when Americans are asked to identify themselves in terms of ideology on a Left-to-Right ideological continuum, they routinely cluster around a "center-right" position, forming a single-peaked distribution with most voters near the middle of the range of views.[1] The single peak near the middle of the ideological spectrum is one index of "centripetal" societies in which the social distances separating the adherents of various political orientations are relatively small and opportunities for compromise often available. In contrast, when French citizens vote, they have historically revealed a different distribution. Rather than forming a single peak, they have divided into two broad peaks, one forming on the left side of the ideological spectrum—currently supporters of the Socialist Party with some Communists to their left—and the other on the right side—currently supporters of the socially conservative RPR, the economically conservative Union for French Democracy (UDF) and the extreme social conservatives of Jean-Marie Le Pen's National Front on the far right.[2] In further contrast to the United States, there have been relatively few citizens in the middle of the ideological spectrum, a hallmark of a centrifugal society.

In addition to the contributions of socially distanced classes and their rival political parties to France's difficulty in maintaining a coherent path of institutional development, French society has also been torn by struggles between relatively well-organized clerical (i.e., Roman Catholic) and anticlerical (i.e., generally secular republican) factions. Analysts of

French society frequently contend that class and party divisions have co-
incided with clerical and anticlerical positions, respectively (Jenkins
2000, 118). Thus they suggest that high-status conservatives tend to be
clerical, while Socialists of more modest social status adopt anticlerical
positions. Lijphart (1984, 145) provides a general model of intrasocietal
conflict in two dimensions that fits better with French reality. He con-
structs a triangle the base of which represents the conflict between the
secular Left (i.e., varying socialists) and Right (i.e., economic conservatives). The tip opposite the base represents the clerical position (social
conservatives).

This model distinguishes the clerical position, not just from the Left,
but from French secular politics generally, which comes in two forms.
The varying lengths of the different sides in Lijphart's model represent
the relative degree of distance or conflict between the Left and Right as
well as between the two secular positions and the clerical view. Since
1789 the lengths of the sides in the French case have varied across time
and issues. But there has been an overall trend toward a shorter triangle
(less secular-clerical conflict) and even some shortening of the base (reduced conflict between Left and Right). Often, in France as elsewhere,
the clerical tip of the triangle has been offset to the right, indicating that
social conservatives have more in common with economic conservatives
than with various forms of socialism on the political Left. But while
France has supported less thorough collaboration between Christian
democracy and social democracy than other European societies such as
Sweden, French social conservatives and socialists do share some common political enterprises such as advancing public social programs.

In spite of these obstacles for maintaining a coherent path of institutional development, the tradition of an active executive, inherited from
the Ancien Régime, has survived—with some intermittent break-
downs—across time. Such an executive was crucial both for France's frequent military conflicts initially in Europe and then—until
recently—across the globe generally as well as for maintaining continuity
of routine public services during periods of republican instability. The institutional foundation of the Fifth Republic (i.e., a powerful independent
president alongside a parliamentary system) draws on and reinforces this
tradition. Additionally, Fifth Republic's executive appears to have contributed to moderating regime and government instability and possibly
even the centrifugal character of French society.

One measure of these changes is the increasing stability of French republican leaders. A contributing element in this regard is the lengthy
(seven-year) term of the powerful president. During the Fifth Republic's

early years, de Gaulle—who served as president until 1969—provided virtually unprecedented central direction to a French republic, countering at least some of the centrifugal tendencies of French society. Repeatedly, he simply overwhelmed parliamentary disagreement and inaction by using the powers of the presidency (including calling national plebiscites) to move issues forward. De Gaulle's immediate successors as president came from his party, (currently) the RPR, or at least from other parties associated with the political Right (currently the UDF). It was not until the election of François Mitterrand (Socialist Party) in 1981 that the constitutional structure of the Fifth Republic received a truly rigorous test with regard to fostering elite stability. Yet the replacement of conservative (initially socially conservative and subsequently—with Valéry Giscard d'Estaing—more economically conservative) elites by Socialist elites went smoothly, and this transition suggests that political conflict in France, while remaining vibrant, is less prone to the centrifugal tendencies for which it was long so infamous. The relative rejection—in the presidential and parliamentary elections of 2002—by voters of both the Left (i.e., Socialists) and the extreme Right (i.e., National Front) with the resulting triumph of what is now called the "Center Right" (i.e., RPR) is an example of this recent trend away from centrifugal politics.

Other factors contributing to elite stability are independent of constitutional restructuring. An example is the increasing influence of the National School of Administration (ENA). While this institution was created in the immediate aftermath of the Second World War, it was not until the Fifth Republic that its graduates were both numerous and prominent enough in government for its influence to be felt. ENA's graduates have included a progressively larger and now a significant proportion of high-ranking national bureaucratic officials. Additionally, they are found in increasing numbers among prominent politicians, including presidents of the Republic (e.g., Giscard d'Estaing). While the school's graduates are hardly cookie-cutter duplicates, the institution's focus on updating and improving traditional French use of a powerful central state for solving societal problems tends to foster economic conservatives who are less prone to bash the state than their American (Reagan) or British (Thatcher) counterparts as well as social democrats with few qualms about using central-state bureaucracies in the service of policies that reduce selective social inequalities. In this fashion, ENA reduces differences in policy preferences among contemporary French political elites from those evident among their counterparts in the Third and Fourth Republics.

Additional factors contributing to the reduction of centrifugal tendencies in French society include gradually growing affluence coupled with a moderate degree of after-tax-and-public-transfer income inequality. While impoverished pockets of hopelessness remain and in some instances have even grown, the competition for control of the French state between more moderate Socialists, who no longer face a significant party on their Left flank, and slightly more moderate conservatives (social and economic) has helped to translate increasing societal affluence into better lives for a substantial portion of the population.

CULTURE

According to Grendstad (1999), France is an example of a "low-group" society. That is, in the population generally, adherents of the low-group cultures (fatalism and individualism) are more numerous than the adherents of egalitarianism and hierarchy (the high-group cultures). (See table 2.1, p. 36.) These proportions and the remarkably high representation of fatalists that Grendstad reports (46 percent) are signs of a long and bitterly divided society. When a democracy's citizenry is composed of a large proportion of fatalists, political stability is particularly dependent on the capacity of the adherents of the three socially interactive cultures (i.e., hierarchy, individualism and egalitarianism) to compromise with one another so as to acquire enduring governing coalitions. Historically, French political cultures have lacked this capacity.

France's unusual division of its citizenry among cultures is likely a consequence of repeated regime changes and republican instability. When shifts from republican to hierarchical regimes occur, what have previously been raised as central political values (e.g., liberty, equality and—in egalitarian regimes—solidarity), become decried as evils. A similar transformation occurs for central hierarchical values (e.g., harmonious order, social stratification, expertise) when varying republican regimes replace hierarchical ones. It is understandable that ordinary members of a society whose leaders periodically shift so sharply in their views on the nature of values—views that are translated into laws and the character of other political institutions—should gradually drift in significant numbers toward fatalism. Persons turn to fatalism when their environments seem unpredictable and uncontrollable. If practicing what is virtuous in one period leads to ordinary persons being pilloried for knavery in another, then adopting fatalistic orientations is an understandable popular reaction. Ehrmann (1983, 57-64, 78-80) shows that many French citizens hold fatalistic views, distrusting public authority but craving order. Other analysts point out a relative absence in France of civil society—few voluntary citizen organizations (Jenkins 2000, 116-17)—which produces circumstances similar to those associated with fatalism in southern Italy (Banfield 1958; Putnam with Leonardi and Nanetti 1993).

But complementing the trends among both the historical and institutional factors discussed above, recent changes in the lines of French social conflict may create less extreme cultural divisions and rivalries. On some contemporary issues, for instance, the traditional French population becomes a group confronting "the other." I offer two brief examples. First, the character of French citizenship has become increasingly unclear. By European standards France has traditionally been relatively open to immigrants who have come mostly from other European societies and members of the French Community. But for the French the appropriate process with respect to such immigrants has been their assimilation as French. That is, the immigrants should acquire the language and social customs of the French and "pass for" French, save in some instances for physiological characteristics. The large influx of North African Muslims over the past few decades has created increasing problems for this view. The Muslims have argued for a right to be different (Weil and Crowley 1994). Many French citizens, from supporters of Le Pen's National Front on the extreme Right of French politics to many members of the Socialist Party on the Left, have taken exception to this stance, so French immigration problems have brought some traditional adversaries in French politics together on an increasingly prominent set of issues (Jenkins 2000, 120). Second, a broad swath of French society made a hero of José Bové, the farmer who damaged a Paris MacDonald's outlet in 1999. From Socialists to the National Front there are many who take pride in France retrieving grandeur as a leader against globalization either in the form of a single global economic market or in terms of the dominance of American popular culture (Meunier 2000).

A summary characterization of the political cultures of the current Fifth Republic seems in order. With respect to political elites, while the adherents of all three of grid-group theory's socially interactive cultures are prominently represented, hierarchists and egalitarians still outnumber individualists. Hierarchists are the most numerous among the political elite as a result of their heavy representation among central-state bureaucrats. As we discussed in chapter 1, fatalists are not found among political elites in contemporary advanced industrial societies, although the numerous fatalists among the French citizenry are probably more comfortable with a thoroughly hierarchical state than with the institutions favored by individualists and egalitarians. With respect to the population generally, Grendstad's 1990 data indicate that fatalism remains the most prominent culture (1999), but it seems likely that recent factors which I mentioned above (i.e., increasing stability of French political leaders, growing affluence, and the rise of issues which bring many French citizens together) have progressively reduced the level of fatalism in French society. Several analysts contend that the French are becoming more individualistic, increasingly finding happiness in individual private, rather than collective public, pursuits (Khilnami 1996). Grendstad's data (1999) suggest that individualism is the second largest culture among the general public. While Grendstad finds that progressively smaller proportions of the population adhere to the egalitarian and hierarchical cultures for which France is famous (i.e., the Revolution and the Ancien Régime), it is not clear that their numbers, as opposed to their strident political activity, are decreasing.

CONTRASTING THE UNITED STATES AND FRANCE

For nearly four centuries France had intermittent yet extensive experience with military conflict on its various frontiers. For instance, during the twentieth century—within the memories of many contemporary French citizens—France experienced German invasion in both world wars and defeat and occupation in the Second World War. These experiences helped to foster a statist tradition in the form of a powerful executive actively involved in society. Although this tradition developed from military exigency, it was expanded early and easily to welfare concerns with domestic policy implications: population enhancement, other aspects of family policy and eventually the broader public social programs associated with the modern welfare state. This tradition, born in the Ancien Régime, was stymied at various junctures from the Revolution of 1789 until the Fifth Republic by sharp regime shifts and government instability, but since 1958 it has been retrieved and enhanced by that Republic's constitutional structure.

In contrast, the United States' historical experiences, particularly those imposed from abroad, have generally threatened less chilling societal consequences. Accordingly, until the twentieth century, actions of the U.S. national government touched the lives of most American communities only at lengthy intervals and then generally briefly. While the structure of the 1787 Constitution did provide greater central-government capacity than the Articles of Confederation, it offered only narrow support for a strong executive and routine state intervention social life and was visibly skeptical of statism. The path of development for political institutions that it carved was shaped by experiences that fostered the idea that most persons were capable of mastering their own fates. In turn, this institutional path helped to sustain this idea.

Before turning to abortion policy, I ought to clarify what may seem to be an incongruity in my characterization of French political culture. In our examination of the United States in chapter 2, we found a society dominated by the low-grid cultures, particularly individualism. The political institutions of the United States—its modestly funded, relatively inactive and highly fragmented public sector—strongly suggest that individualists are also extremely prominent among the American political elite. The situation that we have uncovered with respect to France is different in three respects. First, with regard to the citizenry generally, France appears to be a "low-group," rather than "low-grid," society in which fatalists and individualists comprise the two largest segments of the population. Second, all three of grid-group theory's socially interactive cultures are well represented among the French political elite. I have suggested that hierarchists are the most numerous, followed by egalitarians, with individualists as the least numerous. Hierarchists achieve first place by combining the representatives of hierarchical political parties (e.g., the RPR) and the upper levels of the national bureaucracy, which are predominantly hierarchical. Egalitarians take second place on the basis of extensive electoral support for the Socialist Party.

So, third, in contrast to the United States, in which the mass and elite cultures appear similar, the French political elite might be characterized as "high-group," whereas the mass political culture is predominantly "low-group." How does such an incongruity develop in a democracy? I draw on two factors for an explanation. First, fatalists tend to be relatively inactive politically. They vote in more modest proportions than do the adherents of the socially interactive cultures, and they rarely if ever have fatalistic candidates to vote for. Consequently, the large proportion of fatalists in the population is not reflected in the political elite. Second, while many French fatalists may be shifting to individualism in their orientations toward their private lives (Jenkins 2000, 121; Khilnami 1996), the political preferences of those who remain fatalists are likely to predispose them toward hierarchy. As adherents of a high-grid culture, fatalists are attracted to the central hierarchical idea that sanctioned experts can lead society toward the one best or correct way of doing everything. But as the adherents of a low-group culture, fatalists lack faith in the experts of a society from which they feel alienated. Nonetheless, to the degree that fatalists are politically active, they are apt to support hierarchical leaders and institutions over the low-grid alternatives.

CONTRASTING SOCIETAL APPROACHES TO ABORTION

ABORTION PREFERENCES OF RIVAL CULTURES

Assume again that we have no information about how the United States and France have dealt with abortion. What might we able to deduce about their approaches to abortion knowing that the United States is a "low-grid" society in which individualists are exceptionally influential and France is a society in which the "low-group" cultures predominate among the citizenry in general but the "high-group" cultures, particularly hierarchy, dominate among its political elite?

Because individualists perceive the world from a low-grid perspective, they believe that persons are capable of making their own life decisions. They acknowledge, of course, that there are some persons who do not appear to be able to master their own fates. But they believe that overall persons are better off when society is structured so as to provide systematic incentives for them to strive to run their own lives, thereby minimizing approaches which seek to assign either particularly capable individuals or collectives of equals to make decisions about the lives of ordinary citizens. For individualists, these alternatives, as Hayek famously noted, lead society down "the road to serfdom" (Hayek 1976b). Individualists believe that having a few persons in society who do not make adequate decisions about their lives serves as a reminder to the rest about the perils of individuals failing to live up to their responsibilities to themselves.

From Locke (*Second Treatise*) on, individualists have attempted to enhance persons' abilities to safeguard their interests—by making the decisions that form their lives themselves—through the device of individual rights. Locke argued that careful examination of the way the world was designed to work revealed that it was never appropriate for others to usurp a person's "conscious purposes." That is, we should allow others the right to live their lives as they see fit, exercising their (natural) rights to "life, liberty and the pursuit of property" in the manner best suited to their own peculiarities. While Locke recognized that a few persons would behave as "noxious creatures" in the sense that the agendas which they chose would routinely involve usurping others' conscious purposes, he imagined a more appropriate life for all under a regime which supported humans' natural rights.

Of particular relevance to our topic in this chapter is Locke's view that a person has property in (i.e., owns or minimally holds a long-term lease on) her or his body and the uses to which it is put. Locke used this view to explain how persons might claim an exclusive right to possessions that they could then use to protect real or personal property from the predations of others, including a government's demands for taxes. In Locke's view, persons could claim such a right by mixing their labor with previously unclaimed property (e.g., collecting walnuts from the forest floor) or by making a mutually acceptable voluntary agreement to exchange something to which they had a legitimate claim (e.g., a nugget of gold found in a stream) for something else which was legitimately claimed by another party (e.g., a sack of walnuts). For Locke, persons who lacked the ability to protect the products of their labor became, in effect, slaves. That is, their conscious purposes could be routinely usurped, so that their own agendas for their lives were replaced by the agendas that others imposed on them. They might collect walnuts with the intent of eating them later, only to have a more physically powerful person take them away or (under an illegitimate government) a legally more powerful person extract them in taxation.

Later thinkers in the individualistic tradition have tried to avoid reliance on the natural rights which Locke presumed to represent God's will. Instead, many have focused—similarly to Hayek—on the practical consequences of different social practices. From the views of John Stuart Mill and other early utilitarians on, this vein of individualism has contended that recognizing a broad sphere of individual rights—characteristically what are called civil-political rights today[3]—produces more favorable social, economic and political consequences or circumstances for the vast majority of persons in society.

With respect to abortion, then, individualists are predisposed to argue that a woman has a right to determine how her body will be used. For society to require her, against her will, to use her body for the development of a fertilized egg into an infant represents, in this view, a form of servitude. It amounts to the woman denying her own conscious purposes and delivering her body—her property—over to the purposes of others. This view—as well as two others which follow below—carries certain implicit assumptions (e.g., that the fetus is, at least for a time, not a full-fledged person, with equal and countervailing interests and rights) that are open to argument on various moral and increasingly empirical grounds. Yet in most societies, even today, the moral positions associated with grid-group theory's three socially interactive cultures affect abortion issues more prominently than the knowledge of empirical science. Thus we might anticipate that in a society in which individualists are highly influential, such as the United States, women would have significant legal capacity to acquire abortions on demand and that this ability would be protected by their being accorded certain individual rights.

Hierarchists characteristically disagree with all the crucial points of the individualistic perspective on abortion, and social conflict over abortion policy frequently pits hierarchists against individualists. If, as hierarchists believe, persons' natural capacities for behaving prudently and morally vary sharply with only a relatively few having the ability to make sound decisions, then having capable persons make decisions for others represents a sensible way to organize society. Accordingly, hierarchists are unwilling to leave important decisions in the hands of ordinary persons. If, as hierarchists also tend to believe, there is one correct way of doing everything, then the preferences of ordinary persons are unimportant. The hierarchical approach to virtually all issues of appropriate behavior relies on regulation by experts. Those considered to possess the greatest knowledge about certain areas of social life are granted the legal capacity for defining appropriate behavior within their spheres of expertise. So what is crucial from the hierarchical perspective is what sanctioned experts consider appropriate.

This question, in turn, tends to hinge on the criteria for identifying sanctioned experts. In this regard, the prominent historical bases for social stratification (i.e., discriminating more and less capable persons) have not favored women. These bases have minimally included age, ethnicity, gender and social class. While particularly under contemporary circumstances of advanced industrial societies involving relative socioeconomic affluence and biotechnical capacity, the demand for abortion is not limited to relatively young women, abortion has historically been of primary concern to such women. Given widespread historical patterns of male social dominance, this means that at least two of the four primary bases for social stratification (age and gender) do not favor relatively young women being included among those making decisions about the appropriateness of abortion in hierarchical societies. Additionally, while the demand for abortion is hardly limited to lower socioeconomic strata, it seems likely that having legal access to abortion is of greater concern to women of relatively low socioeconomic status than it is to women in elite families. Wealth and social position facilitate both evading and coping with society's strictures.

So in hierarchical societies women generally need considerable empathy from others—distinguished from them by gender, age and social class—in order for them to have abortion as a legitimate option. This empathy has been forthcoming in a variety of societies across considerable stretches of time, but it has frequently been lacking as well (McFarlane and Meier 2001, ch. 2). While there are certainly exceptions, hierarchists are prone to perceive abortion as attempting to solve problems arising from one irresponsible action by taking yet another irresponsible action. Thus the mature, high-status males who have typically provided pervasive direction for the members of hierarchically organized societies have frequently sought—and continue to seek—to deny the legitimacy of abortion. Their specific reasons have varied from honest abhorrence at the taking of incipient life, through religious convictions that the appropriate purpose of sexual intercourse makes abortion unnecessary, to overt desires to use control over women's sexual lives to hold them in subservient social positions.

So, while the leaders of some hierarchically dominated societies may adopt relatively permissive rules with regard to abortion, the crucial feature common to hierarchical regimes is that socially recognized experts, not ordinary members of society, determine when abortions are permissible. Further, authorities may employ stern measures in their efforts to persuade ordinary persons to follow what the former regard as the correct path with respect to abortion. The precise forms of regulation favored by hierarchists in a particular society (e.g., France) cannot be predicted from culture alone. Hierarchical elites employ different patterns of regulation as a result of their societies' varying historical experiences and paths of institutional development.

While societal struggles over abortion policy tend to make allies of egalitarians and individualists, the former have their own distinctive orientation toward abortion questions. Egalitarians' low-grid perspective, which argues for treating persons as equals, coupled with their high-group perspective, which requires inclusiveness with respect to the concerns of affected persons, leave them reluctant to accept either the hierarchists' tendency to proscribe abortions on the basis of exceptional expertise or the individualists' unfettered-right-to-abortion approach. Until the point at which they consider the development of a fertilized egg to produce a person, coequal with the pregnant woman, contemporary egalitarians are sympathetic toward abortion when, for the woman in question, bringing the fetus to term would produce significant deleterious consequences either for the woman and/or others connected to her—existing children, a spouse, dependent elderly parents. These consequences might include health risks (physical or psychological) for the woman as well as difficulties in acquiring the increased resources—money, time, energy—necessary for adequately caring for an expanded household.

While egalitarians have a tougher time supporting abortion after the point at which the fertilized egg is considered to become a person, abortion may not be precluded for them even under these circumstances. The costs for the woman and other persons associated with her of bringing a given fetus to term might still outweigh the cost of not doing so for a nonconscious fetus. This might particularly be the case if the life of the person-to-be would be blighted by physiological abnormalities which would also place exceptionally heavy demands for care on others or if the household would face serious deprivation.

Yet the juncture at which the development of a fertilized egg is considered to produce a person is clearly important in the egalitarian calculus. There is an additional person to consider after this point, and abortion will mean ending the life of that person. Nonetheless, contemporary egalitarians, particularly feminists, have characteristically pushed this point back in time toward its logical limit: birth. Indeed use of the concept *person* is designed to facilitate this extension. Requiring that the development of a fertilized egg produce a person is more demanding than inquiring as to when a *life* begins, as hierarchists are inclined to do (English 1975). Contemporary egalitarians' tendency to push toward the limit in this regard is likely a consequence of their concern to counter what they view as the pervasive and pernicious influence of hierarchy in social life and, among feminists in particular, to offset what they perceive as the especially destructive effects of gender hierarchy.

Yet the truly distinctive aspect of the egalitarian perspective on abortion questions is the inclusive consideration of affected persons. Individualists are prone to allow a woman to do what she wants with respect to abortion without protecting the concerns of others. For better or worse, one of the consequences of having a right in the individualistic sense, is that one's actions are not constrained by their social costs. These rights are trump cards (Dworkin. 1977). High-group hierarchists are predisposed to consider collective costs which may cut both ways. The potential public costs of birthing infants with physiological abnormalities who would likely become expensive wards of the state may lead them to favor abortion in some instances. Yet they routinely consider as well collective costs, such as societal disintegration, which they often see as resulting from insufficient restraint on what they regard as immoral practices such as sexual promiscuity. So hierarchists frequently oppose abortion as a means for raising the costs of and thus discouraging such activity.

But the combination of low-grid and high-group influences that form the egalitarian perspective produce a unique concern for the full range of individual persons who are significantly affected by particular situations

(Gilligan 1982). What the egalitarian seeks to accomplish is a resolution that does as well as possible by all concerned. This is a worthy but also a demanding and characteristically loosely defined objective. Realizing this objective in particular instances often requires drawing on subjective definitional devices such as requiring personhood rather than the beginning of life or discounting the concerns of those exhibiting noticeable gender hierarchy. Fortunately, since egalitarians usually govern in coalitions involving the adherents of other cultures, they may infuse public policy with constructive aspects deriving from their unique concern for all affected individuals without necessarily being able to impose dubious definitional devices on their coalition partners.

We are now in a position to offer a general—not precise—prediction about French abortion policy that draws on both the hierarchical and the egalitarian portions of the preceding discussion. To recapitulate, we should expect the prominent influence of hierarchists among the French political elite to produce an abortion policy in which elites—not pregnant women among the citizenry—define when abortion is appropriate. This policy will evince skepticism about the appropriateness of abortion, but it may treat what are perceived as significantly varying situations differently. Further, as a result of the influence of egalitarians among the French political elite in the last several decades, we should expect French abortion policy to include consideration of the consequences for the full range of persons affected by particular abortion decisions.

U.S. ABORTION POLICY

American regulation of abortion has varied considerably across time. While regional differences have generally existed, during the colonial period and the early years of the United States, efforts to proscribe abortion were limited and unsystematic. According to Mohr (1978, vii), for instance, abortion was not illegal in any state in 1800. This situation began to change in the 1820s, initially more as a response to the high risk of women's death from prevailing abortion practices than as a principled rejection of the procedure (Sheeran 1987, 54-55). Yet the legal restrictions on abortion of this period were widely ignored and only rarely enforced (Rosenblatt 1992, 86). Formal legal proscription of abortion grew across the next four decades without much affecting social practice. In the early 1860s the American Medical Association (AMA) began supporting laws restricting abortion, partially as a result of changing conceptions about the beginning of life and partially so as to better secure a monopoly on the practice of medicine (Sheeran 1987, 55-56). By the

1870s the Catholic Church began opposing abortion as a result of Pope Pius IX's position on the early beginning of fetal life (Tribe 1992, 32). Some Protestant clergy also began expressing opposition to abortion, but organized religion in America was not a fervent opponent of abortion through the nineteenth century (Sheeran 1987, 56).

Nonetheless, state regulation grew, and by the early twentieth century abortion was legal only in Kentucky (Craig and O'Brien 1993), except when done in order to save the life of the mother.[4] Yet Luker (1984) estimates that during the early twentieth century one-third of pregnancies were aborted. As McFarlane and Meier (2001, 8) suggest, demand for abortion—driven by the social costs of unwanted children—was inelastic with respect to both the legal penalties and even the danger of death associated with the practice. Therapeutic abortions (i.e., those done in order to save the life of the mother) grew in number through the early 1950s, at which point the practice of allowing individual physicians to conduct these operations based on their own judgment began to be replaced by the requirement of advance approval from hospital review boards.

Advocates of abortion responded to this new restriction in part by prompting a new Model Penal Code from the American Law Institute (ALI) which argued for allowing abortion in three types of situations: if continuing a pregnancy would harm a woman's physical or mental health; if the fetus was likely to be born with significant physical or mental abnormalities; and if the pregnancy were due to rape or incest (Tribe 1992, 37). During the early 1960s, epidemics of children born with significant physiological abnormalities—some due to the use of thalidomide, others the consequence of a rubella epidemic—reinforced the ALI's suggestions for liberalizing abortion restrictions (Tribe 1992, 37-38). The AMA contributed to this process by reversing its century-long opposition to abortion in 1967 and coming out in favor of liberalizing restrictions. About 40 percent of American states did ease restrictions on abortion in the late 1960s. Most followed the ALI suggestions, but a few (e.g., Hawaii and New York) decriminalized abortion during the early portion of pregnancy. Women seeking safe legal abortions traveled to these states in large numbers in the early 1970s (Sheeran 1987, 57).

American abortion policy was transformed in 1973 by the U.S. Supreme Court's ruling in *Roe v. Wade* (401 U.S. 113). This decision, in turn, grew out of *Griswold v. Connecticut* (391 U.S. 145—1965), which argued that a right to privacy surrounding marital reproductive activities was antecedent to but supported by the Bill of Rights. In *Roe v. Wade* the Court held that women had a constitutional right to abortion, on the basis of citizens' right to privacy in their personal lives, that state legislation could not contravene. The Court ruled that during the first trimester of pregnancy this right was constrained only by the requirement that abortions be performed by licensed physicians. Restrictions during the second trimester could be more extensive, but were again derived from concern for the mother's health, and additional state regulations contributing to this end were permissible. *Roe v. Wade* let general proscription of abortion during the third trimester stand, arguing that by this stage the protection of developing fetal life overrode the mother's right to privacy about decisions involving her personal life (Tribe 1992, 10-13). By finding a basis for a right to abortion in the U.S. Constitution, the Court effectively blocked legislative efforts to prohibit abortion. Since 1973, the formulation of abortion policy for the United States as a whole has occurred through a number of federal court decisions, which have generally involved rulings on various state efforts to constrain the right, created by *Roe v. Wade,* of abortion on demand throughout the greater portion of pregnancy.

As Glendon (1987) shows, both the conception of a right to abortion and this relatively wide window for abortion on demand are unusual among advanced industrial societies and suggest the firm position of individual rights in American society. This policy stance, lenient in contemporary comparative perspective, has essentially withstood a large number of formal legal challenges. Subsequent major court rulings have refined U.S. policy toward abortion but left a significant area of individual discretion standing.[5] I discuss several categories of rulings, seeking to minimize legalistic jargon and formal case nomenclature. McFarlane and Meier (2001, ch. 4) provide one of many more detailed yet accessible discussions.

Likely the most significant change to *Roe v. Wade* occurred in 1992 (*Planned Parenthood of Southeastern Pennsylvania v. Casey*—510 U.S. 1309), when the Supreme Court discontinued the earlier decision's trimester approach. The latter decision used instead the potentially more lenient yet less clearly defined criterion of "undue burden." That is, the state could not place an undue burden on a woman's right to an abortion during a pregnancy. The protection that this decision offers clearly hinges on how "undue burden" is defined.

We can acquire some sense of the current definition by employing the concept retrospectively to explain a variety of other decisions, generally coming before *Casey.* Some of these cases deal with the question as to whether a woman's right to an abortion can require the use of public sector resources—public (e.g., Medicaid) funds, public hospitals (at the state and local level), state-employed physicians—in the provision of abortions. The court has uniformly supported state and local restrictions on the use of public (including federal, e.g., Medicaid) resources. In light of *Casey*, this category of restrictions might now be viewed as posing no undue burden. While this may be so in some abstract sense, it is surely an interpretation that treats abortion services as commodities available on the basis of consumers' ability to pay. Thus from the perspective of these cases, a woman's right to an abortion is a "negative" right; that is, a right to be free from government restraint if she chooses to have an abortion. It is not a "positive" right; that is, a right encompassing whatever external and likely public resources she may require to realize her preference for an abortion. Negative rights have long represented the heart of the Lockean tradition; whereas positive rights have been associated with both social conservatives and particularly social democrats.

A number of decisions (prior to and including aspects of *Casey*) deal with state's efforts to regulate abortions in terms of gaining concurrence from other persons associated with the woman desiring an abortion. The Court has held, for instance, that the consent of a woman's partner, even his notification, is not required. Even with respect to minors, the Court has offered support for individual rights. For instance, *Casey* allowed a judicial determination of maturity in place of requiring notification of one parent. Further, the decision does not demand this procedure nationally, it simply grants that Pennsylvania (or other states wishing to do so) is not imposing an undue burden to require either parental notification or the judicial by-pass. The Court's positions with respect to various notification issues clearly distinguish the United States' abortion policy from the policies of many other societies (McFarlane and Meier 2001, 23).

A few other Court decisions have held modest implications for a woman's right to an abortion by permitting greater procedural complexity. For instance, the standards that define the "informed consent" of the woman having an abortion have risen across time. The Court, in other words, considers that, when states require women seeking abortions to examine other options, they pose no undue burden. The Court has taken a similar stance with regard to having women wait for a day or two after they formally request an abortion.

By focusing on the principle underlying American abortion policy we can acquire a better accounting of the structure of conflict on this issue in the United States. Establishing a constitutional individual right which allows a woman to make her own reproductive decisions (a "pro-choice" position) affects as well the options of persons who wish to oppose abortion as a matter of personal discretion. Simply passing legislation that constrains the right in various ways will not accomplish this objective. The right often trumps such legislation, which is subsequently invalidated in the courts. A more potentially effective strategy for American opponents of a woman's right to choose has been to create another right—a fetus' right to life—that takes precedence over the right of women to privacy in their reproductive decisions (a "pro-life" position). Establishing such a right represents a prominent effort of the contemporary American pro-life movement in its struggle against abortion. So individual rights are such a politically potent device in the United States that the pro-life movement, many of whose members view individual rights' capacity to trump perceptions of the collective good with great skepticism, has had to adopt this—for its members—uncomfortable tool as a primary weapon for overcoming the United States' permissive abortion policy. The pro-life side to this conflict has also sought to shape the U.S. Supreme Court and the federal judiciary generally so that the right to an abortion will lose judicial support. A constitutional amendment banning abortion would presumably be more effective once the federal judiciary was less favorably inclined toward women's right to privacy with respect to their reproductive decisions.

Across nearly three decades neither of these strategies has been successful, a fact bound to try the patience of those who honestly believe that abortion is a form of murder, and a particularly vile form due to the fetus' utter defenselessness. Accordingly, the American pro-life movement, normally a reliable law-and-order constituency, has torn yet another page from the Lockean book of political strategies: civil disobedience. Members have held peaceful demonstrations, passively allowing themselves to be removed by police from blocking the doorways of abortion clinics, in an effort to raise the consciousness of the population to what they regard as the nefarious practices of the prevailing American policy.

Yet, as these same persons are prone to warn with respect to other issues, the line between civil disobedience and battle in the streets is easy to cross, and public demonstrations against abortion have become progressively less constrained by civil disobedience norms. A number of demonstrations at abortion clinics have involved active protesters, shoving and shouting insults in the faces of staff and patients. These demonstrations prompted the Freedom of Access to Clinic Entrances Act (1994), which has been subsequently upheld by the federal courts. A relative few among the pro-life faction have taken the battle in the streets even further: stalking abortion clinic staff and patients and threatening and assassinating physicians who perform abortions. In conjunction with the civil disobedience sanctioned more widely among the American pro-life movement on this issue, these activities contributed to reductions both in the number of abortions performed each year across the 1990s as well as in the number of American counties with abortion clinics (Mc-Farlane and Meier 2001, 113, 128).

Perhaps the most significant consequences of U.S. abortion policy being couched in terms of a constitutionally protected, individual civil right is that dominant abortion positions become extreme, even nonsensical, and abortion issues admit few possibilities for compromise. In the polarized atmosphere of individual rights, ironic incoherence flourishes. So, American pro-choice activists, who generally follow Hobbes and Locke in accepting that a right to life is fundamental, refuse to take sanctity of life issues seriously with regard to fetuses. Instead, anything which—in their view—places an undue burden on a woman seeking abortion services is illegitimate. The political success of this perspective forces opponents to ironic nonsense: a countervailing trump card in the form of fetuses' right to life. Thus American pro-life activists, many of whom are predisposed to make sharp distinctions among persons, insist on granting all fetuses an equal right regardless of their physiological condition. There is no way to cut the Gordian knot that secures the gate to the path of compromise among factions resting their positions on mutually exclusive inviolable individual rights. Yet, whichever side achieves victory in this struggle produces a policy more extreme than that supported by the views of the vast majority of the American population (O'Connor 1996).

FRENCH ABORTION POLICY

France has a more thorough history of legal proscription of abortion than the United States (Pedersen 1996; Stetson 1986). Some of the factors that have motivated American resistance to abortion—concern for the dangers to women's health associated with the practices of many illegal abortionists, resistance from the Catholic Church and others based on views as to when life begins—appear in French resistance to abortion as well. But for nearly a century—from the early 1870s through the early post–Second World War period—a factor absent from American controversies over abortion became a prominent consideration. This was the French birthrate, particularly in contrast to the birthrate of France's major continental competitor in this period: Germany. During this time span France's birthrate was generally declining and was also usually lower than Germany's. In an era in which national status as well as defensive capacity was closely linked to the ability to field large armies, France's relatively low fertility—in combination with its alarming loss in the Franco-Prussian War—contributed to both French feelings of insecurity and a natalist policy. The latter was clearly at odds with aborting fetuses, so for most of a century, abortion was opposed in France at least in part on patriotic grounds. Women who aborted their fetuses were not doing their part to build the French nation as well as its grandeur and military capacities (McIntosh 1983).

As McFarlane and Meier (2001, 8) alert us to expect, the illegality of abortions, and the stiff penalties for either performing or undergoing an abortion prior to the 1920s, were relatively ineffectual in deterring the practice (Stetson 1986, 278).[6] Abortions are thought to have occurred at a rate of close to a half-million a year across the 1920s and 1930s, and this rate is estimated to have doubled after 1945. According to a report by the French National Institute of Demographic Studies, about half of these abortions occurred in instances of poor married women who performed the procedure themselves. The remaining cases, among women with more resources, were characteristically performed by private physicians (Dyer 1978).

Various private groups began agitating for a much less restrictive legal code with respect to abortion in the 1950s, arguing in particular that the discrepancy between the existing law and social practice demonstrated the inappropriateness of the former. The Gaullist government (i.e., de Gaulle as president and Georges Pompidou as prime minister) of the mid-1960s was sufficiently sympathetic to this general argument to be a silent cosponsor of 1967 legislation which legalized contraceptives. But creating greater access to abortion hinged on the impetus that the demonstrations of May 1968 gave the women's liberation movement in France, de Gaulle's resignation in 1969, and the subsequent presidency, beginning in 1974, of Valéry Giscard d'Estaing, who was more sympathetic to the concerns of the secular Right.

Abortion issues acquired a high profile in France in the early 1970s. Several women's organizations kept related contraception and abortion issues in the consciousness of attentive publics and political elites by demonstrating frequently for less restrictive legislation. One organization, Choisir, was particularly effective in this regard by managing the legal defense of a pregnant adolescent rape victim. The young woman had found a physician who was willing to perform an abortion—but for a substantial fee which the adolescent's poor single mother could not afford—and she had thus engaged in a far more dangerous "back-alley" procedure. Choisir organized demonstrations and witnesses designed to educate attentive publics and political elites about the difficulties that existing abortion legislation imposed on women, particularly those who were poor, and it won acquittal for the defendant in this case. Choisir also proposed legislation which provided for free contraceptive services and abortion on demand during the first trimester of pregnancy (to be paid for by the French national health insurance program) and for abortion in cases in which a woman's health was endangered or the fetus was seriously abnormal during the second trimester (Stetson, 1986, 279, 281).

Measures such as these acquired increasing support from the French Left—the Socialist Party and the Communist Party. But there remained much resistance—from the Church, natalists, and particularly from physicians' organizations stressing that medical ethics respected life from conception. Further, France's socially conservative "clerical Right" was extremely influential among the members of the Gaullist Party, which prior to 1974 held the presidency (Pompidou) and was the major coalition partner in the government it formed with its parliamentary colleagues of the secular Right.[7] Nonetheless, under the public pressures that Choisir and other groups had developed, the Gaullist government, now bolstered by a minister of health from the secular Right, proposed a revised statute in 1973. This initiative was fairly similar to the guidelines that the ALI was recommending in the United States in the 1960s. It allowed abortions if two physicians concurred that the pregnancy threatened a woman's physical or mental health, that the fetus was likely to have serious abnormalities, or that the pregnancy had been coerced. Lengthy public hearings over this proposed legislation raised considerable controversy, and in the end the legislation could not win parliamentary approval. Support among the government parties—particularly the Gaullist clerical Right, whose members considered the legislation too lenient—was limited, and the parties of the Left were tepid in their support of this measure, which they perceived as an insufficiently bold reform.

This impasse was broken by the arrival of new leadership. President Pompidou died in April 1974. The subsequent presidential election was a three-way competition among François Mitterrand (Socialist Party), Chaban Delmas (of the socially conservative, Gaullist, clerical Right) and Valéry Giscard d'Estaing (of the more economically conservative, secular Right). Giscard d'Estaing narrowly won over Mitterrand on a platform of change, which he realized in part by appointing Simone Veil—the first woman to hold a cabinet position in the Fifth Republic—as minister of health. The new president instructed her to produce compromise legislation on abortion less restrictive than the existing law and directed the government to suspend prosecuting persons under the existing abortion law.

Veil's legislative initiative, which was strongly supported by Giscard d'Estaing and provides the basic outline for current French law, reflects a political compromise that stands in sharp contrast to the individual rights–dominated *Roe v. Wade* and *Casey* decisions of the U.S. Supreme Court. The 1975 French law (as modestly revised in 1979) entails the following elements. First, although the French legislation requires that, during the first ten weeks (twelve weeks as of 2000) of a pregnancy, French women can obtain an abortion on demand, the legislation is couched in terms of respect for human life and treats abortion, not as a means of birth control, but as a path to be chosen only by women in particular distress as a measure of necessity. In part, this framing of the legislation represents a symbolic payoff to those on the clerical Right for whom allowing ordinary persons to opt for abortion represented a particularly distressing outcome. Yet it also bespeaks a concern—reinforced in other aspects of the legislation—shared minimally by French adherents of both the clerical Right and the Socialist Left with the various persons touched by a woman's decision to have an abortion.

Second, this concern is reinforced by the legislation requiring two processes designed to: educate women considering abortions on a range of issues; include the concerns of other interested parties in the decision process; and if possible dissuade women from choosing an abortion. Distinct aspects of these three goals appeal particularly to the French clerical Right and to the Socialist Left. The first process requires that physicians explain various physiological and psychological risks associated with abortion to potential patients as well as provide these women with extensive information about agencies which are able to offer them various sorts of assistance. The second process requires that women consult a state-sanctioned family counseling, social welfare or similar service on various ways of coping with the problems associated with giving birth and raising a child.

While in practice these processes may be perfunctory in some instances, they represent a serious attempt to educate women considering an abortion with respect to the moral and practical issues associated with the procedure including the material help available to them in overcoming the challenges of accepting and rearing a child. As Glendon (1987) points out, the factors that state-approved counselors discuss include not only alternatives to abortion such as adoption—as tends to be the focus in the United States—but also the range of French public social programs that are available to assist poor, single, or otherwise unprepared women in dealing with bringing the pregnancy to term and mothering the child themselves. Benefits of these programs include: child allowances, publicly financed medical care, paid maternity leave, child care through the public school system (during the day for preschool-aged children and before and after the school day thereafter) and various social services assisting with pregnancy and child-rearing issues. Thus French policy not only strives to consider the fetus more seriously than do crucial American court decisions, there is as well an effort to show women that they are not alone in facing the difficulties that may be associated with adding a child to their lives. Additionally, French law explicitly encourages, though it does not require, that a woman's partner be included in these consultations and the resulting decision.

Third and reinforcing the skeptical attitude toward abortion found elsewhere in the legislation, abortion operations have to be performed by a physician in a hospital, and neither physicians nor hospitals can be required to offer the service. Additionally women must wait a week from the time that they make their initial request for an abortion and two days (which may be part of the overall week requirement) from the time that they complete their consultation with a state-approved counseling service before they are cleared to undergo an abortion procedure (Glendon 1987, 15-22, 146, 155-57). Fourth, after ten weeks (now twelve), abortion is available only when two physicians—one chosen from a list of publicly recognized experts—certify that an abortion is necessary in order to preserve a woman's health or to avoid the birth of a child with a serious condition considered to be incurable.

While some persons have considered French abortion policy to be permissive by international standards (Stetson 1986), the window that it opens for abortion is far narrower than the one available in the United States. Indeed, among contemporary European Union (EU) societies, France's policy has appeared increasingly restrictive as other societies have become progressively more permissive, and it is reasonable to imagine that several of the obstacles that French legislation purposely places in a woman's path to abortion might be interpreted in the United States as constituting an undue burden. The French requirement that abortion operations occur in hospitals, for instance, was specifically designed to avoid the routinization of the procedure, particularly in a setting like that of many U.S. abortion clinics in which the service becomes an essentially one-stop commercial transaction.

This French legislation, with its substantial window for abortion roughly on demand, is more Lockean than the prediction which I offered above about French abortion policy on the basis of the relative influence of rival perspectives. This discrepancy appears to be due to the policy having been developed under the most economically conservative (indeed the only economically conservative) president that the Fifth Republic has had to date. While the UDF's economic conservatives were uncharacteristically influential during Giscard d'Estaing's presidency, their party governed through a multiparty coalition in parliament. Thus they were not in a position to impose their preferences on a society in which the clerical Right and the Socialist Left remained powerful. The legislation that Veil developed was not only a carefully constructed compromise, it was designed to be provisional as well. It was to be examined after five years of operation and affirmed, altered or rescinded based on parliamentary reactions to that experience. The package was initially passed in late 1974 and given final approval by the Constitutional Council in early 1975. It passed its review in 1979 and with some modifications (e.g., the physicians' cautionary process described above) had its provisional status lifted. Shortly after the Socialist Party won the presidency and formed a government in 1981, abortions were added to the medical procedures covered under French national health insurance.

One index which suggests that this compromise legislation dealt acceptably with concerns crucial to the clerical Right, the secular Right and the Socialist Left is that—in contrast to the American experience—abortion pretty much vanished as a high profile issue for a lengthy period after 1975. For instance, the 1979 renewal of the legislation was not a controversial affair. The French legislation represents the sort of compromise that the juxtaposed-rights approach followed in the United States cannot produce. For this compromise character and the relative social harmony that it produces, the French law represents a sensible model for emulation. The two parties most obviously at odds in abortion issues are the pregnant woman and the fetus. As Glendon suggests (1987, 20), much of the focus of the French procedures with physicians and family counseling is to try to defuse this conflict of interest by educating women that French policy includes numerous programs that make the trials of poor, single or otherwise disadvantaged mothers easier than the uninitiated might imagine.

French abortion policy continues to evolve, and some active resistance to abortion reappeared in France during the last decade. In 1993, parliament passed legislation making it illegal to interfere with women obtaining legal abortions. In 1996, a variety of women's groups were sufficiently upset over France's progressive slippage vis-à-vis other EU societies with regard to the availability of abortions to hold high profile demonstrations. As a result, several Socialist-sponsored and generally modest changes in the law were introduced in 2000. The ten-week window of abortion availability was expanded to twelve weeks. Further, while physicians are required to urge them to gain parental approval, minors in the 16-18 age bracket are now allowed to have abortions without parental consent. They are encouraged to have an adult of their choice accompany them through the process. At about the same time the Ministry of Education directed school nurses to begin dispensing RU-486 on demand to adolescent students, but this practice was later restrained by order of the Council of State. However, the 2000 legislation also allowed adolescents access to contraceptives without parental consent, and RU-486 is available inexpensively in pharmacies without prescription, anyway.

So across the last three decades France has followed an accommodative approach to abortion policy which has generally avoided the impasse and confrontational practices of the United States. This amounts to a surprising reversal of the conventional wisdom about a France that shifts sharply between political extremes and a United States that develops policy through incremental compromise steps.

I conclude this section with a general contrast between the United States and French abortion policies. In so doing I draw on distinctions previously made by Glendon (1987) and Kommers (1985) with respect to the Federal Republic of Germany, which, in the 1980s, had an abortion policy similar to France's. First, U.S. policy focuses narrowly on the pregnant woman as a rights-bearing person. Further, in terms of abortion policy this rights-bearing person is conceived as an isolated, separate, autonomous individual. From this view comes a powerful right to privacy such that: "If the right of privacy means anything, it is the right of an *individual,* married or single, to be free from unwarranted government intrusion into matters so fundamentally affecting a person as the decision whether to bear or beget a child" (*Eisenstadt v. Baird*—405 U.S. 438, 453—1972).[8] In contrast, French policy is animated by clear concern for a social network which spirals out from the pregnant woman and connects her with the developing fetus, her partner, other family members and the broader society which stands ready to help with the difficulties of childbirth and child-rearing. Kommers (1985) characterizes the perspective of the U.S. policy as individualistic, a portrayal with which I agree. Judging from his characterization of German policy, I imagine that he would refer to the perspective of the French policy as communitarian. I would use the term high-group and add that communitarians come in egalitarian (Sandel 1982) and hierarchical (MacIntyre 1988) versions.

Another way of characterizing the contrast between U.S. and French abortion policy is suggested by Glendon (1987) and expands on the contrast of different types of rights raised in a previous section of this chapter. There I noted that the right that women have in the United States with respect to abortion is a "negative" right or freedom "from" state constraint. It is, as Glendon sees it (37), an example of license: the ability to do what one pleases without regard for others. As with negative rights, freedom from external and particularly state constraint has been a moral lodestar of individualism. Again in contrast, while French policy enables pregnant women in distress to choose an abortion (and in practice this may amount to their exercising what Glendon calls license in many instances), French policy also tries to educate these women about the moral importance—the taking of a developing life—that a decision to have an abortion entails as well as to the assistance, both moral and practical, that the social collective extends to them if they choose to follow what the high-group cultures, particularly egalitarianism, argue is a more authentic and meaningful conception of liberty: freedom "to" develop as a person in solidarity with those to whom one is connected. So while the policy formulated under the most individualistic presidency of the Fifth Republic clearly gives women an opportunity to make their own decisions about abortion, the strong high-group influence among the French political elite constructed a relatively dense process through which the policy also seeks to foster women's recognition of their connection to their fetus, their partners, other family and members of a society which generally holds the sanctity of life as a value. Further, French society realizes its responsibilities with respect to connectedness through the provision of public programs which offer various forms of educational and practical material support for women facing the challenges of childbirth and rearing children.

HISTORY, INSTITUTIONS, CULTURE AND CAUSALITY

Since the Second World War, many American political scientists have characterized the American political system as one which has historically produced gradual compromise, in contrast to the French political system's historical penchant for sharp shifts of regime or government and thus of policy as well (e.g., Ehrmann and Schain 1992). What we have found in the instance of abortion policy across the last quarter century stands at odds with this characterization. French politics have produced compromise; whereas American politics have resulted in what—against the background of the policies of other advanced industrial societies—is relatively extreme support for selective individual rights. Glendon (1987) calls for American emulation of the French example in part because it has defused conflict over this issue; whereas in the United States conflict has grown as segments of the stymied pro-life forces have employed ever-more provocative actions in support of their position.

I want to draw on the model that I have been developing across this study for help in explaining these contrasting outcomes. This model involves a causal sequence that begins with exceptionally salient societal historical experiences. These experiences, in turn, influence the character of the developmental path of a society's political institutions. This path then helps to shape both the cultures of society's members—frequently reinforcing the culture that originally chose the path—and the character of specific policies. This sequence does not hold a monopoly on causation, but I will emphasize it for the moment. The brief explanations which follow for the United States and France with respect to abortion policy highlight prominent aspects of this sequence or process rather than providing an exhaustive analysis.

In the instance of the United States, society was initially formed by persons of differing political perspectives who nonetheless disapproved in related ways of various ideas and social institutions that were predominant across much of Europe in the seventeenth and eighteenth centuries. In particular, wariness of powerful central government grew in reaction to British practices in the aftermath of the French and Indian War in the 1760s. The American Revolution strengthened this fear of central authority, both by driving many persons who did not share it to Canada and England and also by producing a political victory for those who subscribed to it. The degree of wariness about a powerful central government was reduced by the experiences giving rise to the 1787 Constitution (Beard 1965), but this less severe version of skepticism was sustained by the Constitution, which—drawing particularly on the ideas of Locke and Montesquieu—delineated a path for the further development of American national political institutions, which was limited and fragmented. The Constitution was a deliberate attempt to preserve the liberty of individuals, thought to be capable of mastering their own fates, from a perceived tendency of political factions to sacrifice the interests of other persons to the pursuit of their own ends.

This view of human capacities and tendencies and the resulting priority on liberty in the sense of freedom from external (especially governmental) constraint has been passed from one generation to another in the United States by both primary group socialization (e.g., families) and the socializing influence of broad social institutions (e.g., the Constitution), which become familiar as persons mature in their midst. Maintaining the preeminence of these individualistic beliefs and values has been facilitated by mild American experiences with socially disruptive historical contingencies and a variety of aspects of social structure such as the ethnic pluralism of the American working class, which has hampered efforts to organize worker solidarity.

Thus Americans are more prone than are the members of other advanced societies to follow Locke and Montesquieu in favoring limited government and to defend citizens against the tendency of those who govern to take advantage of others by developing a robust framework of individual rights. In this light it seems that, once women began to be included in practice among the persons whose rights were to be protected, the development of a right to abortion on demand was a likely possibility. At a minimum, if one were to predict from the perspective of 1970 which society would be most likely to develop a policy toward abortion couched in terms of a constitutional individual right to privacy, particularly from state scrutiny, the United States would have been a good bet. In fact, if all one wishes to do is predict what policy directions are likely to prevail in various societies, it is not necessary to draw on the entire causal sequence under discussion (i.e., societal historical experience, path of institutional development, culture and policy). As I demonstrate in the second section of each of the case study chapters, prediction of central policy features can be achieved from the culture stage which immediately precedes the formulation of specific policies in the sequence. But in order to explain cross-societal cultural differences, we need to draw on societal historical experiences and the paths of institutional development which they help to shape. Yet the American "solution" of the question as to when abortions are legitimate—granting women a constitutional right to abortion on demand—has made compromise with those who disagree with this policy quite difficult. Opponents have been forced to attempt equally intransigent solutions (i.e., a fetus' right to life), and some of them—finding little success in this enterprise—have been driven to increasingly provocative tactics.

France's situation stands in sharp contrast to that of the United States. France's "birthing process" was forged to a considerable degree through military conquest, and its subsequent maintenance on a European continent featuring other great powers required the continued development of a powerful executive served by capable advisors. Indeed, in the seventeenth and eighteenth centuries France became the model for royal absolutism and offered the clearest example of what persons referred to with the phrase "the majesty of the state." The French Revolution (1789) ended the Ancien Régime but exhausted neither perceptions among many citizens of France's continuing need for nor periodic efforts to retrieve a powerful capable executive.

Nonetheless, following 1789 sharp changes in regime between authoritarian and multiple republican types as well as persistent instability among republican governments continued for over a century-and-a-half. The unpredictability and uncontrollable character of this period appears to have driven many French citizens to a culture of fatalism. With many citizens essentially alienated from the political system, cooperation among the elites of grid-group theory's three interactive cultures became particularly important for achieving societal stability and success in various public endeavours (e.g., successful national defense in war). Yet from the early nineteenth century through the mid-twentieth century, French political elites did not cooperate particularly well, and societal stability and the success of crucial national enterprises often suffered.

Against this background, the character of the Fifth Republic, formed in 1958, appears to have been particularly salutary. The Fifth Republic's powerful president became a means for resurrecting France's statist tradition, but the maintenance of the parliamentary system provided for the simultaneous inclusion of more republican orientations. After over four decades of operation, there appears little doubt that the dominant political institution in the Fifth Republic is its presidency, regardless as to whether that position is occupied by a member of the clerical Right (e.g., RPR), secular Right (e.g., UDF) or the Socialist Left. Yet the president cannot simply dictate policy and must regularly compromise with parliamentary leaders, whether they represent the president's political party or another.

Giscard d'Estaing and the party which he led in the 1970s were more individualistic, economically conservative, or representative of the secular Right than other Fifth Republic presidents or political parties. So it is unsurprising that a liberalizing step with respect to abortion policy—long sought by Socialists and portions of the secular Right—came during his presidency. Yet Giscard had to cooperate with his coalition partners of the clerical Right and was anxious to avoid antagonizing potential support on this issue from Socialist MPs. Moreover, even Giscard was more interested in sustaining France's statist tradition than were Margaret Thatcher and Ronald Reagan in the United Kingdom and the United States a few years later.

Stetson (1986: 284) reports that Giscard d'Estaing drew on four principles as guides in formulating the French abortion legislation of 1975, which was explicitly designed to achieve a compromise among the adherents of the secular and clerical Right and the Socialists. These principles were: (1) "respect for life" (for which different practical meanings are important to all three factions); (2) "protection of women from the risks of clandestine abortion" (crucial to the two secular factions); (3) "help to mothers in rearing children" (crucial to the Socialists and the clerical Right); and (4) "freedom of conscience for each doctor" (which was of particular interest to the secular and clerical Right). The relative weakness of the French economic conservatives who initiated this legislation appears to have been a blessing. Rather than trying to impose a victory for the secular Right, Giscard d'Estaing purposely sought a compromise which would meet concerns important to the adherents of all three factions but allow the dominance of none. While all factions are thus incompletely satisfied with the resulting legislation, save for a few zealots in each camp, the adherents of all three realize that the broad structure of the current compromise provides more support for their beliefs and values than viable alternatives. This sort of policy is unlikely in a society in which individualists are frequently preeminent, so preeminent that opposing social conservatives are forced into using alternative versions of the individualists' weapon of choice, trumping rights, to formulate their own positions.

Thus French abortion policy, while creating a significant window through which women may avail themselves of abortions, is explicitly couched as a tool of state-guided education and support. The policy goal is to dissuade women from aborting fetuses by requiring them to go through a multistep process which educates them (and ideally their partners) to the physiological risks, the social and moral costs and the significant array of help that the French state makes available to mothers. While many women who have abortions in France may pay little attention to these efforts, the policy requires a process that is clearly more interventionary and obviously represents more of a compromise among rival political perspectives than a constitutional individual right to abortion on demand.

Let us now return to a question that has been raised in previous chapters: What changes would be required (and how might they come about) for the United States to adopt an abortion policy similar to France's? If—in the aftermath of the 2002 election through which the Republican Party acquired control of all elective elements of the national government—the right of women to abortion on demand were somehow overcome (for instance, by a court infused with new judges who promulgated different decisions), it seems that the most likely immediate alternative policy would be a general ban on abortions supported by another trumping right, a fetus' right to life. Over time this stance might admit some limited exceptions—initiated by legislation in some states that the federal courts left standing—which allowed abortions in the three situations covered by the ALI Model Penal Code of the 1950s: serious danger to the woman's physical or mental health; likelihood that the fetus suffers from grave abnormalities; and instances of rape or incest.[9] The polarization of American politics on this issue might produce either of these two alternatives to existing policy. But neither existing American policy nor either of these two alternatives offers the sort of compromise—satisfying some fundamental concerns of distinct political perspectives and easing the conflict surrounding abortion issues—that French policy represents. Inflexible judicial solutions based on countervailing rights are unrepresentative of the population generally, and on this highly inflamed issue, it is possible that, were the federal courts to step back and allow legislatures (state-level or national) to pursue their craft, representatives would be more responsive to well-organized groups with intense beliefs than to the larger numbers of persons for whom compromises on abortion policy appear sensible.

It is conceivable that time might erode the current polarized rights-based views, and so admit greater compromise such as social conservatives allowing more latitude for abortion early in pregnancies and individualists accepting a process with more extensive cautionary warnings. But as Stith (1987) points out, the sacrifices that society can reasonably ask from women in taking on the burdens of child-rearing surely bear some relation to the degree to which society is willing to assist them in return. And it is on this point that I think the chances for American abortion legislation forming a compromise similar to that of France's crumble.

Public social programs designed to make sound parenting of children more feasible, particularly for mothers with limited private resources, represent a crucial adjunct to French abortion policy. In the highly individualistic United States, divorce is easily attained and child support, both formal and material and particularly informal and intangible, is extremely difficult to assure. Moreover, as we have seen from the previous two chapters, in the short term, only historical contingencies posing extraordinary social dislocations are apt to foster preferences for the higher rates of taxation and the more ambitious social programs that would be required to help many women succeed in rearing additional children well. American social conservatives have been willing to fight individualists on the sanctity of fetal life, but barring such historical contingencies they will be too few in number and too weakly mobilized to effectively overcome individualistic resistance to the larger, more active state which would be necessary for providing greater public social provision for children. Indeed, to date American pro-life activists have virtually ignored how, if women either do not choose or are not allowed abortions, the challenges of rearing their children well will be met in numerous instances. The French public social programs which do respond to this concern complement French abortion policy significantly.

Certainly significant help from American economic conservatives cannot be expected in this regard. If women are the isolated, separate, autonomous individuals that individualists perceive them to be, then they are appropriately responsible for their own lives. From this perspective, government should stand back and not interfere with women's decisions to abort fetuses. But it is far less appropriate for society, through expensive public programs that tax some in order to provide benefits for others, to enter a partnership with women in providing the resources—knowledge about appropriate parenting practices and material assistance with the many expenses that children pose—necessary for rearing children well. For individualists, these too are the responsibilities of isolated, separate, autonomous individuals. Egalitarian pro-choice activists are likely to favor using public programs to assist poor mothers with the challenges of rearing their children, but they represent only a portion of the pro-choice movement. When Glendon (1987) asks why it is that the United States stands alone among advanced industrial societies in cleaving to a conception of persons as isolated autonomous individuals and its accompanying policy implications, she contends that the strength of Americans' individualistic heritage, starting with Hobbes' view of humans, provides the answer. I agree. Further, only sharply different experiences which posed severe social dislocation and thus fostered alternative conceptions of humans—as requiring varying forms of assistance from others—held by American social conservatives and egalitarians would sufficiently increase the numbers, boldness and coalition potential of the adherents of these two high-group cultures. This in turn would prompt American public social program initiatives that would be capable of complementing a compromise policy on abortion as French social programs do.

CHAPTER 5

Immigration and Citizenship in the United States and Japan

Societies differ with respect to how membership in their collectives is acquired and in the degree to which outsiders are allowed to enter and participate in these collectives. The members of some societies are more concerned with the purity of the "Volk," as many Germans would say, than are the members of other societies. Yet among contemporary advanced industrial societies and in times seemingly incongruously characterized by both movement toward economic globalization and refugee-producing, intrasocietal ethnic cleansing, allowing the immigration of temporary workers and refugees has become fairly common. But for a society to allow persons entry, perhaps temporarily to provide needed labor or while life-threatening dangers await them in their societies of origin, is distinct from making them members of this society. Membership in a society or, in the modern world, citizenship tends to be a more closely guarded categorization of persons in virtually all societies, although the importance of having citizenship for accessing certain benefits or avoiding various forms of discrimination may vary across societies.

Historical circumstances, the path of institutional development that these circumstances helped to reinforce and the resulting predominance of an individualistic culture in the United States have fostered a relatively open orientation toward various categories of immigrants across much of American history. As a society composed from the outset of immigrants or the descendents of recent immigrants, there has generally been only limited and often highly focused concern about raising the drawbridge in the face of prospective newcomers. This predisposition has been supported by individualism's relative openness toward, even interest in, the "other." For individualists (e.g., J. S. Mill), surrounding oneself with a broad range of persons having widely varying backgrounds helps to assure one's access to promising innovative suggestions. Periodically across American history varying nativist and related movements have decried the United States' openness to outsiders. Current prognostications about the future ethnic composition of the United States have prompted another episode of relative concern about immigration among American social conservatives in particular.

For Japan, in contrast, historical circumstances, the pattern of institutional development which has evolved from these experiences and the resulting predominance of the high-group cultures, particularly hierarchy, have combined to cultivate a quite different orientation toward outsiders. As representatives of the indigenous (in recorded history at any rate) population of a set of small islands just off the Asian mainland, the Japanese have historically been skeptical about the admission of outsiders, some of whom have been seen—often with good reason—as threatening, and others who have been perceived simply as undesirable. Once again, particular circumstances help to reinforce distinctive cultures. Each of the high-group cultures tends to associate outsiders with pollution of various forms, and these cultures are predominant in Japan. Accordingly, until recently Japan has had remarkably few outsiders in its society, being historically a labor exporting society. While immigration practices have changed in the last few decades as Japan has needed labor, particularly relatively unskilled labor which is in short supply from indigenous sources, contemporary Japanese citizens appear little more willing than they have traditionally been to grant membership to outsiders. Examining Japanese history, institutional development and culture more closely will provide a context for explaining American-Japanese policy differences with regard to immigration and citizenship.

JAPANESE HISTORY, INSTITUTIONS AND CULTURE

HISTORY

For much of the distant past Japan had a relatively low profile among the societies of the Asian mainland. In part, Japanese reclusiveness with respect to other East Asian societies arose from wariness. China, in particular, was threatening on the basis of its sheer size, and the Japanese felt more comfortable drawing little continental attention to themselves. Additionally, the Japanese generally considered their own civilization to be superior to others. Thus they felt little need to draw on the ideas of the continental Asian societies in their region. So traditionally, the Japanese remained behind their oceanic mote with internal matters occupying nearly their full attention (Dower 1975). Internally, Japan experienced periods of both relative order, when a central government was able to establish its supremacy, and near chaos similar to that found in medieval Europe, when regional warlords engaged in lengthy bouts of conflict.

Modern Japan arose from the Meiji Restoration of 1867, which was, in turn, a reaction to the "opening" of Japan by the West. Contact with the United States and European naval forces in the mid-nineteenth century set Japan on a prolonged mobilization for technological, economic and military development. The Japanese were aware that Westerners were using their superior military technology to subjugate, dismember and occupy China. They were fearful of experiencing a similar fate. Against this background, their limited experiences with Western "gun-boat diplomacy" created a prolonged national security "crisis." The emperor, guided by a small but extremely capable bureaucracy, drew on various Western models to begin creating an industrial society and most of the accoutrements then associated with such societies in the West. The Japanese sent students abroad to learn the technologies of the West and employed Western consultants to hasten their construction of modern industrial and military capacity.

These efforts bore fruit when Japan soundly defeated Russia in the Russo-Japanese War of 1904–1905, becoming the first Asian society to defeat a European society in modern warfare. But Russia was only one of the Western powers which the Japanese perceived as encircling them through progressive imperial expansion on the Asian mainland and among some of the island chains off its coast. Western imperial expansion threatened in particular Japan's access to the various raw materials which were essential to its burgeoning industrial production and military power. Japan's growing security fears bolstered the influence of the emperor's military advisors, and Japan initiated its own imperial expansion into Korea and Manchuria.

By the late 1930s Japan had begun implementing the early stages of what it called the "Greater East Asian Co-Prosperity Sphere" by expanding its continental imperialism deeper into China The essence of this sphere involved Japan replacing Western influence in much of East and Southeast Asia and thus gaining exclusive access to the raw materials of these regions. This plan led the Japanese to attempt to destroy the United States' military power in the Pacific with the attack on Pearl Harbor in

December 1941, prompting U.S. entry into the Second World War. By the summer of 1945 the Japanese were clearly losing their struggle with the United States. After the United States dropped atomic bombs on the Japanese cities of Hiroshima and Nagasaki in early August, the Japanese agreed to surrender.

Japan was occupied by the U.S. military for a number of years after the Second World War. Some aspects of this occupation were initially designed to be punitive, but the triumph of the Chinese Communists in the Chinese civil war (1949) and the outbreak of the Korean War (1950) soon shifted American interests in Japan from punishment to reconstruction (Dower 1988). The United States assisted Japan's recovery from the destruction of the war and was involved as well in creating a new Japanese governing framework based on Western democratic models (Pempel 1982; Ishida and Krauss 1989).

INSTITUTIONS

Japan's situation as a "late developer" (that is, a society which began developing an industrial economy later than the Western great powers), in conjunction with Western imperialism in East Asia, created among the Japanese a prolonged security crisis. As occurred even in the United States in the 1930s and early 1940s in response to the Great Depression and the Second World War, this sense of crisis fostered the development of an active national executive, which launched an ambitious mobilization of the society's resources for development. Since Japan was starting from scratch in these enterprises, it was relatively easy for the national executive (an emperor, guided by a modestly sized but capable bureaucracy) to guide the mobilization. Prior to 1890, for instance, Japan had no parliament. Even after the Diet was created, the franchise was highly restricted, political parties objectionable to the emperor were illegal, and the executive was not responsible to the Diet, which was essentially advisory. Japan's swift rise (1870–1940) from a society with features similar to those of Europe in the sixteenth century to great power status occurred largely at the direction of a small skilled central executive.

Japan's defeat in the Second World War brought much formal change (Pempel 1982; Ishida and Krauss 1989). These changes included a new constitution with characteristics resembling Western democracies such as: a range of individual rights; a universal franchise; a popularly elected bicameral legislature; and an executive responsible to the Diet. Pempel (1989) contends that, while Japan has its peculiarities, it is now as democratic as Western societies. Yet a population's long-standing preferences and patterns of behavior do not necessarily change to fulfill the spirit of new formal institutions that have been imposed by outsiders (Tsurumi 1970; Turner 1989, 305, 317; Fukushima 1989, 265).

With respect to what from the early 1950s through minimally the early 1970s was an extremely noteworthy feature of Japanese society (i.e., its remarkable rise from economic destruction to economic "superpower"), Japanese policy formulation has retained aspects of the small but capable and highly interventionary central executive that formerly guided the Restoration. Through the 1980s executives in the Ministry of Finance and the Ministry of International Trade and Industry retained the late developer mindset introduced above (Johnson 1982, 1999). Operating virtually beyond Diet scrutiny, they were preoccupied with expanding economic development, and they worked closely with executives of private industry to achieve this objective. They sought to foster the development of particular industrial sectors, which offered exceptionally good opportunities for Japan to garner new global markets. These sectors characteristically involved Japan importing raw materials, adding great value to them by transforming them into sophisticated consumer goods (e.g., automobiles, electronics) and then exporting huge quantities of these goods.

Central-state executives contributed their knowledge about which Japanese industrial sectors held relative global advantages to the expertise of executives in particular industries for managing value-adding transformations. Ministry officials preferred to keep as much material resources in the private sector and thus available for industry executives, but they actively used public sector expertise to favor the development of some industries, which they believed held greater potential for societal economic development, over others. Thus although the Japanese state is relatively small in terms of the proportion of GDP it consumes in taxes (see table 2.2, p. 42), it is also—from the perspective of Locke-Smith economic conservatives—highly interventionary with regard to the most high-profile Japanese economic activities.

CULTURE

Experts on Japanese society are in accord that Japan is, in grid-group theory terms, a "high-group" society in which hierarchists and egalitarians predominate both among the population generally and within the political elite. According to Ishida: "The individual is submerged in a group-oriented society; minority opinions contrary to established group desire are disregarded by a tradition which values group harmony. This process produces a tendency toward national conformism which in turn leads to discrimination against the minority" (1983, 13). Similar views are offered by Richardson (1974), Tsurumi (1970) and Van Wolferen (1990). Further, both Johnson (1982, 32-37) and Dore (1986, 1) reveal systematic Japanese skepticism about using the individualist's favorite tool, open markets, as a means of organizing various aspects of society, and Japanese reluctance to constrain cronyism in the banking and other industries in the face of economic doldrums across the 1990s reinforces their interpretation. So Japan is clearly a society in which individualistic influence is quite limited.

Gauging relative influence between the two high-grid cultures requires a closer examination. There are several indices of egalitarian influence. For instance, among the various political parties which have—with brief exceptions—been in opposition to the general post–Second World War situation of Liberal Democratic Party (LPD) governance, different strains of egalitarianism (e.g., Green environmentalism, more traditional working-class democratic socialism, and communism) have predominated. Further, some spheres of social life (e.g., primary and secondary education) have been extensively shaped by egalitarian influence (Cummings 1980). Additionally, some analysts contend that class differences are less noticeable in Japan than in many other societies. For example, income is distributed less unequally in Japan than in the United States and in the vast majority of European societies (McKean 1989). Steven (1983) even argues that Japanese social life supports little class consciousness.

In spite of these and other clearly egalitarian characteristics of Japanese social life, it seems difficult to argue with the identification of hierarchy as the preeminent culture. Social stratification is highly developed and pervasive in Japan (Ishida 1983; Tsurumi 1970). Family life, relations among and within industries, the labor market, and the public policy process all illustrate distinctive aspects of this stratification (Pempel 1982; Pempel and Tsunekawa 1979). In fact, the relative absence of class consciousness which Steven discusses is likely a consequence of the relative weakness of the low-grid cultures, egalitarianism included. Class consciousness and the social conflict that arises from it are relatively absent in Japan because hierarchy is the preeminent cultural orientation across most sectors of society. Accordingly, persons generally accept their niches in the series of nested hierarchies (i.e., family, company, nation) which form Japanese society (Verba et al. 1987, 23).

Considerable survey data supports the characterization offered by various experts on Japan of Japanese society as high-group. Flanagan

(1979, 261) shows that, while—as Inglehart (1997) contends—succeeding generations of Japanese citizens are becoming less hierarchical, a clear majority of the general population continues to adhere to a culture valuing economic frugality, pietism, conformity to the attitudes of family and community, and deference to authority. Further, persons adhering to this orientation or culture, which Flanagan labels "traditional" yet speaks of as hierarchical, are predisposed to support the LDP against the opposition political parties which represent various strands of egalitarianism (1979, 268; 1982, 417).

A smaller proportion of the Japanese respondents in Flanagan's studies lie on the opposite end of these four defining tendencies. That is, they are: prone to spend—rather than save—their incomes; more secular; more inclined to experiment with new ideas and practices; and less deferential with regard to traditions and authority figures. Further, they are likely to support the socialist and communist parties against the LDP (1979, 268). Surprisingly in light of their political commitments, Flanagan labels this group of respondents "libertarian" (1982, 409).[1] These persons appear to be becoming more numerous in successive generations. But as election results indicate, they still comprise a minority of the total population.

CONTRASTING THE UNITED STATES AND JAPAN

Canada represents the society which is most similar to the United States among the four other societies considered in this study. Japan arguably represents the society which is most dissimilar. The historical experiences of the United States and Japan, the developmental paths followed by their political institutions and their resulting cultures are all sharply different. As Flanagan's label of "libertarian" for his nontraditional Japanese respondents suggests, some American academics who study Japan—particularly economists (Johnson 1982, 32-37) but also other political scientists (Esping-Andersen 1997)—have difficulty accurately identifying Japanese political and social orientations. One possible basis for confusion among Americans about the identity of Japanese political cultures lies in the common characterization of the LDP as the conservative party of business. This characterization, while accurate in one sense, prompts many observers in the Anglo-American tradition to interpret the "liberal" in LDP as denoting adherence to classical, Locke-Smith, small-state, clear-state-society-boundaries liberalism. In the contemporary United States this sort of liberalism is generally referred to as economic conservatism. Its most salient beliefs foster a disinclination for having the state become involved in regulating economic or other—e.g., religious—aspects of social life.

This orientation is quite similar to the culture that I have referred to as individualism in this study. Milton Friedman represents a high-profile example of such an individualist/economic-conservative/classical Locke-Smith liberal. Friedman prefers to have American society rely as thoroughly as possible, and far more than we currently do, on markets to organize social relations and thus much less on inherently coercive public regulation and other state activity. Friedman is particularly concerned to limit various forms of state intervention on what he perceives as the appropriately autonomous sphere of productive economic activity. So Friedman opposes extensive regulation of business and also active industrial policies which might, for instance, ease the access of "sunrise" industries to capital through publicly subsidized loans. For Friedman, what he perceives as the level playing field of markets fosters better decisions on industrial viability than the favoritism of public bureaucrats.

Yet this sort of active industrial policy has been the hallmark of the "conservative" Japanese state, and Johnson (1982) argues that adroit Japanese use of active industrial policy is responsible for the extraordinary economic development that Japan accomplished from the early 1950s through the early 1970s in particular. So Japan must be conservative in a sense distinct from the economic conservatism synonymous with individualism.

In the United States this other sense is often referred to as "social" conservatism, and it is exemplified by, among others, Pat Buchanan, who has at times found a home for his form of conservatism in one wing of the Republican Party, while another wing of the same party served as home for George Bush Sr.'s economic conservatism. In grid-group theory terms, social conservatism is a form of hierarchy. The most obvious indices of this characterization involve beliefs in gender and ethnic hierarchy and an eagerness to use the state as a moral tool to gain wide social adherence to hierarchy's characteristic belief in "one right way" known to society's experts. Buchanan reveals his social conservatism in his skepticism about the appropriateness of meaningful professional careers for women, his resistance to high levels of immigration for people of color, and his willingness to use public policy both to support religious education and to constrain employers from moving American factories to third-world societies, destroying American communities in the process (Bennet 1995).

While some Japanese "conservatives" likely have what I call "bifocal" cultural biases, with dominant hierarchical and subordinate individualistic lenses to their perspectives, few are predominantly individualistic.[2]

Verba et al. (1987) provide a variety of survey data that support my interpretation that the conservatism most prominent among Japanese political elites is a hierarchical social, rather than an individualistic economic, version. For instance, Japanese and American elites respond quite differently to the question as to whether government should guarantee jobs for all citizens willing to work. Economically conservative American elites (i.e., business executives and elected Republican officials) oppose this idea. Yet Japanese conservatives (i.e., business executives, central-state bureaucrats and LDP members of the Diet) are almost as positive about the idea as are relatively egalitarian American Democratic elected officials (75). These Japanese conservatives represent the other high-group culture, hierarchy, and see themselves as responsible for the welfare of ordinary citizens.

Additionally, on the related questions as to whether government should work to substantially reduce the gap between the incomes of the rich and the poor (e.g., through limits on incomes or more equal earnings) or whether it is fair to tax the rich in order to help the poor, all Japanese respondents—from business to labor—are in a fairly narrow range from mildly to enthusiastically positive (Verba et al. 1987, 78, 81). Their pattern of responses is sharply different from that of American respondents, who are more varied in their views, with the economically conservative respondents (i.e., farm and business elites as well as elected Republican officials) being much more negative than Japanese business executives, central-state bureaucrats and LDP Diet members. These items help to reveal economic and social conservatives as individualists and hierarchists, respectively.

Further, on the question of whether the interests of employers and employees are inherently opposed, Japanese elites across the social and political spectra react with a relatively tight pattern of considerably more optimistic responses than their American counterparts (Verba et al. 1987, 83). This is the pattern that we should expect from the elites of various social sectors in a society in which hierarchy is influential across most sectors. Rather than perceiving antagonistic class interests as their American counterparts do, Japanese socialist elites on one hand, and farm, elected LPD officials and business elites on the other, are both more inclined to interpret employers and employees as contributing to the same overarching social collective in complementary ways. They recognize, of course, conflicts of interest, but they perceive as well much common ground and thus bases for cooperation.[3]

Exceptionally high influence for social conservatives means that formally equal Japanese are, for citizens of an advanced industrial society, immersed to an unusual degree in hierarchical social relations. In this vertical social context they routinely relate to one another, not as relative equals, but as social superiors and subordinates (Ishida 1983; Verba et al. 1987, 23).

CONTRASTING SOCIETAL APPROACHES TO IMMIGRATION AND CITIZENSHIP

IMMIGRATION AND CITIZENSHIP PREFERENCES OF RIVAL CULTURES

Once again, assume that we do not know much about American and Japanese approaches to immigration and related citizenship practices. What can we deduce in advance about these practices from knowing that the United States is a "low-grid" society with a predominant culture of individualism; while Japan is a "high-group" society with a dominant culture of hierarchy? Basically, while individualists are much more hesitant than adherents of the high-group cultures with respect to the public revenue and social program activities that we examined in chapters 2 and 3, they are—similarly to our experience with abortion policy in chapter 4— apt to be considerably less concerned about a range of legitimacy issues, including immigration and citizenship, than are the adherents of these high-group cultures.

Their low-grid position reinforces individualists' skepticism with respect to the regulation of immigration and citizenship. If persons are roughly equal in broad capacities such as rationality and able to be the masters of their own fates, then what difference should it make whether they reside in or "belong" to a particular society? For individualists, the exclusionary implications of immigration and citizenship regulations rest in ill-founded conceptions that persons from one locale are significantly different from or perhaps superior to others. Since in practice these conceptions are reciprocal (i.e., some Chinese see Westerners as inferior; and some Germans regard persons of color as disreputable), individualists tend to conclude that some if not all of these conceptions are flawed. For individualists, these conceptions are to be numbered among the many unfortunate manifestations of parochial minds.

Individualists' low-group position leads them to favor shifting networks of associations—which meet their concerns of the moment—over membership in stable groupings of persons arising from ascription. Persons who subscribe to the bumper stickers reading, "You can choose your friends," are almost certainly individualists. For these persons, ascriptive groupings such as family and nation are arbitrary and confining. They are more comfortable with associations of choice, persons whom they have encountered through their preferred activities and who fulfill particular needs that they are experiencing. From such a perspective immigration restrictions simply represent nonsensical impediments on transactions of mutual benefit to the contracting parties. Similarly, intricate and exclusionary citizenship processes are simply archaic. For persons whose interpersonal associations rest on others' achievement capacity, such regulations have their roots in outmoded ascriptive social patterns (Schuck 1998, 241).

Individualists thus favor minimal restrictions regarding immigration and citizenship. So, we should expect the United States, a society in which individualists have long been preeminent, to be fairly open with respect to immigration and to have accessible citizenship procedures.

Adherents of both of the high-group cultures (i.e., egalitarianism and hierarchy) are more concerned about group purity and thus with the "pollution" that they perceive outsiders as representing. For egalitarians, the central pollution concern involves admitting persons who may be committed to social practices that are different from and perhaps disruptive of or contrary to the practices which specific egalitarian communities have chosen for themselves. Whereas individualists (e.g., J. S. Mill) seek to foster such diversity of practice, hoping thereby to find improved ways of accomplishing various objectives, egalitarians are loath to accept similar diversity, which they regard as a polluting influence on their group's procedures, adopted after careful deliberation. Further, egalitarians are fearful that alternative practices will provide the vulnerable youth of their communities with alternative models for emulation and will, in due time, contribute to the destruction of their way of life. Thus egalitarians are more prone than individualists to restrict human and other traffic (e.g., ideas) across their borders. Further, those outsiders who are granted permission to enter are normally considered visitors rather than candidates for full community membership or citizenship.

Yet egalitarians share with the other low-grid culture, individualism, a sense of human equality. Thus, among them, outsiders who gain entrance to their communities and who demonstrate protracted credible adherence to community practices can generally become full-fledged members. These former outsiders may in time become more central to their adopting communities than some indigenous members who are remiss in their practice of the community's procedures. So for the combination of high-group and low-grid which forms the egalitarian position, initial hesitancy about accepting particular outsiders can be overcome if these persons demonstrate their dedication to the gradually shifting body of practices which the community produces through extensive deliberation among its members.

Hierarchists represent the opposing positions from individualists on both the grid and group dimensions, and among them we find the greatest motivation to regulate immigration and membership in society. Hierarchists share a concern with the other high-group culture (egalitarianism) about the pollution of their social collectives' purity. Yet in the instance of hierarchy this concern is reinforced, even instigated, by pressures arising from their high-grid position. Hierarchists are believers in pervasive human inequality, anxious to differentiate—and thereby to organize or order—persons on the basis of ethnicity, gender, social class and a host of more subtle criteria as well. Thus social collectives in which hierarchy is the predominant culture are apt to exhibit a sense of the superiority of their indigenous members over outsiders. In the case of hierarchists, the concern that outsiders might fail to follow the practices favored by societally sanctioned experts and so disrupt social harmony is overlain by a sense that outsiders are simply inferior persons (Buchanan 2002). So their mixing with members of the indigenous community may be thought quite literally to lower the level of (pollute) this community.

Perceptions of this sort appear to underlie some of the most egregious examples of ethnic conflict and cleansing in recent history. Under Milošević, for instance, Serbia sought to expand its territory at the expense of nationalities who were regarded as inferior, treating them in the process with an extraordinary level of violence that could only signal disdain for what Serbian officials considered their subhumanity. Further, the Serbs treated those members of adjoining nationalities who were unfortunate enough to have been isolated within the enlarged Serbian state with even greater ferocity. The fear of social disruption from the presence of inferior persons can clearly prompt remarkable levels of inhumane behavior from hierarchists.

So it comes as no surprise that hierarchists are perhaps even more concerned than egalitarians about regulating human traffic across their borders and allowing outsiders permission to linger in their societies. The most rigorously controlled societal frontiers on the planet (e.g., the former Soviet Union and its former client states in Eastern Europe, China, and North Korea) are associated with societies in which hierarchy is the dominant culture of the political elite and frequently the general population as well. These societies are also reluctant to harbor the few outsiders to whom they grant admission for lengthy periods or to grant them membership in society. In contrast to egalitarians, who may come to genuinely appreciate outsiders who accept their adopting community's practices as their own, hierarchists are more apt to remain skeptical of the generally "inferior" humans from other societies. The primary rationale for allowing outsiders lengthy residence among hierarchists is the ability of exceptional outsiders to provide specialized services less available from the social collective's indigenous population (e.g., the Western technical experts who provided the Japanese with instruction during the early phases of the development mobilization of the Meiji Restoration).

Accordingly, we should expect that Japan, as a "high-group" society in which hierarchy both has been and remains extremely influential, should be relatively restrictive with regard to immigration and especially citizenship issues. In particular, we should anticipate that most migrants will be allowed entry only for the short term (e.g., tourists, students, trainees, workers offering specific capacities which are in demand in the Japanese economy). Sophisticated outsiders who are capable of serving some important need recognized by Japanese central-state executives may be allowed to stay longer. But it would be surprising if any significant proportion of even these persons were granted full membership in society in terms of being allowed citizenship. Citizenship might be extended to a select few on the basis of assimilation. That is, persons who could "pass for" Japanese in both appearance and behavior (e.g., language) would be more likely candidates for citizenship than others.

U.S. IMMIGRATION AND CITIZENSHIP POLICY

American policies toward immigration have varied across time (Archdeacon 1983; Jones 1992). Overall, however, regulation of immigration has been fairly modest. Prior to the mid-1870s there were virtually no restrictions on entry into the United States. Some restrictions were initiated in 1877, but they were focused narrowly on what various nativists viewed as particularly "undesirable" persons (e.g., convicts, prostitutes, Asian workers).[4] More systematic restrictions were introduced in the early 1920s in the aftermath of particularly high levels of immigration. For over a quarter-century thereafter, the overall level of immigration allowed varied with social dislocations outside the United States and responding peaks in American nativist reaction. Across this period, restrictions fell much more heavily on non-European immigrants, particularly Asians who—while admitted in limited numbers as unskilled laborers—were not permitted to bring family members with them. During the first two decades following the Second World War, regulation of American immigration became much more even-handed. Through the Immigration and Nationality Act of 1965, for instance, immigrants from different societies were accorded much more similar formal treatment. Immigrants from Europe continued to dominate numerically into the early 1970s. Since then, levels of immigration from Asia and particularly Latin America have each risen above the European numbers.

While the United States continues to try to regulate the total number of immigrants accepted per year, as table 5.1 shows, relative to many other societies—and particularly other societies with large populations—it remains a relatively open society in terms of allowing outsiders entrée. (See table 5.1.) American policy does not treat all persons in an even-handed fashion, but the favoritism employed today is generally more rational than the historical aversion to persons of color. In the contemporary period selected categories of refugees, close relatives of persons already in the United States, persons with skills currently in demand in the American labor market and those willing to invest significant sums of capital in the American economy are all granted varying degrees of preference.

Table 5.1 Percentage of "Foreign-Born" Persons in the Populations of Selected Advanced Industrial Societies (various years from the mid-1980s to the mid-1990s)

Luxembourg (highest among OECD societies)	34.1
Australia	22.7
Switzerland	19.0
Canada	15.6
Austria	9.0
Belgium	9.0
Germany	8.9
United States	7.9
France	6.3
Sweden	6.0
Denmark	4.7
Netherlands	4.4
Norway	3.6
United Kingdom	3.4
Ireland	3.2
Italy	2.0
Portugal	1.7
Finland	1.4
Spain	1.3
Japan (lowest among OECD societies)	1.1

Source: Gurowitz 1999, 421; Iguchi 1998, 294–95

In practice, the U.S. Immigration and Naturalization Service is a large, poorly coordinated organization with low employee morale. Thus a variety of mistakes or minimally seemingly arbitrary decisions occur among the nearly one million immigrants who legally enter the United States each year. According to Freeman (2002), nearly as many migrants enter the United States illegally each year, including many Canadians and Irish, still greater numbers of Asians and even more numerous Latin Americans. While it would be practically impossible to seal American borders in terms of illegal immigration (Andreas 2000; Chiswick 1982), a society more worried about immigration than the United States would surely adopt more strenuous steps than the recent American upgrading efforts (e.g., increasing the border patrol personnel along the U.S.-Mexican border) in order to reduce the current levels of illegal immigration.

Schuck summarizes several decades of American public opinion data with regard to immigration by noting a consistent refrain. While generally favoring immigration, Americans frequently think that the levels of immigration prevailing in their own time are too high, exacerbating various social problems (e.g., unemployment). Nonetheless, they are quick to point out their own immigrant roots and tend to be proud of similarly high levels of immigration in the past. They are generally unaware that previous generations have held similar views. That is, earlier generations have also been distressed by some consequences of immigration in their own time but pleased with the results of previous immigration (1998, 248).

As Weiner (1998) suggests, even more indicative of an open attitude toward immigration than this history of regulatory leniency, is the manner in which Americans have seen immigrants fitting with a collective identity. "The widely held American view is that individuals admitted as immigrants ought to be and can be incorporated into the American society, economy and polity. This is an assumption of human pliability, that foreigners can become American by living in the United States, and that their children, through the impact of the educational system and popular culture, can become Americanized" (6). Further, Huntington (1981) contends that what it means to become Americanized is the adoption of certain principles. That is, rather than essentially ascriptive characteristics such as ethnicity, language, religion or traditional patterns of cuisine or attire that, for instance, distinguish members of many societies, becoming an American involves adopting certain political beliefs and values—democracy, liberty, equality of opportunity, individualism and limited government—which are potentially universal. As Weiner puts it: "others can be like us" (1998, 7). So persons from other societies can retain all their ascriptive characteristics and become American. Indeed,

Weiner argues Americans have held a "widely shared ideology that believed diversity could be a source of creativity" (8).

Many persons applying for entry into the United States have as their long-term objective achieving American citizenship. This goal is so common that it is incorporated into the presuppositions implicit in American immigration policy as well as the perceptions of many Americans about migrants as future citizens. If one's historical perspective is long enough, the inhabitants of all but perhaps a few East African societies have emigrated from somewhere else. Yet the United States has been and continues to be a society of immigrants in a much more immediate sense than many others. As table 5.1 suggests, the proportion of American citizens who are foreign born has persistently exceeded that of most other societies, particularly other societies with large populations. Further, the individualistic belief that diversity will spawn creativity has much evidence to support it. Migrants or their children have been disproportionately represented among captains of industry, Nobel prize winners and prominent political officials, including a few presidents.

Over a span of time—say a decade—American citizenship is obtained by numerous persons from an extraordinary range of societies. Many of these persons have had to endure a lengthy wait for an immigration visa. Once in the United States, potential citizens have to stay out of legal difficulties during a probationary period, fill out forms, pay a modest fee, and pass a relatively simple exam. These limited restrictions weed out some who aspire to be citizens, but a rainbow of persons from a remarkable array of backgrounds succeed in this endeavor. Further, children born in the United States are citizens regardless of their parents' citizenship status. There remain, of course, large numbers of persons—particularly in South Asia and Africa—who are so poor that emigration to the United States simply transcends their capacities. Even in an era of increasingly global mass culture, it is likely that emigration to the United States transcends the cognitive horizons of many such persons as well. There are as well persons who live in societies that do not allow emigration (e.g., North Korea). Nonetheless, by the standards of most other societies (particularly Japan), American citizenship is relatively available.

As we saw in chapters 2 and 3, the United States does not offer the array of public services (e.g., medical care) that many other advanced societies do. Further, some American public assistance services (e.g., TANF—Temporary Assistance to Needy Families) are joint federal-state programs which offer varying benefits on the basis of somewhat different eligibility rules in various states. The United States also has a mixed record about allowing immigrants access to the public benefits it does offer prior to their becoming citizens. The most obvious example of open acceptance involves children's access to public education. As Weiner (1998) suggests, this access has been thought of as a tool for developing adherence to the set of values which Huntington (1981) contends define "the American creed." Immigrants' access to those public medical benefits which the United States offers have varied with time and place, although American-born children of noncitizen immigrants are eligible for Medicaid on a basis similar to other citizens. As assuring access to emergency medical care has become nearly universal in the United States across the last quarter-century, immigrants have generally benefited. Similarly, immunization of children is generally open to immigrants. But few states provide benefits for medical care in other contingencies to noncitizens. Immigrants' access to benefits such as food stamps and public assistance cash have varied across time and region. The long-term trend, however, is toward according migrants rights increasingly similar to those of citizens. Even when political leaders such as Governor Pete Wilson in California (1994) or subsequently President Bill Clinton attempt to restrict migrants' access to public services, the courts have been increasingly prone to negate their actions (Freeman 2002).

JAPANESE IMMIGRATION AND CITIZENSHIP POLICY

Since any substantial flow of persons across Japanese borders began with the modern (i.e., Reformation) era, Japan has been—until quite recently—a nation of emigrants. Japanese seeking work have migrated all over the world, but particularly to the Americas (e.g., the United States and Brazil). Thus until the period leading up to the Second World War, Japanese society had extraordinarily few resident foreigners, and there was virtually no transformation of citizens of other societies into Japanese citizens.[5] Japan annexed the Korean peninsula in 1910, and during the 1930s many Koreans—and some Chinese from adjacent areas—came to Japan seeking work. Just prior to the Second World War, the Japanese government forcibly moved many more Koreans to Japan in order to acquire the laborers needed to replace the Japanese workers conscripted into the armed forces. During the early 1940s there were over a million Koreans resident in Japan, and they comprised the vast majority of foreigners living in Japan. After the war the number of foreigners—and particularly Koreans—resident in Japan dropped considerably and remained below the level of the Second World War for several decades. While the recent size of the Korean population of Japan has remained relatively stable, the total number of foreign residents began rising sharply again in the 1980s as Japan's continued economic development created a need for laborers that the indigenous population could not support.[6] In the early twenty-first century there are more foreigners, coming from a more diverse array of societies, living in Japan than at any previous point in its history (Cornelius 1994, 376).

Analysts frequently divide the foreign population of Japan into three groups (e.g., Kajita 1998). One is the aforementioned Koreans (and some associated Chinese), many of whom are now fourth-generation Japanese residents. Following the Second World War this group lost its Japanese citizenship—acquired inadvertently through the annexation. They were initially treated as aliens, losing the new rights that Japanese citizens acquired under the postwar constitution and having to carry registration cards, endure fingerprinting and suffer deportation for criminal behavior. In terms of physical appearance "they cannot easily be distinguished from Japanese" (133), but their names reveal them as Korean, and they have continued to suffer systematic discrimination in Japanese society. A 1965 treaty between Japan and South Korea granted Koreans living in Japan who identified with the South permanent resident status. As Gurowitz (1999) shows, under pressure from the United Nations covenants on human rights (to which Japan is a party) and related sources, the Japanese government has slowly and grudgingly restored some rights and recently discontinued the practice of fingerprinting permanent residents.

While taking Japanese citizenship is increasingly common among third- and fourth-generation Korean residents in Japan, the bulk of the current Korean population living in Japan has not sought Japanese citizenship (Gurowitz 1999, 430). The formal process of applying for citizenship is not terribly difficult, but the government's decisions have been highly discretionary, favoring, for instance, those Koreans willing to assimilate to the degree of taking Japanese names.[7] While taking Japanese names makes ethnic Koreans virtually indistinguishable in Japanese society, it also signifies capitulation to a frequently mean-spirited host and entails considerable loss of one's previous identity. Less than 1 percent of the Korean population resident in Japan—numbering over 600,000—acquires Japanese citizenship annually (430).[8] Kajita (1998, 131)—following Weil (1991)—refers to the Korean residents of Japan as "sociological Japanese." He means that, in addition to being difficult to distinguish in physical appearance from the Japanese, they generally speak Japanese and can behave consistently with most Japanese social customs. This population could, if it so chose, blend into Japanese society by holding its ethnic Korean identity implicit. Kajita argues that many third- and fourth-generation Koreans are likely to do this once their parents die, although he acknowledges that Korean residents of Japan who identify themselves with the North (about a quarter of the Korean residents of Japan) are less likely to do so than Korean residents of Japan identifying with South Korea. Japan's poor relations with North Korea mean that these northerners remain technically "people who are not qualified to reside in Japan but allowed to remain" (French 2002a).

A second smaller group of foreigners living in Japan (numbering about 200,000) are ethnic Japanese who are citizens of various Latin American societies, particularly Brazil, with smaller numbers from Peru, Argentina, Bolivia and Paraguay. Kajita (1998, 127) refers to these persons as "ethnic Japanese" immigrants. By this he means that although they are, for the most part, as ethnically Japanese as indigenous citizens of Japan, they generally do not speak Japanese, nor are they able to act consistently with Japanese traditions across a variety of social situations. Whereas the long-term Korean residents of Japan have assimilated in these respects, the Latin American Japanese, or *Nikkeijin,* are clearly foreigners in spite of their ethnicity. For the most part, these persons come to Japan to work, typically on three-years visas, which can be renewed indefinitely. Their contacts among the Japanese population are limited, and they generally pay labor brokers to find them jobs and housing. The brokers, in turn, typically have contracts with large industrial corporations. So the *Nikkeijin* frequently work for large corporations and live in "company towns" provided by or through the brokers, hence their minimal contact with the indigenous Japanese. Yet they generally earn relatively high wages—considerably higher than they might expect in Brazil or Peru. Some *Nikkeijin* workers bring their families with them, and their children's attendance in Japanese schools increases the contact these foreigners have with the indigenous Japanese.

While there may be a growing proportion of *Nikkeijin* who are considering settling in Japan (Kajita 1998, 127), the vast majority continue to follow a pattern of relatively short-term visits to Japan for the purpose of gaining access to good wages. The *Nikkeijin* currently hold, by virtue of their Japanese ethnicity, an important advantage vis-à-vis most other nonresident foreigners. They are officially permitted to work full-time, indeed increasingly encouraged to do so, in the mainstream Japanese economy. While they typically take relatively modest positions which the indigenous Japanese workers are reluctant to accept, they often work overtime and acquire hefty total wages. If the Japanese government were to allow non-ethnic Japanese foreigners similar opportunities (to be discussed shortly), the *Nikkeijin* would lose their relative advantage and with it most of their incentive for traveling to Japan.

A third category of foreigners in Japan is much more varied than the previous two groupings. Since the mid-1980s the Japanese economy, even during persistent recession, has been a beacon for a large population of relatively young workers from Asia's southern rim. They come from Taiwan, the Philippines, China, Vietnam, Malaysia, Thailand, Bangladesh, Pakistan, Iran and other societies. Because a growing number of these persons overstay their legal period of visitation in Japan, there is likely no accurate estimate of their current number, but in combination the legal and illegal members of this category in Japan may number as high as 700,000 (Lie 2001, 3-5; see also Kuwahara 1998, 357-60; Koshiro 1998, 155). Most of these persons are attracted by Japan's wage levels, which are considerably higher than those in their home societies, and by the ease with which unskilled employment, even under conditions of recession, can be found. In part, this ease arises from the growing reluctance of successive generations of progressively better-educated Japanese to accept unskilled employment.

For the most part these foreigners enter Japan on visas that prohibit or limit their accepting employment. Many enter on tourist or student visas, but once in Japan, they find work easily, and many simply stay on—working in Japan—past the expiration of their visas. Others enter through various industrial training programs.[9] As with those who come on tourist or student visas, once in Japan or at least once their training is over, they frequently remain in Japan, working full-time. Clearly, the Japanese government could, if it so chose, make some progress against the presence of illegal overstayers, which many Japanese consider an important social problem. But government at all levels, particularly the local, finds itself torn between the complaints of Japanese citizens that the law be followed and illegal foreigners be sent home, and the needs of employers for labor, especially inexpensive unskilled labor.

Japan has a low birth rate, and its population is rapidly aging. Further, Japan's largely urban population retains little in the way of its historical labor reserve from rural regions on which to draw. Additionally, young Japanese workers are increasingly reluctant to accept "3K" jobs (i.e., dirty, dangerous and difficult[10]), and the government has been trying to reduce the hours worked by the Japanese population (Cornelius 1994, 378). In combination, these factors create a growing need for relatively unskilled labor. Yet Japanese sensitivity toward the presence of outsiders contributes to a social environment in which, in contrast to the United States

and Western Europe, a remarkably low proportion of the foreign laborers in the broad category we are currently considering work in service occupations (e.g., live-in maids or child-care providers, restaurant
buspersons, store clerks, street sweepers, garbage collectors). Shopkeep-
ers are afraid of offending their Japanese customers if they employ foreigners in visible positions. And, as Cornelius relates: "Having a foreigner
working in the home could be regarded as a particularly egregious form
of impurity" (385).

Instead, the first wave of these workers was composed of females,
many of whom are formally categorized as "entertainers," but who frequently work as bar hostesses and in related jobs. Subsequently, a large
wave of male workers entered Japan. Many of these persons find employment in the construction industry in remote areas. The infrastruc-
tural development that these construction projects represent is an
activity crucial to the political fortunes of many LDP Diet representatives. While in many respects the Japanese government as well as the
population have been ill-disposed toward the increasing numbers of legal
foreigners and illegal overstayers that these successive waves of immigration have entailed, several factors suggest that even increased immigration and overstaying is likely across the near future. The Asian continent
has a huge labor surplus, and Japan is the closest society which combines
a demand for labor with relatively high wages. Further, various solutions
to the Japanese labor shortage that draw on the indigenous population—
making the traditionally hierarchical labor market more appealing to
women, extending the retirement age and relying more heavily on automation (Koshiro 1998, 170-72)—do not seem to offer sufficient
promise.

Japan's restrictive orientation toward immigrants generally is reflected as well in its policy toward refugees and asylum seekers. Japan
contends that it is too small and densely populated to cope with refugees,
regardless of the legitimacy of their status or the desperation of their
need. Accordingly, Japan screens persons claiming such status extremely
carefully and deports the vast majority. For instance, Japan has accepted
only about 1 percent of the number of Indo-Chinese refugees that the
United States has accepted as permanent settlers. From 1982 (just after
it signed the 1951 United Nations Convention on Refugees and the 1967
Protocol Relating to the Status of Refugees) to 1995, Japan accepted 208
of the 1,141 applications for asylum that it received (Takeda 1998, 432-33;
see also Cornelius 1994, 392). Recognizing that this seemingly heartless
orientation holds the potential for a public relations disaster, Japan has
offered significant financial support to the United Nations High Com-

missioner for Refugees and other organizations dealing with refugee problems. Japan has also sent medical teams to provide assistance to societies which are receiving large numbers of refugees. Japan's restrictive practices with respect to refugees and asylum seekers are widely supported among the Japanese population which favors helping these persons to move on to other societies but is extremely reluctant to have them settle in Japan (Weiner 1998, 23; Takeda 1998, 444-48).

In addition to an increased population of foreigners, Japan has some—albeit extremely limited—indigenous diversity. The Ainu are an aboriginal people of the northern islands of Japan. They were driven from the Asian mainland long ago and were originally distinguishable from ethnic Japanese by Caucasoid features such as more body hair. But generations of intermarriage with Japanese have reduced these visual distinctions among many Ainu. There are, at most, 300,000 persons of Ainu descent in Japan (Lie 2001, 3-5). The Burakumin are ethnically Japanese but suffer discrimination even today as a result of caste or social-class distinctions arising in the distant past. The population of Japan includes two to three million Burakumin. While, as Gurowitz relates, the Ainu and Burakumin both continue to suffer a variety of forms of social discrimination in Japan, official government statistics incorporate both into the Japanese nation so as to better portray a homogenous society without minorities.

In spite of Japan's resistance to immigration, its hard-nosed approach to refugees and extremely limited indigenous ethnic minorities, Lie contends that Japan is "multiethnic." Including relatively generous estimates for all of the groups of persons mentioned above in this section (and a few more—e.g., mixed ancestry children), he derives a figure of roughly 4 percent of the population of Japan as non-Japanese—but not all "foreign" (2001, 3-5). Even if we used this figure rather than the smaller "foreign born" datum in table 5.1 (p. 138), Japan would rank as a relatively homogeneous society and still represent a sharp contrast with the United States in this regard. But we may obtain a better indication of the Japanese orientation, and its distinctiveness from the American orientation, by explicitly considering citizenship in addition to migration. It is on the question as to what eventually happens to foreigners who enter Japan that Japanese society most sharply distinguishes itself from the United States.

As Weiner (1998) points out, Americans and Japanese (and likely most other societal populations as well) think of their societies as unique. But their uniqueness is viewed in quite contradictory ways. As I indicated in the previous section, Weiner characterizes the American conception of uniqueness as a "principled universalism" (7). That is, others can be assimilated—regardless of their ethnicity, religion or whatever—by adopting the "American creed" of democracy, liberty, equality of opportunity, individualism and limited government (Huntington 1981). In this sense adherents of these values all over the world are Americans—or at least potential Americans. But the Japanese sense of uniqueness represents a "particularistic exclusiveness" (8). For many Japanese, there is something primordial and significant about being born of ethnically Japanese parents, holding a Japanese name, learning the Japanese language and associated customs, and living from birth in Japan that cannot be assimilated. Persons lacking these experiences and characteristics are forever outsiders.

Additionally, the relatively high degree of ethnic homogeneity that results from this view is widely held to be important for fostering a variety of other desirable aspects of Japanese society. Most significant in this regard is the often-voiced perspective that the extraordinary postwar Japanese rate of economic development was facilitated by Japan's exceptional "collective spirit and group harmony" (Weiner 1998, 8-9; see also Gurowitz 1999, 415, 420; Cornelius 1994, 404). Some Japanese even point (almost assuredly incorrectly) to the growing influx of foreigners in the late 1980s as the source of their economic doldrums across the 1990s (Gurowitz 1999, 435). Similarly, Mitsunobu reports that a 1980 policy advisory council appointed by the (then) prime minister Ohira Masayoshi attributed Japanese national superiority to "harmony, consensus, and complementarity" (1988, 264).

These three characteristics, widely perceived among the Japanese as contributing to exceptional Japanese postwar economic development, are argued to hold as well other benefits for Japanese society. Government officials (e.g., former prime minister Nakasone and former foreign minister Watanabe) have publicly stated that the relatively low crime rate in Japan (vis-à-vis the United States) is attributable to the relative absence and presence, respectively, of racial minorities in the two societies (Gurowitz 1999, 443). Official government reports also blame the recent rise in criminal behavior on the increased presence of foreigners among the Japanese (Hanami 1998, 230). While this is true in a strict sense (migrants contribute disproportionately to the rising rates of some categories of crime), this view ignores the (relatively) low wages, difficult working and living conditions, as well as the pervasive discrimination that immigrant workers experience in Japan (Weiner 1998, 13). Collectively, these experiences surely contribute to natural human feelings of resentment. Additionally, it is common for the

Japanese to compare themselves favorably with Germany in particular in that they have avoided what they see as the high social and public economic costs endured by the Germans as a result of the much higher rates of foreign workers allowed to enter and frequently to remain in German society (Gurowitz 1999, 435; Iguchi 1998, Berger 1998, 339-45; Weiner 1998, 13).[11]

The relative German propensity for allowing foreign workers to remain in Germany and having their families join them marks a crucial distinction between what is tolerable and what is not for the Japanese. While older citizens routinely voice negative views about the mere presence of foreigners in Japan, higher proportions of younger citizens understand that this presence provides a significant boost to the economy. That is, the existing economy would be much attenuated in the absence of foreign workers. Yet even these younger persons are repelled by the idea that individual foreign workers might become permanent fixtures in the Japanese economy. They think that the longer individual workers remain in Japan, the more likely they are to agitate for having family members join them. Further, they fear that adding family members would be the first step along a path that would eventually lead to a permanent resident status (similar to that currently held by the South Koreans) for workers holding a range of nationalities. Such a path might even pose issues of Japanese citizenship for such workers or their children born in Japan. All these steps are widely feared and opposed in Japan.

Accordingly, the orientation of the general public, government officials and formal public policy are all arrayed against this possibility. The results of a society-wide survey conducted by the office of the prime minister in late 1990 found surprising support for the admission of unskilled foreign workers (70 percent) but only under specified conditions, which most frequently involved strictly limiting their time in Japan (Cornelius 1994, 395). The greatest support for admitting unskilled workers to Japan comes from younger persons, who are increasingly unwilling to take unskilled jobs themselves and also recognize more clearly the labor shortage that Japan is experiencing. Nonetheless, a substantial majority of Japanese respondents express a reluctance about having foreigners in their neighborhoods or familial interaction such as having a child marry a foreigner (402). However, the reservations of ordinary citizens are couched more in terms of practical day-to-day problems (e.g., rising crime rates, unemployment of indigenous Japanese and community conflict) than in terms of "the threat to Japan's unique culture" (403). But Weiner argues that the term "internationalization," which acquired popularity in Japan in the 1980s, "meant learning English, traveling abroad, keeping up with advanced industrial societies, acquiring the latest state-of-the-art technology, and fully participating in the global economy and in international institutions. What it did not mean was the incorporation of foreigners into Japanese society and becoming ethnically diverse" (1998, 10). Kajita agrees: "the Japanese people have become more receptive to the employment of foreign workers, including unskilled workers, although they do not welcome their permanent settlement in Japan" (1998, 145).

Gurowitz characterizes Japanese officials' attitudes toward migrant workers in terms of "avoiding them when possible and maintaining a policy of non-integration when necessary, in order to avoid compromising the ideal of the homogeneous nation" (1999, 433). According to Weiner, "the Ministry (of Labor) is particularly concerned with the political and social consequences of a more heterogeneous labor force and the pressures that would arise for admitting spouses and children were foreign workers permitted to stay in Japan for any extended period. The Ministry of Justice is similarly opposed to admitting foreign workers, arguing that immigrants have a higher crime rate than Japanese" (1998, 12).[12]

With respect to formal public policy, Cornelius argues that the "three fundamental tenets" of contemporary Japan's immigration policy are that: the admission of foreign workers should be a last resort; unskilled workers should simply not be admitted; and foreign workers should be admitted only for specified limited periods (1994, 386-87—see also Freeman and Mo 1996). These somewhat inconsistent principles are reinforced in theory both by constraining visa issuance and a recent law which punishes the employers of illegal migrants with prison sentences and heavy fines. But enforcement of these rules, which lies largely in the hands of local officials, is extremely lax. Local officials are confronted directly with the crucial contributions that illegal foreign labor makes to specific businesses and the Japanese economy generally. Consequently, they are more willing than central-state executives to make informal accommodations (Cornelius 1994, 391, 394; see also Gurowitz 1999, 441).

But even if Japan's immigration practice is less strict than its policy, few outsiders gain Japanese citizenship. The formal requirements for Japanese citizenship resemble those of the United States (e.g., having lived—legally—in Japan for five years without having seriously violated the law; meeting certain requirements with respect to age, income and holding acceptable political views). But in practice, Japanese citizenship is more difficult to acquire (Hanami 1998, 221-22). First, as we have already seen, only the Korean population in Japan, the *Nikkeijin* (i.e., foreign nationals of Japanese ancestry), and small numbers of highly skilled workers (e.g., journalists, business executives, etc.; see Hanami, 213) can live in Japan legally for a five-year period.[13] Second, in contrast to the United States, children born in Japan of foreign parents are not accorded Japanese citizenship. Third, Japanese law does not allow dual nationality. So a South Korean who is a permanent resident of Japan must relinquish South Korean citizenship in order to acquire Japanese citizenship, and this requirement acts as a significant disincentive, both for the Koreans and particularly for the roughly 60,000 Westerners (Cornelius 1994, 376) who live for lengthy periods in Japan. Fourth, while Japan may be moving toward greater routinization of citizenship decisions, the decision process employed to date has supported broad discretion on the part of public officials. In particular, successful applicants have generally had to be willing to adopt Japanese names (Gurowitz 1999, 430).

HISTORY, INSTITUTIONS, CULTURE AND CAUSALITY

I turn once again to the model that I have developed and employed in previous chapters to trace a causal sequence that holds fairly broad currency among contemporary American political scientists. It begins with the unique combinations of salient historical experiences confronted by various societies. These experiences help to carve out the varying paths along which societal political institutions develop. The general character of their broad national political institutions, in turn, helps to socialize persons to particular cultures. Through this process the adherents of some cultures become more numerous and influential than the adherents of their rivals. The institutional designs favored by the adherents of dominant cultures, then, help to explain the character of specific policies (e.g., immigration and citizenship policies).

This sequence, while worthy of our attention, is not exhaustive. Madison and his colleagues, for instance, drew on sources of socialization exogenous to their adult experiences with the British Empire and the Articles of Confederation in constructing a new fork on the path of development for American political institutions with the Constitution in 1787. Further, the sequence is not determinate. While similar situations often elicit related responses, persons may respond differently to comparable experiences. For example, when the United States experienced significant internal and external threats during the 1930s and early 1940s, it shifted away from its exceptional, Lockean, limited government tradition and quickly adopted a much larger and more active national government which more closely resembled the institutions that many other societies have constructed to meet related threats. Further, some late-nineteenth-century Swedes reacted to extremely difficult labor-market conditions by attempting to organize workers more effectively; while others emigrated to North America or deferred to societal leaders for solutions to their problems. In spite of these limitations I draw on this sequence to explain U.S.-Japanese immigration and citizenship policy differences. The explanations below are not exhaustive; they highlight particularly salient factors

I emphasize three such factors in the Japanese instance. First, prior to the Meiji Restoration, Japan had a lengthy tradition of largely ignoring the world beyond its island domain. This orientation appears to have arisen both from fear of the larger civilizations on the Asian mainland and from a sense of Japanese qualitative superiority. It would be an exaggeration to say that Japan was completely cut off from the rest of the world, but it was routinely selective about the persons and ideas it admitted to its territory and to stood aloof from most mainland conflicts (Dower 1975). While the Japanese had their own internal conflicts among regional warlords, their shared orientation toward the outside world as well as—for the most part—common ethnicity, language and religion gave the Japanese population a relatively strong sense of being a distinct group as well as a feeling about the outside world as the "other." Japan has, in other words, long been a high-group society with significant group boundaries.

Japan's isolation from the outside world underwent a change of revolutionary proportions with the Meiji Restoration. The Restoration's mobilization of Japanese resources was prompted by the so-called opening of Japan to Western ideas and imperialism across the 1860s. As leaders of a "late-developing" society, the Japanese elite was fearful of experiencing the division and subjugation that China was enduring. It replaced the long-standing policy of security through isolation with a prolonged, centrally directed effort to acquire security through technological, economic and—until 1945—military emulation of the Western powers. Restoration leaders felt threatened by their relative inferiority in these regards and transmitted these feelings to many ordinary citizens. At crucial junctures during this mobilization, these leaders produced policies designed to foster social harmony among the Japanese population (Calder 1988; Shinkawa and Pempel 1996). So, second, and in spite of the revolutionary character of the Restoration, it reinforced for about a century—from the early 1870s to the early 1970s—the sense among the Japanese that their society was not only a relatively homogeneous distinct group, but it was also engaged more or less as a group in catching up to the "other."[14]

Third and less significantly for immigration and citizenship policy than for some other sectors of policy, the path of institutional development which the Restoration carved out—governance by a small, especially capable executive elite—acquired such a deep-seated niche in Japanese political life that it continues—in spite of the post–Second World War democratization—to dominate the formulation process for policy in particular sectors, including the high-profile economic policies which helped to spark Japan's meteoric rise from postwar destruction to economic superpower status (Johnson 1982, 1999). So, Japan's most salient experiences with the world have given it, not only a high-group perspective, but also a reliance on expert political institutions which are sheltered to an unusual degree—among advanced industrial societies—from popular and parliamentary pressures (Johnson 1982, 1999).

Contemporary Japanese orientations and policy toward immigration and citizenship follow straightforwardly from these experiences with the world and the fundamental institutions and basic beliefs and value priorities that these experiences have cultivated. Many contemporary Japanese perceive high boundaries separating them from other nationalities. The concern that these Japanese have for living among persons with Japanese ethnicity and names who speak Japanese and follow Japanese social customs are indicative of these boundaries. Japanese fear of the "other" is bolstered by tainting the "other" as dangerous—an unclean polluter. This orientation helps to explain why, even in an era in which the Japanese desperately need foreign labor, they are so unwilling to allow foreigners to settle among them.

Against this experience, a hierarchical orientation that is careful about admitting foreigners and extremely reluctant about allowing them to become permanent residents is both distinct from more individualistic American views but understandable. It is difficult to imagine how the contemporary Japanese could hold orientations toward immigration and particularly citizenship similar to those of Americans, although some analysts suggest that population decline may prompt them (French 2002b). But if cultural orientations are shaped by experience with the world, then they ought to gradually change if historical contingencies produce long-term shifts in experience. While the future is always in doubt, there are some signs that Japanese opinion has already begun to change with the status that Japan has acquired over the last quarter century.

In the aftermath of the oil shocks of the 1970s, Japan's economic growth rates declined from the extraordinarily high levels of the 1950s and 1960s. Nonetheless, the cumulative impact of those earlier rates was substantial, and by the 1980s Japan had "arrived" as an economic superpower, with the world's second largest economy. While Japan's economy did not experience much growth during the 1990s, economic difficulties were sufficiently widespread across societies during this decade that

Japan retains its relative status into the early twenty-first century. Unsurprisingly in light of Japan's transformation from "late developer" to economic superpower, a variety of authors find clear evidence of intergenerational attitude change in Japan (Cornelius 1994; Flanagan 1979; 1982; Gurowitz 1999; Takeda 1998). The changes that Flanagan picks up are the broadest. He notices a progressive intergenerational decline in the proportion of Japanese citizens whose views mark them clearly as socially conservative hierarchists (1979, 268; 1982, 417). The increasing electoral difficulties that the generally egalitarian opposition parties have posed for the once-dominant, socially conservative LDP reinforce my view that the proportion of egalitarians among younger generations is likely growing. But it is possible that a culture of individualism is also developing among younger Japanese. Certainly young Japanese workers tend to be less ill-disposed toward foreign workers than are their elders (Cornelius 1994, 395). Yet they are still concerned that these workers stay in Japan only for specified limited periods.

Berger (1998, 340) argues that if Japan continues to be an economic leader in Asia, it will face increasing pressures to relax its stance toward foreign workers. Particularly if Japan overcomes its current economic doldrums, its need for labor will act like a magnet for the huge and largely unskilled labor surpluses in most other Asian societies. The age structure of Japan's current population offers little hope of a larger population from which more numerous indigenous workers might be drawn in the near future. Persistent sharp discrimination reduces the likelihood of luring more Japanese women into the labor market. More extensive automation is generally seen as freeing fewer workers than Japan will need in the future. Further, the nature of Japan's most pressing labor needs (i.e., for dirty, dangerous and difficult work *in Japan*), in combination with an increasing reluctance of younger Japanese workers to accept such jobs, reduces the efficacy of having Japanese companies expand the exportation of work through direct foreign investment in other Asian societies in which labor is less expensive.

Berger (1998) finds it difficult to imagine that these factors will fail to combine to place great pressures on Japan to draw more extensively on migrant labor. If the Japanese government continues to try to strictly limit the duration of these migrants' legal work periods in Japan, increasing numbers of these workers will inevitably overstay their visas. As the population of foreign workers essentially living in Japan grows, so too will both internal (340) and external (Gurowitz 1998) pressures on Japan to legalize their status, allow their relatives to join them and grant eligibility of all concerned to Japanese public social programs.

But in order for continued Japanese economic success to actually spawn these policy changes, Japanese citizens and their leaders would have to adopt different cultural orientations. Changing experience with the world might cultivate something like the following shifts in perspective. Increasing numbers of Japanese might come to see their society as a prominent node in a global economy. Thus they might begin to see themselves more as "citizens of the world" than as members of a society largely insulated from outsiders. Further, their society's obvious global economic importance might relax the traditional Japanese anxieties arising from late-developer status and ease Japanese concerns about the social costs associated with allowing increasing numbers of foreigners to live among them. If so, then in effect, progressively larger portions of the Japanese population might move from relatively high-grid, high-group positions minimally "down-grid" toward the low-grid cultures and likely as well "down-group" toward individualism. It is not clear that such a series of changes will occur. But it is difficult to imagine what other set of changes might produce the result of the historically insular Japanese allowing a broad range of immigrants to live among them on a more or less permanent basis.

It also strains the imagination to try to depict a societal history, institutional structure and resulting set of cultural orientations more dissimilar— particularly in terms of their implications for immigration and citizenship policy—to the Japanese than the American. While migrant flows have waxed and waned, the United States has always been a society of immigration. A few Americans emigrate to other societies, but—since the Tory exodus to Canada before, during and immediately after the Revolutionary War—there have been no systematic patterns to U.S. emigration, and immigration has always exceeded emigration. More importantly as Huntington (1981) relates, American identity or, more formally, citizenship has been highly accessible. It has involved adopting the American creed of democracy, liberty, equality of opportunity, individualism and limited government. Numerous successive generations of immigrants from a shifting array of societies have entered the United States, adopted these values and become as American as their predecessors.[15] As Weiner suggests, the essence of the American collective identity is the "principled universalism" (1998, 7), encapsulated in this creed. And, at least retrospectively, successive waves of immigrants are viewed as having provided the United States with the human resources necessary for overcoming the challenges posed by various historical contingencies (e.g., industrialization, the Second World War). In comparison to the Japanese instance, the United States long looked abroad—to continue a traditional pattern—in order to find the human resources for building a continent-spanning society. The diversity of American immigration from early on has obviated any sustained fear of the "other" comparable to that exhibited by the Japanese.

In comparison to a number of other policy areas, the United States' path of institutional development, similarly to the Japanese instance, seems less centrally involved in shaping orientations and policies toward immigration and citizenship than societal historical experiences. Nonetheless the limited and fragmented character of American national government has been and continues to be ill-suited to tight regulation of these issues.

Where could the initiative come from to prompt a society with this history and path of institutional development to think and act "outside the box" of this causal sequence and practice restrictiveness, similar to the Japanese with regard to immigration and citizenship? Given the United States' lengthy land frontiers and the huge labor surplus in Latin America, it could probably never be as successful as the Japanese in limiting access. But what might prompt Americans to try? In the current post–World Trade Center–attack period it is not difficult to envision such circumstances. If attacks of similar magnitude on American targets—arising from whatever source—continued, Americans would likely begin to adopt a "siege mentality." This orientation would lead to a variety of changes in public policy: further restricting civil liberties; increasing the financial resources for the public sector generally and its law enforcement, intelligence and national defense activities in particular; and almost assuredly making immigration and possibly acquiring citizenship more difficult.

However, the public officials who made these decisions and the citizens who elected them, like their counterparts in the era of the Great Depression and the Second World War, would represent a cultural mixture distinct from the one which predominated across the 1980s and 1990s. They would have to reject Ronald Reagan's idea that bigger government is the problem, not a solution, and adopt in its place something similar to Franklin Delano Roosevelt's conception of more active government as a solution to the nation's problems. In order to make this transition, they would have to move both "up-grid" and "up-group." That is, persons who were relatively individualistic would have to become more hierarchical in the face of continuing threats to their own security and that of their society. Further, according to my dual process pattern of political change, in order for shifts in the cultural orientations of significant portions of the American citizenry to have noticeable public policy consequences, they would have to be augmented by changes in the American political leadership. Thus the relatively individualistic orientation of the Reagan and George W. Bush administrations would have to evolve into a coalition of hierarchical and individualistic influences similar to that of the New Deal.

So, finally, I have located a policy area in which American attempts at emulation (likely not full emulation) of the practices of a sharply distinct society (Japan) can be envisioned. Why does such emulation seem more possible here than in the other instances which I have examined? The crucial difference is that a significant historical contingency (a series of devastating terrorist attacks on the American homeland) can be envisioned. This contingency, in turn, would be likely to set in motion a pair of cultural change processes. First, as their social environments became more threatening, many Americans would be apt to alter their cultural perspectives. In particular, they would be likely to perceive themselves as less self-reliant and more in need of assistance from public bureaucracies (e.g., police, intelligence and military) than they had been previously. For instance, prior to the World Trade Center attack, most American business executives lived in a world in which it was easy for them to view public bureaucracies more as hindering their activities than as assisting them. Executives of businesses that operated in the World Trade Center likely now see their economic fortunes as more dependent on state security services. If similarly high-profile attacks continue, their numbers will surely grow.

Second, shifting attitudes among ordinary citizens do not themselves create the changes in public policy by which we recognize the practical effects of cultural change. Rather, there must be changes in the composition of a society's political elite as well. If the electoral fortunes of candidates favoring extensive civil liberties and a relatively inactive public sector declined and the fortunes of candidates favoring more restricted liberties—including immigration and citizenship practices—as well as more extensive police, intelligence and defense capacities improved, the cultural mixture of governing American political elites would change as well. The results at the national level of the 2002 election are consistent with the early stages of such a transformation. As the culture of the political elite shifts, the new elites will make some of the innovations in American public policies which grid-group theory predicts for a hierarchically dominated coalition.

I say some of the changes, because it is not clear that attacks on the United States from foreign terrorists would prompt the same range of policy innovation as was induced by the combination of the Great Depression and the Second World War. Rather, it seems likely that restrictions on civil liberties as well as on immigration and related issues might be even greater, but the buildup of state coercive capacities— while extensive—would not be proportionate to that entailed by the Second World War. Further, it would be surprising if terrorist attacks on their own prompted an expansion of public social programs similar to that of the Great Depression, although repeated attacks on the order of the one on the World Trade Center and Pentagon might have sufficiently significant economic effects to foster a modest expansion.

CHAPTER 6

Conclusions

S o far, I have contrasted four U.S. policies with their counterparts in
other societies. I turn now to examining more extensive configurations of cross-societal policy variation and also patterns of intrasocietal policy consistency. That is, while the differences among the policies
of various societies in certain substantive areas are not always as sharp as
those which distinguish the United States from other advanced industrial
societies, different societies' unique historical experiences, distinctive
paths of institutional development and the resulting disparities in the influence of rival cultures within them routinely produce cross-societal
variations in particular policies. But within each society, policies directed
at different substantive areas tend to evince similar basic characteristics.
That is, each society produces distinctive multipolicy patterns that consistently reflect that society's unique historical, institutional and cultural
influences.

EXAMINING AND EXPLAINING THE DISTINCTIVE
MULTIPOLICY PATTERNS OF DIFFERENT SOCIETIES

THE UNITED STATES

I examine first the situation of the United States, for which this study
has provided the fullest data. The four American policies that we have
encountered in this study form a consistent pattern. That is, a modestly
extractive and minimally progressive tax regime, limited public financing of medical care (and limited public social programs generally), an
abortion policy which locates decision-making in the hands of ordinary
women, and policies of relative openness with regard to immigration

and inclusiveness with respect to citizenship all share a relative willingness to allow ordinary persons to manage their own lives, based on a conception of roughly equal capable persons. Consequently, in comparison to the citizens of other societies that we have examined, American citizens overall pay a lower proportion of their incomes in taxes, have a less thorough array of public social programs available to assist them with the vicissitudes of life, enjoy more freedom with respect to their reproductive decisions and share their collective life with a more rapidly growing number of new immigrants and citizens.

In light of certain salient unique aspects of American history, the path of American institutional development and the resulting relative influence of rival cultures among both ordinary Americans and particularly political elites, this pattern should come as no surprise. The immigrants who populated the territories which later became the United States shared—for distinct reasons—an unusual degree of skepticism about powerful central authority (Lipset 1990, 1996). These views were whetted by new British regulations in the aftermath of the French and Indian War in the 1760s. These regulations constrained the degree of local self-government which had developed across the colonies for over a century. Increased constraint prompted a successful Revolution, which drove significant segments of the population loyal to England out of what became the United States. The governing principles of the revolutionary period and its immediate aftermath (The Articles of Confederation) honored to an extraordinary degree the limited and local government aspects of what Huntington (1981) calls the American creed.

A new fork in the developmental path of American national political institutions came from the Constitutional Convention of 1787. This meeting produced a new set of governing principles, which was ratified by the requisite nine states in less than a year. While forging a more capable central government than the one allowed by the Articles, these principles drew on Locke and Montesquieu in assuring a large private sphere for individual action in which government could not intrude, maintaining considerable government decentralization and requiring a degree of fragmentation of authority within the national government that is relatively high by comparative standards both past and present. This governmental structure was designed to preserve the liberty of relatively equal and capable citizens to master their own fates, by constraining the abilities of various (particularly majority) factions to use government to serve their interests at the expense of others.

While the size and activity level of the American government has grown, particularly in the twentieth century, through episodic responses to crises (i.e., the Progressive Movement, New Deal/Second World War, and the Civil Rights Movement/rediscovery of poverty), the United States remains a society for which—in comparative perspective—government institutions are relatively small (in terms of the percentage of GDP that they consume) and inactive. These characteristics have been maintained across time in part through the influence of certain accidental characteristics of American social structure and other historical contingencies. Some particularly salient examples in this regard included the long-standing diversity of the American population, which has hindered various movements instrumental to the development of more ambitious welfare states in Europe (Katznelson 1986) and the relative mildness of American experiences with social dislocation stemming from wars and economic depressions. Particularly in the twentieth century, fresh in the minds of many contemporary Americans, the United States has suffered more modestly from economic depression and particularly from war than many other advanced industrial societies. Thus the circumstances under which its citizens have lived have provided more support for the individualistic view that persons are capable of and should be the masters of their own individual fates, relatively free from both constraining public regulation of abortion, immigration and citizenship issues as well as high taxes and supportive public programs such as the public financing of medical-care services.

THE OTHER FOUR SOCIETIES

I have not provided any basis so far in this study for demonstrating that the public policies of other societies also reveal complementary multi-policy patterns, but configurations indicative of historical, institutional and cultural influences different from those of the United States. I now draw on limited data from the other four societies which will at least suggest that different patterns of program consistency, revealing the influence of contrasting historical experiences, institutional paths and cultures, characterize these four societies. In examining the policies of these other societies, I will be concerned particularly with the direction in which these policy configurations vary from the baseline offered by the United States' example.

Sweden. In chapter 2 we found that Sweden regularly ranks at or near the top of OECD societies in terms of public sector revenues as a percentage of GDP. (See table 2.2—p. 42.) Concomitantly, Sweden has been the exemplar of the so-called third way (i.e., between the individualistic United States and the authoritarian former Soviet Union). This path has involved parliamentary democracy along with a broad range of civil-political rights and a competitive economy driven by private capital on one hand and an extensive array of public social programs on the other. Indeed, the expenses of these public social programs are the primary driving force behind the extensive and moderately progressive Swedish tax regime. So, in the case of Sweden, these two central political-economic aspects of contemporary advanced industrial societies (i.e., taxing and public social program spending) are both mutually complementary and much more extensive than their counterparts in the United States.

But what about Sweden's policies with respect to the two "legitimacy" (i.e., abortion and immigration/citizenship) issues that we have examined? Sweden follows a policy of abortion on demand through the first 18 weeks of pregnancy. A woman seeking an abortion after the twelfth week must have a session with a government-approved counselor. So far the Swedish approach resembles the lenient policy found in the United States. But thereafter abortion is strictly regulated, and the presumption against it can only be overcome by a positive decision on the part of the National Board of Health and Welfare on the basis of "substantial grounds" (Glendon 1987, 14, 23, 153). Further, the Swedish abortion law of 1974 was part of a package which emphasized adolescent education with respect to birth control and fostered the increasing availability of contraceptives. The aim of the package has been to make abortion a less frequent option of last resort. This objective has been realized to a significant degree in substantial reductions in the rates of both abortions and births among Swedish teenagers (23). So Swedish abortion policy also reveals several aspects similar to the French approach to abortion, involving a compromise among rival political perspectives that I related in chapter 4.

Swedish policies with respect to immigration and citizenship also differ predictably from their American counterparts. The proportion of "foreign born" persons in Sweden is smaller than for the United States (6 percent and 7.9 percent, respectively—table 5.1, p. 138), but much larger than for Japan (1.1 percent). However, the character of a large portion of Sweden's "foreign born" population reduces the significance of Sweden resembling the United States more closely than Japan on this criterion. A substantial portion of Sweden's "foreign born" population comes from adjacent Nordic societies (i.e., Norway, Denmark and Finland), which have much in common with Sweden (i.e., ethnicity, language, religion). Thus these persons are minimally "foreign," frequently intermarry with Swedes and may become Swedish citizens. In other respects Swedish immigration policy distinguishes itself clearly from that of Japan. After the Second World War, Sweden sought workers from southern Europe as immigrants, and it has also been more open to refugees. Sweden has accepted groups of refugees in the aftermath of specific high-profile social dislocations in various regions over the last few decades. So, while Swedish immigration policy has not been as open as that of the United States, it has been more inclusive than Japan's.

Overall, then, Sweden is more predisposed to actively employ public policy—across both political economy and legitimacy issues—than is the United States. It funds its public sector more generously and uses these funds far more expansively to help citizens confront various social hazards such as aging, illness and single parenting. Further, it is more prone to regulate legitimacy issues such as abortion and immigration/citizenship than is the United States. Drawing on Sweden's history, path of institutional development and the resulting influence of rival cultures that these factors have helped to produce, enables us to formulate a compelling explanation of these systematic Swedish-U.S. differences.

For a lengthy period of Swedish history, the most high-profile activity of the Swedish state was the management of frequent warfare with other European powers. While some of these conflicts arose from Swedish monarchs' desires for personal aggrandizement, others were necessary to defend the Swedish population from the predations of foreign powers or to better secure the commerce which supported this population. In the course of several hundred years of this experience, Sweden developed a relatively capable central executive which relied on a sophisticated bureaucracy nearly two centuries before the United States followed suit in this latter regard. Further, Sweden became accustomed to using this state to solve problems (e.g., attack by foreign powers) which were social rather than individual, in that they transcended the capacity of individuals to resolve. Prolonged, high-profile national security issues produced both a capable and active executive as well as mass and elite high-group cultures which were predisposed to use this societal resource to solve social problems. Related though briefer experiences created similar but more modest tendencies in the United States in response to the Great Depression of the 1930s and the Second World War.

Thus in the late nineteenth and early twentieth centuries, when systematic disparities between Swedish population growth and the employment capacities of the Swedish economy replaced national security issues as leading societal problems, the capable Swedish state was able to redirect its attention and resources from managing warfare toward these new challenges, with little resistance from persons who perceived these new problems as individual rather than social. Swedish historical experience had created both the public institutions and the cultural predispositions to use them to help resolve the social dislocations the new economic difficulties posed.

Against a background of prolonged fears about national security and economic disaster, the conception of individuals as capable of being the masters of their own fates has simply been less realistic and—accordingly—less credible among the Swedish population than among the American. Thus the relative concern for having public sector support for physical and economic security as opposed to individual freedom from public regulation (and support) has been higher among the former population than the latter.

Canada   Canada's public sector extracts more heavily from its private sector than does the United States (43.1 and 32.2 percent of GDP, respectively—table 2.2, p. 42). Further, as I have already shown in chapter 2, selected aspects of Canadian public social programs are considerably more ambitious than their counterparts in the United States. Overall, however, Canadian social program expenditures have not differed sharply from those of the United States across the last few decades (OECD 1985; 1995). In fact, the single most significant variation between Canada and the United States in terms of public social programs is likely the difference in public financing of medical care on which we focused in chapter 2.

Canada's differences from the United States on the legitimacy issues present a predictable outcome and a surprise. The predictable outcome involves abortion. As we might expect for a society sharing some important similarities with the United States, Canadian abortion policy has followed—somewhat more hesitantly—a path broadly similar to the one that American abortion policy has traveled. Until 1988 Canada regulated abortion strictly as the United States had done prior to 1973. Technically, a board of three physicians had to certify that an abortion was necessary for sustaining the life or health of the pregnant woman in order for an abortion to be legal (Glendon 1987: 14, 145). Across the 1980s a series of court decisions opened loopholes in this regulatory edifice by, for instance, broadening the definition of a pregnant woman's health to include psychological maladies, and in 1988 the Canadian Supreme Court essentially decriminalized abortion. Technically, Canadian law allows for public financing of abortions, but the governments of five of Canada's ten provinces have—so far—effectively resisted federal pressures to fund this service (*Toronto Star* 2001). Private abortions are available but expensive, and the waiting lists for publicly funded abortions are characteristically long, so abortions are not as readily available in Canada as their formal legal status implies. Additionally, the Canadian Alliance, a regional political party of the Canadian West with a largely socially conservative constituency, made the legal status of abortion a prominent issue in the 2000 Canadian parliamentary election (*Toronto Star* 2000). While the party and its allies failed to take control of parliament, in the election's aftermath the status of abortion continues as a more high-profile issue in Canada than it was across most of the 1990s.

Canada shares with the United States a tradition of relative openness with regard to immigration.[1] Yet Canada's degree of openness to and recent experience with immigration represents something of a surprise for a society with a history of more extensive socially conservative or Tory as well as social democratic influence than the United States. Across the 1990s, immigration to Canada—predominantly from Asia—was sharply higher than it had been previously. While Canada admitted only about a quarter of the immigrants that the United States did across this period, its population base is so much smaller that the proportion of foreign-born persons living in Canada now is nearly twice (15.6 percent) that of the United States (7.9 percent—see table 5.1, p. 138). In comparison to the United States, a more modest proportion of immigrants to Canada acquire Canadian citizenship.

These Canadian-American policy differences are smaller than the Swedish-American contrasts, but in three of the four policy areas Canadian policies differ in the same direction as do Sweden's. Tax extraction is higher than in the United States, and Canadian public social programs (e.g., public financing of medical care) are more extensive. Further, Canada has moved more hesitantly than the United States to deregulate abortion. The exception involves immigration policy. Canada has recently been more open to immigrants than the United States.

Canada's experiences with historical contingencies resemble those of the United States in some important respects. A major exception to this similarity of experience comes in the form of differences between the early populations of Canada and the United States. Immigrants to the areas of North America which became Canada were somewhat more diverse, with a larger proportion of French, and—at least by the late eighteenth century—were decidedly more loyal to England than their United States' counterparts. Canada has shared, perhaps even exceeded, the United States' good fortune across the last two centuries in remaining free from major foreign attacks or even warfare arising from internal disputes on its territory. Canada has been more dependent on foreign trade than the United States. The United States has been Canada's leading trading partner for a lengthy period. So, while throughout much of the twentieth century Canada shared the United States' insulation from some of the economic problems of Europe and Asia, its fortunes have been closely tied to those of the much larger American economy.

Greater Canadian loyalty to the United Kingdom is captured by the structure of several of Canada's most basic institutions. These include: use of the British North America Act (1867) as Canada's foundational document until 1982; active membership in the British Commonwealth, including recognition of the English Queen as Canadian head of state; and the development of a parliamentary—rather than a presidential—system. Acceptance of monarchy and even parliamentarianism evince a greater tolerance for human inequality and central authority and correspondingly less concern for individuals' liberty from state regulation than have historically been evidenced in the United States.

Canadian-U.S. differences with regard to historical contingencies and paths of institutional development are not as sharp as those separating the United States from Sweden, France or particularly Japan. Nonetheless, they appear to arise partially from and have continued to support more hierarchical and egalitarian influence among both the general public and the Canadian political elite. We found particularly telling examples of greater high-group influence in Canada in chapter 2, both in the basic beliefs and value priorities underlying the Canadian national health insurance system and in the popularity of this system among Canadians.

France.   France's Fifth Republic supports a substantial tax regime (46.1 percent of GDP—see table 2.2, p. 42). Further, it represents a classic example of what Esping-Andersen (1990) calls a corporatist welfare-state regime. That is, France supports extensive public social programs which differentiate among social strata. France spent 33.1 percent of its GDP on social programs in 1990 (OECD 1995). Thus France is more prone to intervene on private society through taxation and is more active in providing public social and related programs than is the United States.

As I explained in chapter 4, France's abortion policy is less extreme in terms of favoring one political perspective than is the United States' policy. French abortion policy represents an artful compromise among secular economic conservatives, clerical social conservatives and socialists. The economically conservative component was prompted by the government of Valéry Giscard d'Estaing. His presidency created the most economically conservative government of the Fifth Republic to date. But France's two secular constituencies (i.e., the economic conservatives and the socialists) have remained influential enough to maintain Giscard d'Estaing's 1975 legislation and even to expand it slightly in 2000.

In contrast to a number of other major continental European societies, France has long had a reputation for openness to immigrants willing to assimilate (Freeman 1995). That is, the egalitarian internationalism of French socialists, in conjunction with the diversity-favoring attitudes of economic conservatives, have predominated over the social conservative perspective with respect to immigration. Historically, most French immigrants have come from other European societies. Over the last half-century increasing numbers have come from members of the French Community (i.e., former French colonies). Many of these persons have become French citizens. Islamic immigrants from Algeria and Morocco have dominated the flow of migrants into France during the last few decades. They have shown a disinclination to assimilate, demanding instead a right to be different. This change in immigrants' attitudes has created a significant issue in France (Weil and Crowley 1994). Overall, France has a somewhat smaller proportion of foreign-born persons in its population than does the United States (6.3 percent as opposed to 7.9 percent—see table 5.1, p. 138).

Thus all four aspects of French policy included in this study differ from their U.S. counterparts in the same direction as do Sweden's. Taxation and public social provision are more extensive than in the United States. Moreover, abortion and immigration/citizenship policies represent more obvious compromises among rival political perspectives than their straightforwardly individualistic American counterparts. Across these four policy areas, French citizens are more heavily regulated (e.g., taxation and abortion) and supported (public social programs) than are their American counterparts. This general tendency arises in part from more widespread skepticism in France about the fitness of individuals for mastering their own fates.

As one of the first nation-states, France has been a major European power for over 500 years. During the seventeenth and eighteenth centuries in particular, France provided the model for success in the then regular military conflict, in which such a power engaged, by developing a well-financed absolute monarchy served by a relatively capable group of advisors. The French Revolution of 1789 ended this Ancien Régime, and for over a century and a half France struggled with shifts between authoritarian and republican regimes and instability among the latter. France's internal divisions held costly consequences for its position among the European powers. France's defeat in the Franco-Prussian War of 1871, in particular, ushered in nearly a century's insecurity. Germany's population and military strength was expanding while France's appeared to be in relative decline. In these circumstances, the French birthrate became a national security issue. Accordingly, the French state, which had been built to focus on conventional national security concerns, began to develop what became known as "family policy" (e.g., child allowances) in the hope of rejuvenating the French birthrate and the society's military resources. It also welcomed additions to its population in the form of immigrants.

France's experience with European warfare in the twentieth century was sobering indeed. France was the seat of much of the Western Front in the First World War. While France emerged on the victorious side in this conflict, it suffered much loss of life and other destruction, and this victory was achieved only with significant help from France's allies. In an effort to counter its relative decline France continued to develop its family policy as well as related public social programs. In spite of all France's efforts to improve its situation vis-à-vis Germany, France was defeated early in the Second World War and partially occupied by the Germans. Enduring modern warfare on French soil and the German occupation are experiences unsupportive of beliefs that individuals are capable of mastering their own fates. They are more apt to foster adherence to the high-group cultures, which are more prone to construct collective responses to widespread difficulties or to strengthen the ranks of fatalists.

Charles de Gaulle's melding of a strong presidency onto the French parliamentary system in the Fifth Republic of 1958 has secured more stability among French political leaders and, even more surprising, what appears to be a less centrifugal society. In these improved circumstances, compromise—which long eluded rival French political factions—has become possible. French abortion policy represents an excellent example of the benefits of these more secure, stable and generally less volatile circumstances.

Japan.   Japan presents two anomalies in terms of the direction of its deviations from U.S. policy. For one, in spite of relying heavily on executive leadership, only marginally constrained by popular pressures or parliamentary scrutiny, to overcome a lengthy security crisis and being the most high-group—and the most hierarchical—society among the five considered in this study, the size of Japan's public sector—in terms of the proportion of GDP that its public revenues represent—is, like that of the United States, routinely at or near the bottom of the range of variation

offered by advanced industrial societies. (See table 2.2—p. 42.) As I explained above,[2] this is the result of competition between and shifts in the
relative influence of two factions of contemporary Japanese social conservatives. Both factions share a predisposition toward an active, socially
interventionary state, and this preference clearly distinguishes their hierarchical perspectives from the individualism which produces a modestly
sized public sector in the United States. But the contrasting institutional
socialization of these two factions prompts distinct views on how to
achieve the goals that many other advanced industrial societies address
through extensive public social programs.

Parliamentary Japanese hierarchists, prominent LDP Diet members
in particular, have come increasingly to accept expensive public social
programs (and the extensive public revenues that they require) both as
devices of electoral competition and as vital means for realizing central
hierarchical values such as social harmony. Yet bureaucratic Japanese hierarchists, particularly executives in the ministries that have historically
been charged with overcoming Japan's "late-developer" status (i.e., the
Ministry of Finance and the Ministry of International Trade and Industry), favor instead an active industrial policy for meeting these goals. In
their view, this policy choice provides the resources (i.e., particularly
jobs) that households—many of which are still multigenerational
(Hashimoto 1996)—require in order to help themselves. Moreover, by
avoiding the extraordinary expense of extensive public social programs,
this policy leaves more of society's material resources in the private sector and thus available to capable corporate executives who, with guidance
from expert central-state bureaucrats, are able to use them in fostering
societal economic development.

During the period in which Japan was rebuilding its economy from
the destruction of the Second World War (i.e., from the late 1940s into
the late 1950s), bureaucratic hierarchists dominated Japanese social policy formulation. Accordingly, across this period spending on public social
programs was modest. As relative prosperity was achieved in the late
1950s, popular pressures for improved public social programs began to
build. From the late 1950s through the mid-1970s parliamentary hierarchists acquired increasing influence on social policy formulation, and
Japanese social program development was extensive. Indeed, in 1973 the
LDP declared its commitment to a "vigorous welfare society" (Pempel
1982, 142). However, in the aftermath of the "oil shocks" and resulting
economic difficulties as well as the appearance of discouraging long-term
demographic trends (e.g., population aging) in the mid-1970s, bureaucratic hierarchists began reacquiring control of social policy formulation,

and this shift ushered in a period of social program retrenchment (Lockhart 2001b: chs. 3, 8; 2001c).

With a relative modest tax regime, Japan is necessarily limited with respect to the proportion of GDP that it can spend on public social programs. Its "national effort" (i.e., the proportion of GDP spent on public social programs—see Wilensky 1975) is roughly similar to that of the United States. But with regard to the particular social program on which this study has focused—the public financing of medical care—the situation is different. With respect to what we might generically call national health insurance, Japan is much more similar to most other advanced industrial societies than is the United States. Japan has one system of public medical-care insurance for employees of relatively large-scale employers, dating from the prewar period, and a second system for other citizens that was developed in 1959.

Abortion policy provides a second Japanese anomaly from the predictions offered by the combination of historical, institutional and cultural variables employed in this study. One would think that a society which has experienced significant social dislocation for which it has relied heavily on relatively unscrutinized public executives, and in which hierarchy is the predominant culture, ought to place abortion decisions in the hands of experts.[3] Nonetheless, Japan legalized abortion during the period of the U.S. occupation (1948), and in comparison to the United States there has been little controversy over abortion since. Other aspects of fertility policy in Japan frequently display amazing degrees of hierarchical influence. For instance, the Ministry of Health did not approve birth control pills for use in Japan until 1999—34 years after the pills were first submitted for approval and also after the Ministry had hastily approved use of Viagra. Even now the use of birth control pills is low. According to a member of the Diet: "Many men dislike giving women the right to choose" (Magnier 2000). Instead, Japan continues to have what in cross-societal perspective is an extraordinarily high rate of condom use. Additionally, many Japanese women feel that a stigma is associated with getting a prescription for contraceptive pills, and the mostly male Japanese gynecological profession is apparently reluctant to provide their patients with information that would counter many irrational fears regarding the use of contraceptive pills (Magnier 2000).

Yet it is surely sobering to the potential of deductive theory in the social sciences that a society which exhibits high levels of societal disruption, relatively unconstrained public executives and gender hierarchy as pervasively as does Japan, placed decisions on abortion in the hands of ordinary women earlier and more thoroughly than the other societies in-cluded in this study. There were, of course, mitigating circumstances: widespread destruction attributable to the war and associated social dis-location heightened concerns about unwanted children; the methods of contraception extant in 1948 were less reliable than those available today, etc. Nonetheless, the 1948 Japanese decision and particularly the relative absence of controversy that it has engendered in the ensuing half-century are surprising. In the social sciences, deductive theories are apt to be less powerful than in the physical sciences, which study inanimate particles and other more rule-respecting phenomena.

As I discussed in chapter 5, Japan has a restrictive orientation toward immigration and a particularly exclusive perspective toward granting im-migrants citizenship. So on this second legitimacy issue, Japan clearly conforms to the deviation from U. S. policy that the explanatory variables employed by this study predict.

For Japan, the pressures on institutions and policy exerted by the last century-and-a-half's experiences are particularly obvious. "Late devel-oper" status in a region of active Western imperialism created a long-term security crisis, and the formation of a capable, relatively unfettered national executive focused on a development mobilization. Overall, this state has sought less to extract material resources from the private sector than to expertly direct the use of private resources in support of societal development aims. In spite of a general preference for leaving material resources in the private sector where corporate executives can use them (with state guidance) for national development, Japanese leaders' peri-odic concerns for social order among a population experiencing signifi-cant social dislocation (Calder 1988), for better health among young men subject to military service (Shinkawa and Pempel 1996) and for continued LDP postwar electoral success (Calder 1988) have led to the introduction of new social programs or the expansion of existing ones. One consequence of the social disruption of the immediate postwar pe-riod is an abortion policy of surprising permissiveness. Yet experiences with massive destruction from Western attacks on Japanese cities and foreign occupation reinforced both long-standing Japanese preferences for keeping the number of foreigners in their midst to a minimum and restrictive policies toward immigration and citizenship. As a result of these experiences and the path of institutional development which they have spawned, few contemporary Japanese subscribe to the view that in-dividuals are generally capable of mastering their own fates, and Japanese policy in the four areas that we have examined reveals their skepticism.

ISSUES IN EXPLAINING AND
PREDICTING SOCIETAL POLICY PATTERNS

SPECIFICATION OF A CAUSAL MODEL

Throughout this study I have drawn on three distinct categories of variables—historical, institutional and cultural—to explain policy differences between the United States and other advanced industrial societies. I have fit these variables into a progressively more explicit causal model similar to the one employed by historical institutionalists (Steinmo 1995). The institutionalists' version appears to accept a society's unique experiences with the world as the initial step of the causal sequence, and this category of variables forms an explicit causal step in this study. These experiences then influence the path along which the society's broad political institutions develop. These institutions, in turn, help to shape both the culture(s) of a society's citizens and political elites as well as the design of the specific policies that the latter introduce. This study generally follows this sequence of causal factors in explaining the distinctive multipolicy patterns of various societies in the preceding section.

Yet this study has also suggested some changes to the model favored by many institutionalists. First, the model is indeterminate in a couple of important respects. For one, as we have witnessed, persons may react differently to similar situations. Some of the late-nineteenth-century Swedes who faced severe labor-market difficulties reacted by organizing workers in Sweden. Others emigrated to the United States, where conditions were less severe. Numerous factors influence these differences. For instance, young Swede males probably found emigration a more viable strategy than did older Swedish women. Another factor which influences how persons react to specific situations is their culture. Egalitarians are predisposed to develop collective remedies with their peers; whereas individualists are more inclined to negotiate independent solutions for themselves (e.g., Atlantic passage) with specific other persons.

Another sense in which this model is indeterminate is that we cannot expect to be able to predict in any detail the specific character of the policies that societal elites develop. Policy details are too contingent on numerous random contextual features and social interactions that are too complex for social science to have much hope of modeling in the foreseeable future. Yet some predictions can be made. For instance, the variables on which this study draws support the prediction that U.S. policies across a range of substantive areas will—in comparative perspective— evince relatively high degrees of faith in the capacities of, and place considerable responsibility on, individual persons. Further, we can predict that the policies of the four other societies included in this study will generally support greater collective, as opposed to individual, responsibility and be less generous in their assessment of the capacities of ordinary persons to master their own fates. As the direction of the cross-societal "capacities-responsibilities" differences of the various policies that we examined in the previous section showed, using these variables enables us to make accurate predictions in 17 out of 20 instances (85 percent of the time). More refined predictions may be possible, too, but the prediction of the nearly infinite detail of specific policy designs lies beyond the reach of current models.

Second, it appears as if, at least with respect to specific policies, the influence of certain historical accidents or contingencies may sometimes exert itself directly on culture and policy design. That is, historical experience may influence these variables without important contributions from the developmental path of more general political institutions. For instance, Japanese hesitancy to admit foreigners and, particularly, to allow them to remain, to have their relatives join them and become citizens and the policies created pursuant to this hesitancy do not appear to be highly dependent on the development in Japan of highly capable central-state executives, some of whom—even in the contemporary period—enjoy remarkable independence from parliamentary constraint. Rather, these cultural preferences and the policies supporting them appear to flow from historical experiences such as the lengthy early insular period, during which Japanese attentions were focused internally, and the long-standing security fears arising initially from Japanese contact with the West in the mid-nineteenth century.

Third, the paths along which general political institutions develop may sometimes be as much the result of culture and its cause. Two distinct possibilities merit consideration in this regard. For one, the different paths of development for American and Canadian political institutions are not attributable to the sorts of sharp differences in national experiences that led Sweden, France or Japan to develop powerful active national executives. Both the United States and particularly Canada have had relatively mild experiences in the past couple of centuries with military or economic havoc within their own borders. Canada's greater acceptance of colonial status, monarchy and parliamentary—as opposed to separation-of-powers—democracy does not stem from more severe experiences with the world as in these other three societies. The contemporary forms taken by both Canada and the United States developed largely after England was already embroiled in the Tory-Whig controversies which gave birth to what became liberal democracy. In this regard they are both exceptional in comparison to the other three societies included in this study. But Canadians and Americans made different *choices* with regard to this controversy, the former more favorable to the Tories, the latter more inclined toward the Whigs. We can label this difference a historical accident: e.g., Tories were more predominant among early Canadians. But a cultural difference clearly lies at the heart of this explanation. Early Canadians were comfortable with more hierarchical political institutions than were their American counterparts, who favored more individualistic and egalitarian institutions.

Another way in which culture acts as a cause of the developmental paths of general political institutions appears when sets of beliefs and value priorities arising from socialization exogenous to this path are crucial in reshaping it. The actions of Madison and others in developing and gaining ratification of the Constitution of 1787 provide an example of this process. In the mid-1770s Madison rejected the socialization arising from his participation in the hierarchical British Empire by supporting independence through the Articles of Confederation. Just over a decade later he took an equally significant step. Madison's experience with life under the Articles raised for him numerous concerns about various weaknesses in and problems stemming from the basic structure of the government the Articles sustained (*Federalist Papers;* Beard 1965). Thus he took steps perhaps less to carve out a new path than to shift the existing path in a new direction. The nature of this new direction drew less on Madison's adult socialization by existing political institutions than on the ideas of Locke and Montesquieu, which he had encountered in the education of his youth.

Madison employed these ideas to build a considerably more powerful national government than the one afforded by the Articles, a government that violated the limited and local characteristics popular among the anti-Federalists. But the replacement that Madison developed with others was replete with safeguards reflecting the self-interested conception of humans associated with Locke and the liberal revolution generally. Madison sought to replace the power of local governments responsible to popular majorities that were so congenial to egalitarians with a more capable and centralized but still constrained government which found more favor among individualists and even hierarchists.

Major shifts in the direction of the developmental paths of societies' broad political institutions are relatively rare. But when they do occur—

as in the American Revolution or the Constitution of 1787; the French Revolution or the Fifth Republic; and the Meiji Restoration or the postwar Japanese democracy—the character of the institutions defining the new direction is based on sets of beliefs and value priorities that are sharply different from those on which the previous institutions rested. These significant social changes grow out of deep frustration with the beliefs and values underlying the former institutions, so these institutions do not represent a positive source for the culture animating the new institutions. Rather, the source of these beliefs and values is distinct from the former institutions. So in these situations, culture arising exogenously from participation in the prevailing institutions of the past provides the standards for reshaping the developmental path of society's broad political institutions.

Fourth, in combination, shifting historical contingencies and culture may prompt significant policy changes less deep-seated but more frequent than the shifts of revolutionary magnitude just discussed. Across this study, Roosevelt's New Deal has repeatedly provided an example of a "dual-process" pattern of policy change. One process involves new socially dislocating experiences (e.g., the Great Depression or the Second World War) moving ordinary citizens "up-group" and possibly "up-grid" from relative individualism toward adherence to one of the high-group cultures (i.e., egalitarianism and hierarchy). That is, new domestic economic or foreign military threats pose problems which persons cannot master individually. So, instead of emphasizing individual freedom from state regulation, citizens become more concerned that the state provide various forms of collective security. A second process, requisite to significant policy change, involves the replacement of existing political leaders beholden to one culture with others animated by a culture evincing greater sympathy for the collective remedies becoming more popular among the general citizenry. One group of leaders may replace another, or new members may be added to a governing coalition. In either case, the new political leadership will likely revise the character of public policy in ways that would not have seemed possible in the past.

Valéry Giscard d'Estaing's introduction of a more lenient compromise with respect to abortion policy represents another example of this dual-process pattern, although the French were moving toward, rather than away from, a relatively individualistic position. Cox (2001) offers additional examples of changes of this latter sort. During the 1980s both Denmark and the Netherlands engaged in forms of retrenchment in their public social programs that required greater individual responsibility from program recipients. These changes thus occurred in societies with long-standing welfare-state traditions which supported exceptionally generous public social program benefits. The dual-process pattern of policy change originated in growing ire among ordinary citizens over what were widely perceived as various forms of beneficiary abuse of specific public social programs (e.g., able-bodied persons opting for living on generous public program benefits rather than accepting jobs). These shifts in citizens' orientations toward public programs that had virtually defined the public sphere in these societies (Cox 2001, 479) altered the fortunes of various political parties either in terms of electoral success and/or revised parliamentary coalitions. New governments then made policy changes designed to shift the way public social programs weighed citizens' rights against their obligations.

RELATIVE EXPLANATORY AND PREDICTIVE CAPACITIES

At various points in this study I have modified the causal sequence I employ due to one or more of the considerations discussed in the previous section. But all my variations locate culture as the last step prior to policy formulation.[4] Thus, as I have illustrated in the "Policy-Preferences-of-Rival-Cultures" section in each of the four case study chapters, fairly effective predictions for the nature of particular societies' policies in varying substantive areas can be obtained from knowing the cultures that predominate among the society's relevant organized political elites. Minimally, these predictions are sufficient to ascertain the direction in which other societies' policies will differ from those of the United States with regard to matters such as the citizen-capacity-and-responsibility issues that we discussed earlier in this chapter. Sometimes—as with the focus of French abortion policy on considering the concerns of all interested parties—these cultural orientations support prediction of more fine-grained policy design features. In short, proximity to policy in the causal sequence makes the cultural orientations of dominant political elites reasonably effective predictors of policy design.

As Toulmin (1961) points out, however, explanation is a more demanding task. We can explain cross-societal policy variation in terms of efforts on the part of dominant political elites, the adherents of rival cultures in various societies, to realize their contrasting sets of beliefs and value priorities through distinctive institutional designs. But doing so offers an explanation that begs the question as to why, for instance, American political elites are predisposed toward a culture different from the one that attracts Swedish elites. Including historical and institutional variables in our efforts to account for these policy differences produces broader, likely deeper, and surely more satisfying explanations.

Yet we need to keep in mind that—for practical purposes—*all* explanations leave something unexplained. Explanations of policy design that draw on historical, institutional and cultural factors are likely to be more thorough than those which draw only on culture. But identifying one of our variable categories as historical contingencies acknowledges a willingness to accept the Great Depression or the greater predisposition of early Canadian immigrants to defer to royal authority as "given." Thus this study does not seek to explain the sources of these factors which have, nonetheless, been the focus of inquiry for other scholars. Placing limits on inquiry is essential for successfully studying any question. An assignment to explain everything asks too much of any particular scientific inquiry.

So the important practical issue seems to be how broadly to cast one's net in terms of including explanatory variables. Quantitative researchers can gain useful perspective on this question by calculating statistically how much of the total variance in their dependent variable is accounted for by a particular set of explanatory variables. Qualitative researchers have no similarly clear measure. Frequently in the past researchers have employed or at least focused primarily on only one of the three categories of variables on which this study draws. More recently, historical and institutional variables have been explicitly distinguished and used in conjunction with one another (e.g., Steinmo, Thelen and Longstreth 1992). This study explicitly adds distinct cultural variables to the pool of explanatory variables. The denseness of interaction between both historical experience and institutional structure on one hand and culture on the other provides an initial argument in favor of this addition. But many historical and institutional analysts perceive culture as a residual explanatory variable in the sense that historical and/or institutional factors are capable of carrying so much of the explanatory load that there is little left for culture to contribute.

I have four bases for disagreeing with this contention. First, as I have stressed from the outset of this study, historical experiences and institutional structure rarely, if ever, determine persons' responses completely.[5] Late-nineteenth-century Swedes reacted differently to difficult labor market conditions, and Madison's adult experience with the British Empire and the Articles of Confederation caused him to discard both before constructing his preferred government, via the Constitution of 1787, from scratch on the basis of his early education.

Second, as Elkins and Simeon (1979) suggest, relations between culture and historical or institutional variables are sometimes quite tight and involve complex interaction. It is often difficult to separate the consequences of these three types of factors, and efforts to do so are frequently highly arbitrary. For instance, in this study I have considered the more favorable predispositions of early Canadian immigrants toward monarchy as a historical accident. But the explanatory force of this variable rests on distinctive beliefs and value priorities and thus culture; early Canadian immigrants, in effect, preferred colonial imperialism and monarchy to independence and republicanism. Similarly, I have accorded a society's broad political institutions a significant explanatory role as socializers of successive generations and as facilitators of some courses of action over others. Yet these institutions have been constructed—perhaps more clearly in the United States than in other societies—purposely to realize particular sets of beliefs and value priorities rather than others. Moreover, at least some—and likely the most politically active—portions of the citizenry socialized by these institutions recognize this cultural message. So an element of the explanatory power of institutional structure for explaining policy design draws inherently on the culture that the institutions embody.

Third, in some instances culture acquired from general experience with the world offers an explanation of policy without having its effects filtered through the intervening general political institutions which define a society's developmental path. One example of this phenomenon among the cases included in this study involves the long-standing Japanese concern to limit pollution of their social life by restricting foreigners' access to and especially membership in Japanese society. It is not clear that the character of the developmental path of general Japanese political institutions plays much of a role in fostering the policies supporting these goals. Similarly but more significantly, as we have found at several junctures in this study, sharp changes in historical experience may cause citizens to shift their cultural orientations. In reaction to these changes, new political elites—drawing on socialization exogenous from the society's existing path of institutional development—may produce substantially revised policies (e.g., the New Deal) which are sharply at odds with the policy designs that the influence of this developmental path might be expected to produce. In some instances new elites even introduce changes in the direction of this developmental path (e.g., the U.S. Constitution, the French Revolution, the Meiji Restoration).

Fourth, including culture in analyses of policy design aids, minimally by simplifying, prediction. By explicitly considering culture, even in the potentially residual position of the last category in a causal sequence prior to the dependent variable (i.e., policy design), researchers are able to isolate a potentially powerful predictor. Certainly the influence of historical experiences and—in most cases—the developmental path of broad political institutions are important in shaping the proportions of various societal populations and political elites which adhere to rival cultures. But the relative influence of rival cultures among the relevant organized members of a society's political elite appears to be a good predictor of important aspects of policy design. This is so because the contrasting sets of basic beliefs and value priorities that characterize grid-group theory's rival cultures foster what we could call "institutional/policy formation imperatives." That is, politically active adherents of each of the three rival socially interactive cultures that grid-group theory distinguishes strive to construct contrasting policies through which they seek to realize distinctive sets of beliefs and value priorities.

RIVAL INSTITUTIONAL/POLICY FORMATION IMPERATIVES

In an immediate sense, the varying multipolicy patterns of the societies that I have contrasted with the United States are the result of the dominance in different societies of various combinations of the socially interactive cultures that grid-group theory distinguishes. Adherents of each of these cultures display instrumental rationality. That is, they all seek to realize consistent ends efficiently. But the ends of these rival ways of life are distinct, even contradictory. Humans routinely turn to institutions in order to realize their persistent objectives. However, since the ends of rival cultures differ, their adherents have to construct contrasting institutions to realize them, and this means that their institutional/policy formation imperatives differ. Hierarchists cannot realize their belief in the inequality of important human capacities or their resulting value of expertise by supporting grass-roots movements. Egalitarians cannot further their belief in human equality and their resulting value of equal respect by fostering expert-dominated hierarchies. Individualists cannot embody their belief in humans capable of mastering their own fates and the resulting value of liberty through the construction of extensive centralized state bureaucracies. To realize their contrasting objectives, these cultures require expert-led bureaucracies, grass-roots citizen participation and markets, respectively.

Thus in longer-term perspective, the varying experiences that different societies confront help to shape populations predisposed toward different developmental paths for general political institutions and favoring distinctive policy designs for dealing with specific problems common among societies. So variations in the cultures or cultural coalitions which dominate among political elites foster imperatives to construct contrasting policies which embody disparate sets of beliefs and value priorities. I turn now to profiling these distinctive institutional/policy formation imperatives.

Individualism. Individualism arises among persons whose experiences foster beliefs in the bounty and resilience of humans' natural and social environments. Americans' comparatively greater predisposition toward individualism rests in part on the relative mildness of American experience with these environments. Against such encouraging contexts for social interaction, the specific variations that differentiate persons tend to appear insignificant. In particular, they pale before common characteristics such as capacities for rational deliberation and planning. Thus individualists are prone to see most persons as having roughly equal broad capacities of this sort and as capable of mastering their own fates or being self-reliant.

Given these fundamental beliefs about humans and their world, individualists emphasize the value of liberty in its Lockean (*Second Treatise*) "freedom-from-external-constraint" sense, as well as related values such as personal autonomy. As did Locke, they tend to emphasize the material acquisitiveness aspects of freedom and accordingly also value economic efficiency and material success. Since they perceive humans as equal in significant respects, they also value the version of equality of opportunity that Fishkin (1983) refers to as "procedural fairness." Individualists sometimes see the values of other cultures as worthy, but they develop their own specific conceptions of them. For instance, with respect to order and duty—high priority values among hierarchists—individualists favor the limited conception of order that is produced by market coordination and duty to others with whom they have explicit contractual relations, rather than the hierarchists' broader conceptions of these two values.

Individualists will seek to construct paths of general institutional development consistent with these values and thus emphasizing: civil rights against the state; political rights offering control of the state (Macpherson 1973); various markets in goods (Smith, *Wealth of Nations*) and ideas (J. S. Mill, *On Liberty*); as well as related competitive relations among political parties (Schumpeter 1950) and governing institutions (Madison, *Federalist 51*). They prefer limited, and sometimes local, government and can be counted on to oppose growth in the capacities of central governing institutions to exert what they perceive as coercive constraints on individuals. Accordingly, individualists have a predisposition or imperative to strive to construct particular policy designs: e.g., modest and relatively flat-rate tax regimes; only limited public social programs; and minimally restrictive abortion and immigration/citizenship policies. In short, individualists seek to construct particular policies which are designed to realize efficiently the range of human beliefs and values to which they subscribe. Their instrumental rationality is culturally constrained by the specific character of these beliefs and values and fosters a motivational imperative to strive to construct distinctive institutions and policies.

Egalitarianism.   Egalitarianism has its roots in strikingly different experiences with the world. Persons adopt egalitarianism as a result of experiences engendering beliefs in the fragility of the life-supporting aspects of human natural and social environments. Ephemeral contexts prompt persons to cling together, utilizing the collective resources of all for coping successfully with various environmental threats. Though egalitarians perceive humans as roughly equal in broad capacities and needs, they recognize differences in various persons' specific skills. The varying specific skills of all persons are likely to be useful in the face of one contingency or another, so roughly equal sharing of the limited bounty that can be gleaned from fragile environments makes sense as a means for assuring that the most important needs of all vital contributors are met.

Given these fundamental beliefs about humans and their world, egalitarians emphasize varying aspects of equality as their central value. The importance of a broad range of specific skills fosters equality of respect as well as a predisposition that inequalities of material condition should not grow so large as to jeopardize persons' access to "primary goods" (Rawls 1971) that are essential to any life plan. Efforts to achieve rough equality of respect and material goods benefit from social relations in which humility is valued and fostered. Humility cultivates as well the social solidarity that egalitarians perceive as crucial for meeting the various demands that their environment will pose across time. As do individualists, egalitarians occasionally view the values of other cultures as encouraging, but they also develop their own specific conceptions of them. For example, egalitarians favor the limited conception of order that is produced by what they see as voluntary consensus. Further, they think each member of the community has a duty to "own" the consensus to which she or he has contributed.

Because they hold beliefs and values that differ from those of individualists, egalitarians follow a distinctive institutional/policy formation imperative. They seek to construct social institutions consistent with their own values, institutions necessarily distinct from—even at odds with—those which are the object of individualists' veneration. Egalitarians are the major advocates for including a variety of participatory opportunities within the developmental path of societies' broad political institutions. Egalitarians champion active membership in political parties, labor unions, consumer associations and a variety of other grassroots organizations. These institutions help to shift the locus of decision-making in society from a social elite to the ordinary citizens who must bear the bulk of the consequences of societal decisions (Downey 1986; Zisk 1992). In the social contexts of advanced industrial societies, egalitarians are especially prone to strive to shape paths of broad institutional development focusing on socioeconomic rights. For them, the public social programs which realize these rights ease the personal burdens of persons facing particularly difficult social circumstances. Accordingly, egalitarians favor relatively ambitious tax regimes and particularly progressive taxation; broad, accessible and high-quality public social programs; orientations toward abortion that take the concerns of all affected parties, perhaps particularly the pregnant woman's, into consideration; and acceptance of those migrants willing to fully assimilate with their adoptive community. As was the case for individualists, egalitarians want to realize a (different) select range of beliefs and values efficiently, and the institutions and policies that they strive to construct are designed to embody their distinctive preferences in these regards.

Hierarchy.   Hierarchy arises among persons whose environments, both natural and social, have cultivated more differentiating reflection on their experiences. The human contexts that hierarchists perceive include elements similar to those of individualists and egalitarians. Similarly to the individualistic perspective, the hierarchist's view supports both some degree of experimentation with social environments and some degree of exploitation with natural environments. But hierarchists believe that at some point the boundaries of salutary experimentation/exploitation will be surpassed, and persons will confront various forms of environmental failure and social disaster similar to those envisioned by egalitarians. This perspective on human contexts places a high premium on the talents of persons who are able to discern where these crucial "tolerant/perverse" (Thompson, Ellis and Wildavsky 1990) boundaries lie and/or who know how to constrain human activities from transcending them. Accordingly, hierarchists perceive specific sorts of expertise as socially and morally significant. Those who possess this expertise are accorded exceptional status. Indeed, varying capacities with regard to different specific areas of human endeavor create hierarchies of human inequality, with those below dependent on the superior capacities of those above.

Given these beliefs about humans and their world, hierarchists emphasize the values of expertise and the harmonious social order that can be derived from its appropriate application. This order is conceived by societally recognized experts and developed through central political direction. This conception of order typically assigns all persons various niches in the resulting social stratification, and so long as they continue to perform their specialized duties to the broader social collective, these niches are generally secure. Each position in the stratified collective is associated with some degree of honor, but social harmony requires that subordinates act with deference toward their superiors.

Thus hierarchists adopt a third set of distinctive beliefs and values which they strive to embody through yet a different institutional/policy formation imperative. In terms of the path of general institutional development, hierarchists favor a strong central state complete with a set of formal bureaucracies capable of guiding, monitoring and correcting social activity in all significant sectors of social life. This preference contrasts particularly with the individualists' desire for limited government that allows social organization to emerge from less formal market interactions. Another hierarchical institutional favorite is the sectoral "peak association." By organizing various sectors of civil society in this fashion, experts subject the untutored preferences of ordinary persons to a series of creative compromises, which edit their content and strive for better harmonization among competing societal interests. This preference contrasts particularly with the egalitarians' penchant for maximizing the influence of ordinary citizens in the construction of the societal rules which constrain their lives.

These ambitions of the hierarchical state require particular policies, including an extensive tax regime, but likely not the degree of tax progressivity that egalitarians would prefer. Hierarchists are supportive of a broad range of accessible public social programs for helping less-capable ordinary persons with the vicissitudes of life, but these programs are likely to treat varying social strata differently. Particular hierarchical groups may vary in their attitudes as to when abortion is a legitimate practice, but they will likely want to keep the decision in the hands of socially recognized experts rather than allowing ordinary persons to do what they wish in this regard. Hierarchists' beliefs in human inequality leave them more prone than the adherents of the low-grid cultures to regulate immigration and citizenship strictly. So the beliefs and values that hierarchists strive to realize efficiently, prompt them to construct institutions and policies distinct from those preferred by either egalitarians or individualists.[6]

SO, WHY DOES THE UNITED STATES NOT EMULATE THE POLICIES OF OTHER SOCIETIES?

In an immediate sense, the answer to this question is that, while the situations with regard to policies in various substantive areas differ in their specifics, insufficient proportions of the general citizenry of the United States or, particularly, its relevant organized political elite are intensely supportive of a more extensive and perhaps more progressive tax regime, a universal public system for financing medical care, an abortion policy constructed through compromise among rival political perspectives, or more restrictive policies with respect to immigration and citizenship. In many instances, conscious perceptions may be couched in terms of personal self-interest. That is, few American citizens want to pay higher personal taxes. Some Americans have excellent private health insurance and want to keep it. Many American women who may want an abortion in the future wish to maintain the right to choose this procedure for themselves. And many Americans may want to have overseas relatives join them in the United States.

But in terms of self-interest, Americans are not so unusual. Swedes do not volunteer to pay more taxes. Canadians want, and many think that they have, excellent health insurance. French feminists have pushed for—and in 2000 gained modestly—more lenient regulation of abortion, but many accept that, given the divisions in French society on this issue, policy in the area of the current compromise is the best that they can realistically expect to achieve. And many Japanese young adults want the economic benefits that increased numbers of foreign unskilled laborers would help to provide.

All persons are self-interested, but the interests that persons think acceptable for themselves vary depending on which culture shapes their beliefs, values and principles. For instance, in contrast to many Swedish citizens, but similar to the frequent comments of President George W. Bush, American citizens are inclined to believe that income is better left with the persons who earn it rather than transferring this resource to the public sector. They subscribe to the principle that the persons who earn the income will use it more wisely than would public officials if this resource were taxed more heavily in order to provide more extensive public policy benefits such as a national health insurance program.

As the pattern common to American policies across the four substantive areas that we examined in the initial section of this chapter indicates, Americans are more predisposed than are the citizens of other societies to perceive humans as relatively equal individuals who are capable of mastering their own fates if only government will leave them free to look after themselves. These beliefs in relative equality and capacity and the resulting priority of liberty—particularly from public sector regulation—as a value are the hallmarks of individualism, and they provide a persuasive immediate explanation as to why Americans are taxed less, have less extensive public social programs available to them, are more free to make their own decisions with regard to fertility issues and accept less extensive restrictions on both immigration and citizenship than do the citizens of most other advanced industrial societies. If individualists were not more politically influential in the United States than minimally the other four societies that we have examined, it would seem exceedingly difficult to explain why the United States maintains policies across a broad range of substantive areas that differ so sharply—in a direction consistent with individualism—from the policies of these other societies.

What remains to be explained is why both American citizens and their political leaders are more thoroughly individualistic than their counterparts in other societies. I have emphasized two categories of factors as relevant to explaining this distinctive American characteristic. First, I have drawn on historical contingencies in two ways. For one, American society has a more discrete starting point in European immigration of the early seventeenth century than do many other societies. Moreover, while these immigrants differed in their perspectives, they shared related reservations about royal absolutism and various social practices associated with it that were then preeminent in major European societies.

In the New England region, dissenters from the central religious orthodoxy of the Church of England predominated. These persons favored more congregational social structures (relatively small and unstratified egalitarian collectives) than the model offered by the Church of England or the Crown. Over time the Middle-Atlantic area became a refuge particularly for entrepreneurs (individualists) whose fortunes had been constrained by the close regulation of commerce in England and generally on the European continent as well. The southern regions of what became the United States were from the start dominated by persons who were less opposed to hierarchy as a principle of social organization. But many of the persons who immigrated to this region lacked a secure or at least satisfactory niche in the tightly regulated social structure of seventeenth- and eighteenth-century England. While as Madison famously argued (*Federalist* 10), the interests, as well as the cultures, of these regions differed, residents of all three held related reservations about their experience with European practices that fostered shared values (e.g., respect for "self-made" men—the masters of their own fates) and institutions such as generally allowing property-owning males (the vast majority of the male population—in contrast to Europe) political voice on local issues. This historical accident—involving what in cross-societal perspective were the unusual beliefs of early American immigrants—helped to initiate a developmental path for broad political institutions that was distinct from the European experience.

Before turning to this developmental path, I want to consider the other way in which historical contingencies are relevant to the explanation of American policy distinctiveness. In brief, the United States has, until fairly recently, been better insulated from severe social dislocations arising from attacks by foreign powers or the contagion of economic disasters abroad. This has been true across American history but perhaps especially important in the twentieth century, which from 1914 to 1945 was consumed by world war, global economic depression and then world war again. While the United States shared in these experiences, it did not suffer hardship to the same degree as most of the other major participants. Thus an orientation, present—indeed prominent—at the creation, that citizens were capable of mastering their own fates, was not tested as harshly in the United States as in these other societies, and thus retained greater credence. In spite of the relative mildness of the American experience, the combination of the Great Depression and the Second World War did contribute to a major upgrading of the size and activity level of the U.S. government in both domestic and foreign policy.

I now turn to the contributions of social structure in explaining American policy distinctiveness. In chapter 1, I introduced two types of structural variables. One involved various aspects of what we could call general social structure (e.g., the ethnic diversity of the American population, the relative ease of social mobility). While I have mentioned factors in this category from time to time across this study, I have not relied heavily on them, for two reasons. First, these factors—while certainly relevant—seem more distant to explanations of specific cross-societal policy differences than the factors on which I have drawn more extensively. Second, various authors propose a broad range of different aspects of American social structure as indices and/or causes of American exceptionalism (Kingdon 1999, 68-74). There is currently no consensus on the limits of these factors and thus little parsimony or theoretical leverage to their use. Neither is there an overarching argument as to how widely recognized factors vary in importance. Accordingly, drawing on individual factors in this group as they fit conveniently into an explanatory narrative seems ad hoc.

Another type of structural variable involves more clearly the result of purposeful political action: the developmental path of a society's general political institutions. I have portrayed these paths as arising in part from societal experience. Early prolonged warfare, for instance, prompted the Swedes and the French to adopt a dominant active executive. Much less threatening societal circumstances allowed the United States to successfully resist turning to a similar executive until the period of the Great Depression and the Second World War. Avoiding the development of such an executive was facilitated by the tradition—born in American experience with the English monarchy—of skepticism about powerful central authority.

Thus the initial path of development—even in the context of mounting a revolution—for broad American political institutions involved an extremely high degree of decentralization through the Articles of Confederation. This path was shifted in the late 1780s by the adoption of the current Constitution, which created a more capable—though initially Congress-dominant—central government. The separation-of-powers structure of this government, however, made the adoption of new policies more difficult than in parliamentary regimes, and the Bill of Rights reinforced limits on government action by sustaining a substantial private sphere. Subsequent Americans have been socialized to accept limited fragmented government as normal and preferable to alternatives. Additionally, the relative ease with which modest but committed factions can derail legislative initiatives which they find objectionable has meant that American reformers have experienced great difficulty gaining the adoption of policies (e.g., a national health insurance program) that have generally had an easier time in European societies, in which large active states have long been accepted.

It is certainly true that the United States shares a public political-economy trajectory with other advanced industrial societies (Wilson 1998). The American tax regime extracts much more today than it did a century ago, and the United States spends the largest single portion of these enhanced revenues on a range of public social programs which it did not support a century ago. Nonetheless, as we have seen, the American state remains both smaller in terms of the percentage of GDP it extracts and less active—particularly with regard to public social programs (e.g., the public financing of medical care)—than are other advanced industrial societies. It is possible that, as the United States continues to follow this common trajectory, the policy differences distinguishing it from other societies will gradually diminish over time.

In the short-term, however, what would have to change—and how might these changes come about—to prompt the United States to adopt policies more similar to those of other societies? The most open-ended variable in the discussion of this section is societal experience. If American experience were to change sharply so that social dislocations similar to those that other societies have experienced from warfare on their territory or severe and prolonged economic depressions became integral to American history, other changes would likely follow. Under these revised circumstances, numerous citizens would find it much more difficult to continue to believe that they were capable of mastering their own fates. They would, in effect, move "up-group" to egalitarianism and possibly "up-grid" to hierarchy as well. If this process were sufficiently pronounced, the cultural composition of the American political elite would change as well. New leaders, more sympathetic to the beliefs and values of these high-group cultures, would replace existing, more individualistic officials. Replacement of relatively individualistic political elites by persons more sympathetic to hierarchy and egalitarianism would surely lead to the adoption of some new policies, and some of these innovations would likely move particular aspects of U.S. public policy in the direction of policies frequently found among other advanced industrial societies.

In only one of the four policy areas that we have examined in this study have we encountered any sign of shifting historical contingencies which actually seem capable of producing American policy changes of this sort. The 2001 attacks on the World Trade Center and Pentagon have already produced some procedural changes with regard to immigration and citizenship. If multiple attacks of similar magnitude were to occur over the next few years, they might well have a cumulative effect of shifting American orientations toward immigrants in a less favorable direction and fostering policies with respect to immigration and perhaps even citizenship that were more restrictive than current policy.

References

Aaron, Henry J., ed. 1996. *The Problem That Won't Go Away: Reforming U.S. Health Care Financing.* Washington, DC: Brookings.

Adams, Orvill. 1993. "Understanding the Health Care System That Works." In *Looking North for Health: What We Can Learn From Canada's Health Care System,* eds. Arnold Bennett and Orvill Adams, 113–41. San Francisco: Jossey-Bass Publishers.

Almond, Gabriel A. and Sidney Verba. 1963. *The Civic Culture: Political Attitudes and Democracy in Five Nations.* Princeton, NJ: Princeton University Press.

Anderson, Gerard F., Jeremy Hurst, Peter Sotir Hussey and Melissa Jee-Hughes. 2000. "Health Spending and Outcomes: Trends in OECD Countries, 1960–1998." *Health Affairs* 19(3): 150–57.

Anderson, Gerard and Peter Sotir Hussey. 2001. "Comparing Health System Performance in OECD Countries." *Health Affairs* 20(3): 219–32.

Andersson, Krister. 1987. "Sweden." In *Comparative Tax Systems: Europe, Canada, and Japan,* ed. Joseph A. Pechman, 33–90. Arlington, VA: Tax Analysts.

Andreas, Peter. 2000. *Border Games: Policing the U.S. Mexican Divide.* Ithaca, NY: Cornell University Press.

Anton, Thomas J. 1980. *Administered Politics: Elite Political Culture in Sweden.* Boston: Martinus Nijhoff.

Archdeacon, Thomas J. 1983. *Becoming American: An Ethnic History.* New York: Free Press.

Armstrong, Pat and Hugh Armstrong with Claudia Fegan. 1998. *Universal Health Care: What The United States Can Learn From the Canadian Experience.* New York: The New Press.

Atwood, Margaret. 1972. *Survival: A Thematic Guide to Canadian Literature.* Boston: Beacon Press.

Baker, Kendall L., Russell J. Dalton and Kai Hildebrandt. 1981. *Germany Transformed. Political Culture and the New Politics.* Cambridge, MA: Harvard University Press.

Banfield, Edward D. 1958. *The Moral Basis of a Backward Society.* Glencoe, IL: Free Press.

Beard, Charles A. 1965 [1913]. *An Economic Interpretation of the Constitution of the United States.* New York: Free Press.

Beatty, Perrin. 1993. "A Comparison of Our Two Systems." In *Looking North for Health: What We Can Learn From Canada's Health Care System,* eds. Arnold Bennett and Orvill Adams, 28–39. San Francisco: Jossey-Bass Publishers.

Beauregard, Karen M., Susan K. Drilea and Jessica P. Vistnes. 1997. "The Uninsured in America—1996." *Medical Expenditure Panel Survey Highlights* 1. Washington, DC: Agency for Health Care Policy and Research, U.S. Department of Health and Human Services.

———. 1998. "Health Insurance Coverage in America—1996." *Medical Expenditure Panel Survey Highlights* 4. Washington, DC: Agency for Health Care Policy and Research, U.S. Department of Health and Human Services.

Becker, Gary S. 1976. *The Economic Approach to Human Behavior.* Chicago: University of Chicago Press.

Bennet, James. 1995. "Buchanan, in Unfamiliar Role, Is Under Fire As a Left-Winger." *New York Times.* December 31: 1, 10.

Berger, Thomas U. 1998. "The Perils and Promise of Pluralism: Lessons From the German Case for Japan." In *Temporary Workers or Future Citizens? Japanese and U.S. Migration Policies,* eds. Myron Weiner and Tadashi Hanami, 319–54. New York: New York University Press.

Berlin, Isaiah. 1969. "Two Concepts of Liberty." In *Four Essays on Liberty,* 118–72. Oxford: Oxford University Press.

Blendon, Robert J., John Benson, Karen Donelan, Robert Leitman, Humphrey Taylor, Christian Koeck and Daniel Glitterman. 1995. "Who Has the Best Health Care System? A Second Look." *Health Affairs* 14(4): 220–30.

Bok, Derek. 1997. *The State of the Nation: Government and the Quest for a Better Society.* Cambridge, MA: Harvard University Press.

———. 2001. *The Trouble With Government.* Cambridge, MA: Harvard University Press.

Brady, Henry E. and David Collier, eds. 2003. *Rethinking Social Inquiry: Diverse Tools, Shared Standards.* Lanham, MD: Rowman and Littlefield.

Brown, E. Richard and Roberta Wyn. 1996. "Public Policies to Extend Health Care Coverage." In *Changing the U.S. Health Care System: Key Issues in Health Services, Policy and Management,* eds. Ronald M. Andersen, Thomas H. Rice and Gerald F. Kominski, 41–60. San Francisco: Jossey-Bass Publishers.

Bryce, Cindy L. and Kathryn Ellen Cline. 1998. "The Supply and Use of Selected Technologies." *Health Affairs* 17(1): 213–24

Buchanan, Patrick J. 2002. *The Death of the West: How Dying Populations and Immigrant Invasions Imperil Our Country and Civilization.* New York: Dunne Books/St. Martin's.

Calder, Kent E. 1988. *Crisis and Compensation: Public Policy and Political Stability in Japan, 1949–1986.* Princeton, NJ: Princeton University Press.

Callon, Scott. 1993. *Divided Sun: MITI and the Breakdown of Japanese High-Tech Industrial Policy, 1975–1993.* Stanford, CA: Stanford University Press.

Campbell, John Creighton. 1992. *How Policies Change: The Japanese Government and the Aging Society.* Princeton, NJ: Princeton University Press.

Center for the Study of Human Rights. 1994. *Twenty-five Human Rights Documents.* New York: Center for the Study of Human Rights, Columbia University.

Charles, Catherine A. and Robin F. Badgley. 1999. "Canadian National Health Insurance: Evolution and Unresolved Policy Issues." In *Health Care Systems in Transition: An International Perspective,* ed. Francis D. Powell and Albert F. Wessen, 115–50. Thousand Oaks, CA: Sage.

Clark, S. D. 1962. *The Developing Canadian Community.* Toronto: University of Toronto Press.

Congressional Budget Office. 1983. *Changing the Structure of Medical Benefits: Issues and Options.* Washington, DC: Congress of the United States.

———. 1987. *The Changing Distribution of Federal Taxes: 1975–1990.* Washington, DC: Congress of the United States.

Cornelius, Wayne A. 1994. "Japan: The Illusion of Immigrant Control." In *Controlling Immigration: A Global Perspective,* eds. Wayne A. Cornelius, Philip L. Martin and James F. Hollifield, 375–410. Stanford, CA: Stanford University Press.

Coughlin, Richard M. and Charles Lockhart. 1998. "Grid-Group Theory and Political Ideology: A Consideration of Their Relative Strengths and Weaknesses for Explaining the Structure of Mass Belief Systems." *Journal of Theoretical Politics* 10: 33–58.

Cox, Robert Henry. 2001. "The Social Construction of an Imperative: Why Welfare Reform Happened in Denmark and the Netherlands but Not in Germany." *World Politics* 53: 463–98.

Coyle, Dennis J. and Richard J. Ellis, eds. 1994. *Politics, Culture, and Policy: Applying Grid-Group Analysis.* Boulder, CO: Westview.

Craig, Barbara H. and David M. O'Brien. 1993. *Abortion and American Politics.* Chatam, NJ: Chatam House.

Crossette, Barbara. 2001. "Canada's Health Care Shows Strains: Universal Coverage Inspires Pride, But Its Expenses Increase." *New York Times.* October 11: 12.

Cummings, William K. 1980. *Education and Equality in Japan.* Princeton, NJ: Princeton University Press.

Dake, Karl and Aaron Wildavsky. 1990. "Theories of Risk Perception: Who Fears What and Why?" *Daedalus* 119: 41–60.

Dawson, William Harbutt. [1890] 1973. *Bismarck and State Socialism: An Exposition of the Social and Economic Legislation of Germany Since 1870.* New York: Howard Fertig.

Derbyshire, Ian. 1988. *Politics in France: From Giscard to Mitterrand.* Cambridge, UK: Chambers.

Devine, Donald. 1972. *The Political Culture of the United States.* Boston: Little, Brown.

Dore, Ronald. 1986. *Flexible Rigidities: Industrial Policy and Structural Adjustment in the Japanese Economy, 1970–80.* Stanford, CA: Stanford University Press.

Douglas, Mary. 1978. *Cultural Bias.* London: Royal Anthropological Society.

———. 1982a. *In the Active Voice.* London: Routledge and Kegan Paul.

———. 1986. *How Institutions Think.* Syracuse, NY: Syracuse University Press.

———. 1992. *Risk and Blame: Essays in Cultural Theory.* London: Routledge.

Douglas, Mary, ed. 1982b. *Essays in the Sociology of Perception.* London: Routledge and Kegan Paul.

Dower, John W. 1988. *Empire and Aftermath: Yoshida Shigeru and the Japanese Experience, 1878–1954.* Cambridge, MA: Harvard University Press.

Dower, John W., ed. 1975. *Origins of the Japanese State: Selected Writings of E. H. Norman.* New York: Random House.

Downey, Gary L. 1986. "Ideology and the Clamshell Identity: Organizational Dilemmas in the Anti-Nuclear Power Movement." *Social Problems* 33: 357–73.

Dumont, Louis. 1980. *Homo Hierarchicus: The Caste System and Its Implications,* translated by Mark Sainsbury, Louis Dumont and Basia Gulati. Chicago: University of Chicago Press.

Durkheim, Emile. 1951 [1897]. *Suicide: A Study in Sociology,* translated by J. A. Spaulding and G. Simpson. Glencoe, IL: Free Press.

Dworkin, Ronald M. 1977. "Taking Rights Seriously." In *Taking Rights Seriously,* 184–205. Cambridge, MA: Harvard University Press.

Dyer, Colin. 1978. *Population and Society in Twentieth Century France.* London: Hodder and Stoughton.

Easton, David. 1965. *A Systems Analysis of Political Life.* New York: Wiley.

Eckstein, Harry. 1988. "A Culturalist Theory of Political Change." *American Political Science Review* 82: 789–804.

Ehrmann, Henry R. 1983. *Politics in France,* 4th ed. Boston: Little, Brown.

Ehrmann, Henry R. and Martin A. Schain. 1992. "Politics in France." In *Comparative Politics Today: A World View,* 5th ed., eds. Gabriel A. Almond and G. Bingham Powell, Jr., 188–237. New York. HarperCollins.

Einhorn, Eric S. and John Logue. 1989. *Modern Welfare States: Politics and Policies in Social Democratic Scandinavia.* New York: Praeger.

Elkins, David J. and E. B. Simeon. 1979. "A Cause in Search of Its Effect, or What Does Political Culture Explain?" *Comparative Politics* 11: 127–45.

Ellis, Richard J. 1993. *American Political Cultures.* New York: Oxford University Press.

Ellis, Richard J. and Fred Thompson. 1997. "Culture and the Environment in the Pacific Northwest." *American Political Science Review* 91: 885–97.

Elstob, Eric. 1979. *Sweden: A Political and Cultural History.* Totowa, NJ: Rowman.

English, Jane. 1975. "Abortion and the Concept of a Person." *Canadian Journal of Philosophy* 5: 233–43.

Esping-Andersen, Gøsta. 1990. *The Three Worlds of Welfare Capitalism.* Princeton, NJ: Princeton University Press.

———. 1997. "Hybrid or Unique? The Japanese Welfare State Between Europe and America." *Journal of European Social Policy* 7: 179–89.

Estill, Jerry R. 1993. "From Inside the System: A Physician, Hospital Administrator, and Business Executive Talk About Their Work in Canada." In *Looking North for Health: What We Can Learn From Canada's Health Care System,* eds. Arnold Bennett and Orvill Adams, 40–60. San Francisco: Jossey-Bass Publishers.

Etzioni, Amitai. 1988. *The Moral Dimension: Toward a New Economics.* New York: Free Press.

Evans, Robert G. 1992. "'We'll Take Care of It for You': Health Care in the Canadian Community." In *Understanding Universal Health Programs: Issues and Options,* eds. David A. Kindig and Robert B. Sullivan, 159–72. Ann Arbor, MI: Health Administration Press.

———. 1993. "Health Care in the Canadian Community." In *Looking North for Health: What We Can Learn From Canada's Health Care System,* eds. Arnold Bennett and Orvill Adams, 1–27. San Francisco: Jossey-Bass Publishers.

Evans-Pritchard, E. E. 1940. *The Nuer: A Description of the Modes of Livelihood and Political Institutions of the Nilotic People.* Oxford: Oxford University Press.

Fishkin, James S. 1983. *Justice, Equal Opportunity, and the Family.* New Haven, CT: Yale University Press.

Fiske, Alan P. 1993. *Structures of Social Life: The Four Elementary Forms of Human Relations.* New York: Free Press.

Flanagan, Scott C. 1979. "Value Change and Partisan Change in Japan: The Silent Revolution Revisited." *Comparative Politics* 11: 253–78.

———. 1982. "Changing Values in Advanced Industrial Societies: Inglehart's Silent Revolution From the Perspective of Japanese Findings." *Comparative Political Studies* 14: 403–44.

Fooks, Catherine. 1999. "Will Power, Cost Control, and Health Reform in Canada, 1987–1992." In *Health Care Systems in Transition: An International Perspective,* eds. Francis D. Powell and Albert F. Wessen, 151–72. Thousand Oaks, CA: Sage.

Franzwa, Gregg and Charles Lockhart. 1998. "The Social Origins and Maintenance of Gender: Communication Styles, Personality Type and Culture." *Sociological Perspectives* 41: 185–208.

Free, Lloyd A. and Hadley Cantril. 1967. *The Political Beliefs of Americans: A Study of Public Opinion.* New Brunswick, NJ: Rutgers University Press.

Freeman, Gary P. 1995. "Modes of Immigration Politics in Liberal Democratic States." *International Migration Review* 29: 881–902.

———. 2002. "Toward a Theory of Migration Politics." Paper presented at the Council of European Studies, Conference for Europeanists, Chicago, March 14–17.

Freeman, Gary P. and Bob Birrell. 2001. "Divergent Paths of Immigration Politics in the United States and Australia." *Population and Development Review* 27: 525–51.

Freeman, Gary P. and Jongryn Mo. 1996. "Japan and the Asian NICs as New Countries of Destination," In *Trade and Migration in the Asian Pacific,* eds. Peter Lloyd and Lynne Williams, 156–73. Melbourne: Oxford University Press.

French, Howard W. 2002a. "North Korea Has a Hold on Hearts in Japan." *New York Times* March 29: A8.

———. 2002b. "For More Japanese, Love Is a Multiethnic Thing." *New York Times* July 31: A3.

Fukushima, Glenn S. 1989. "Corporate Power." In *Democracy in Japan,* eds. Takeshi Ishida and Ellis S. Krauss, 255–79. Pittsburgh: University of Pittsburgh Press.

Furniss, Norman and Timothy Tilton. 1977. *The Case for the Welfare State: From Social Security to Social Equality.* Bloomington: Indiana University Press.

Gaffney, John. 1991. "French Political Culture and Republicanism." In *Political Culture in France and Germany: A Contemporary Perspective,* eds. John Gaffney and Eva Kolinsky, 13–33. London: Routledge.

Galbraith, John Kenneth. 1958. *The Affluent Society.* Boston: Houghton, Mifflin.

George, Alexander L. and Timothy J. McKeown. 1985. "Case Studies and Theories of Organizational Decision Making." *Advances in Information Processing in Organizations* 2: 21–58.

George, Alexander L. and Richard Smoke. 1974. *Deterrence in American Foreign Policy: Theory and Practice.* New York: Columbia University Press.

Gewirth, Alan. 1978. *Reason and Morality.* Chicago: University of Chicago Press.

Gilligan, Carol. 1982. *In a Different Voice: Psychological Theory and Women's Development.* Cambridge, MA: Harvard University Press.

Glendon, Mary Ann. 1987. *Abortion and Divorce in Western Law: American Failures, European Challenges.* Cambridge, MA: Harvard University Press.

Greenstein, Fred I. 1992. "Can Personality and Politics Be Studied Simultaneously?" *Political Psychology* 13: 105–28.

Grendstad, Gunnar. 1999. "A Political Cultural Map of Europe: A Survey Approach." *Geojournal* 47:463–75.

Gurowitz, Amy. 1999. "Mobilizing International Norms: Domestic Actors, Immigrants, and the Japanese State." *World Politics* 51: 413–45.

Hanami, Tadashi. 1998. "Japanese Policies on the Rights and Benefits Granted to Foreign Workers, Residents, Refugees and Illegals." In *Temporary Workers or Future Citizens: Japanese and U.S. Migration Policies,* eds. Myron Weiner and Tadashi Hanami, 211–37. New York: New York University Press.

Harrington, Michael. 1962. *The Other America: Poverty in the United States.* New York: Macmillan.

Hartz, Louis. 1955. *The Liberal Tradition in America.* New York: Harcourt, Brace.

Hashimoto, Akiko. 1996. *The Gift of Generations: Japanese and American Perspectives on Aging and the Social Contract.* New York: Cambridge University Press.

Hatcher, Gordon H., Peter R. Hatcher and Eleanor C. Hatcher. 1984. "Health Services in Canada." In *Comparative Health Systems: Descriptive Analyses of Fourteen National Health Systems,* ed. Marshall W. Raffel, 85–132. University Park: Penn State University Press.

Hayek, Friedrich A. 1976a. *The Mirage of Social Justice,* vol. 2 of *Law, Legislation, and Liberty.* Chicago: University of Chicago Press.

———. 1976b. *The Road to Serfdom.* Chicago: University of Chicago Press.

Heckscher, Gunnar. 1984. *The Welfare State and Beyond: Success and Problems in Scandinavia.* Minneapolis: University of Minnesota Press.

Heclo, Hugh. 1981. "Toward a New Welfare State." In *The Development of Welfare States in Europe and America,* eds. Peter Flora and Arnold J. Heidenheimer, 383–406. New Brunswick, NJ: Transaction Books.

Heclo, Hugh and Henrik Madsen. 1987. *Policy and Politics in Sweden.* Philadelphia: Temple University Press.

Hirschfield, Daniel S. 1970. *The Lost Reform: The Campaign for Compulsory Health Insurance in the United States from 1932 to 1943.* Cambridge, MA: Harvard University Press.

Hirschman, Albert O. 1970. *Exit, Voice and Loyalty: Responses to Decline in Firms, Organizations, and States.* Cambridge, MA: Harvard University Press.

————. 1982. *Shifting Involvements: Private Interest and Public Action.* Princeton, NJ: Princeton University Press.

Hockin, Thomas A. 1975. *Government in Canada.* New York: W. W. Norton.

Huntington, Samuel P. 1981. *American Politics: The Promise of Disharmony.* Cambridge, MA: Harvard University Press.

Iguchi, Yasushi. 1998. "What We Can Learn from the German Experiences Concerning Foreign Labor." In *Temporary Workers or Future Citizens? Japanese and U.S. Migration Policies,* eds. Myron Weiner and Tadashi Hanami, 293–318. New York: New York University Press.

Inglehart, Ronald. 1997. *Modernization and Postmodernization: Cultural, Economic and Political Change in 43 Societies.* Princeton, NJ: Princeton University Press.

Ishida, Takeshi. 1983. *Japanese Political Culture: Change and Continuity.* New Brunswick, NJ: Transaction.

Ishida, Takeshi and Ellis S. Krauss, eds. 1989. *Democracy in Japan.* Pittsburgh: University of Pittsburgh Press.

Jencks, Christopher. 1990. "Varieties of Altruism." In *Beyond Self-Interest,* ed. Jane J. Mansbridge, 53–67. Chicago: University of Chicago Press.

Jenkins, Brian. 2000. "French Political Culture: Homogeneous or Fragmented?" In *Contemporary French Cultural Studies,* eds. William Kidd and Sian Reynolds, 111–125. New York: Oxford University Press.

Jenkins-Smith, Hank C. and Walter K. Smith. 1994. "Ideology, Culture, and Risk Perception." In *Politics, Policy, and Culture: Applying Grid-Group Analysis,* eds. Dennis J. Coyle and Richard J. Ellis, 17–32. Boulder, CO: Westview.

Jervis, Robert. 1997. *System Effects: Complexities in Political and Social Life.* Princeton, NJ: Princeton University Press.

Johnson, Chalmers. 1982. *MITI and the Japanese Miracle.* Stanford, CA: Stanford University Press.

————. 1999. "The Development State: Odyssey of a Concept." In *The Developmental State,* ed. Meredith Woo-Cumings, 32–69. Ithaca, NY: Cornell University Press.

Jones, Maldwyn Allen. 1992. *American Immigration,* 2nd ed. Chicago: University of Chicago Press.

Kajita, Takamichi. 1998. "The Challenge of Incorporating Foreigners in Japan: 'Ethnic Japanese' and 'Sociological Japanese'." In *Temporary Workers or Future Citizens? Japanese and U.S. Migration Policies,* eds. Myron Weiner and Tadashi Hanami, 120–147. New York: New York University Press.

Kane Rosalie A. 1993. "Delivering and Financing Long Term Care in Canada's Ten Provinces." In *Looking North for Health: What We Can Learn From Canada's Health Care System,* eds. Arnold Bennett and Orvill Adams, 89–101. San Francisco: Jossey-Bass Publishers.

Katznelson, Ira. 1986. "Working-Class Formation: Constructing Cases and Comparisons." In *Working-Class Formation: Nineteenth-Century Patterns in Western Europe and the United States,* eds. Ira Katznelson and Aristide R. Zolberg, 3–41. Princeton, NJ: Princeton University Press.

Kelman, Steven. 1981. *Regulating America, Regulating Sweden: A Comparative Study of Occupational Safety and Health Policy.* Cambridge, MA: MIT Press.

Khilnani, Sunil. 1996. "Individualism and Modern Democratic Culture: Recent French Conceptions." *Economy and Society* 25: 282–89.

Kirchheimer, Otto. 1966. "The Transformation of the Western European Party Systems." In *Political Parties and Political Development,* eds. Joseph LaPalombara and Myron Weiner, 177–200. Princeton, NJ: Princeton University Press.

Kingdon, John W. 1999. *America the Unusual.* New York: Worth Publishers.

Kolata, Gina. 2001. "Medical Fees Are Often More for Uninsured." *New York Times.* (April 2): 1, 13.

Kommers, Donald. 1985. "Liberty and Community in Constitutional Law: The Abortion Cases in Comparative Perspective." *Brigham Young University Law Review* 1985: 371–409.

Kornberg Allan and Harold D. Clarke. 1992. *Citizens and Community: Political Support in a Representative Democracy.* New York: Cambridge University Press.

Koshiro, Kazutoshi. 1998. "Does Japan Need Immigrants?" In *Temporary Workers or Future Citizens? Japanese and U.S. Migration Policies,* eds. Myron Weiner and Tadashi Hanami, 151–176. New York: New York University Press.

Kreps, David M. 1990. "Corporate Culture and Economic Theory." In *Perspectives on Positive Political Economy,* eds. James E. Alt and Kenneth A. Shepsle, 90–143. New York: Cambridge University Press.

Kronenfeld, Jennie J. 1993. *Controversial Issues in Health Care Policy.* Newbury Park, CA: Sage.

Kudrle, Robert T. and Theodore R. Marmor. 1981. "The Development of Welfare States in North America." In *The Development of Welfare States in Europe and North America,* eds. Peter Flora and Arnold J. Heidenheimer, 81–121. New Brunswick, NJ: Transaction Books.

Kuttner, Robert. 1997. *Everything for Sale: The Virtues and Limits of Markets.* New York: Knopf.

Kuwahara, Yasuo. 1998. "Japan's Dilemma: Can International Migration Be Controlled?" In *Temporary Workers or Future Citizens? Japanese and U.S. Migration Policies,* eds. Myron Weiner and Tadashi Hanami, 355–83. New York: New York University Press.

Lane, Jan-Erik, Tuomo Martikainen, Palle Svensson, Gunnar Vogt and Henry Valen. 1993. "Scandinavian Exceptionalism Reconsidered." *Journal of Theoretical Politics* 5: 195–230.

Legro, Jeffrey W. 1996. "Culture and Preferences in the International Cooperation Two-Step." *American Political Science Review* 90: 118–37.

Lichbach, Mark Irving. 1995. *The Rebel's Dilemma.* Ann Arbor: University of Michigan Press.

Lie, John. 2001. *Multiethnic Japan.* Cambridge, MA: Harvard University Press.

Light, Paul. 1995. *Still Artful Work: The Continuing Politics of Social Security Reform,* 2nd ed. New York: McGraw-Hill.

Lijphart, Arend. 1977. *Democracy in Plural Societies: A Comparative Exploration.* New Haven, CT: Yale University Press.

————. 1984. *Democracies: Patterns of Majoritarian and Consensus Government in Twenty-one Countries.* New Haven, CT: Yale University Press.

Limerick, Patricia Nelson. 1997. "The Startling Ability of Culture to Bring Critical Inquiry to a Halt." *Chronicle of Higher Education* October 24: A76.

Lindbeck, Assar. 1997. *The Swedish Experiment.* Stockholm: SNS Foerlag.

Lindblom, Charles E. 1977. *Politics and Markets: The World's Political-Economic Systems.* New York: Basic.

Lipset, Seymour Martin. 1977. "Why No Socialism in the United States?" In *Radicalism in the Contemporary Age.* Vol. 1 of *Sources of Contemporary Radicalism,* eds. Seweryn Bialer and Sophia Sluzar, 31–149. Boulder, CO: Westview.

————. 1990. *Continental Divide: Values and Institutions of the United States and Canada.* New York: Routledge.

————. 1996. *American Exceptionalism: A Double-Edged Sword.* New York: Norton.

Lockhart, Charles. 1991. "American Exceptionalism and Social Security: Demonstrating Complementary Cultural and Structural Contributions to Social Program Development." *Review of Politics* 53: 510–29.

————. 1994. "Socially Constructed Conceptions of Distributive Justice: The Case of Affirmative Action." *Review of Politics* 56: 29–49.

————. 2001a. "Political Culture, Patterns of American Political Development and Distinctive Rationalities." *Review of Politics* 63: 531–62.

————. 2001b. *Protecting the Elderly: How Culture Shapes Social Policy.* University Park, PA: Penn State University Press.

————. 2001c. "Using Grid-Group Theory to Explain Japan's Distinctive Political Institutions." *East Asia: An International Quarterly* 19(3): 51–83.

————. 2003. "Obstacles on the Road to an Overlapping Consensus on Human Rights." In *Constructing Human Rights in the Age of Globalization,* eds. Mahmood Monshipouri, Neil Englehart, Andrew J. Nathan and Kavita Philip, 259–87. Armonk, NY: M.E. Sharpe.

Lockhart, Charles, Richard M. Coughlin, Richard J. Ellis and Gunnar Grendstad. 1998. "Measuring and Applying Grid-Group Theory: An Alternative to Liberal-Conservative Ideology and Inglehart's Schema." Proposal to the National Science Foundation.

Lovejoy, Arthur O. 1961. *Reflections on Human Nature.* Baltimore, MD: Johns Hopkins University Press.

Lubitz, James. 1990. "Use and Costs of Medicare Services in the Last Year of Life, 1976 and 1985." Washington, DC: Health Care Financing Administration.

Lubitz, James and Ronald Prihoda. 1984. "Uses and Costs of Medicare Services in the Last Two Years of Life." *Health Care Financing Review* 5 (Spring): 117–31.

Luker, Kristin. 1984. *Abortion and the Politics of Motherhood.* Berkeley: University of California Press.

Macpherson, C. B. 1973. *Democratic Theory: Essays in Retrieval.* Oxford: Oxford University Press.

McClosky, Herbert and John Zaller. 1984. *The American Ethos: Public Attitudes Toward Capitalism and Democracy.* Cambridge, MA: Harvard University Press.

McFarlane, Deborah R. and Kenneth J. Meier. 2001. *The Politics of Fertility Control: Family Planning and Abortion Policies in the American States.* New York: Chatham House.

McIntosh, C. Alison. 1983. *Population Policy in Western Europe.* Armonk, NY: M. E. Sharpe.

McIntyre, Alasdair C. 1988. *Whose Justice? Which Rationality?* Notre Dame, IN: University of Notre Dame Press.

McKean, Margaret A. 1989. "Equality." In *Democracy in Japan,* eds. Takeshi Ishida and Ellis S. Krauss, 201–24. Pittsburgh: University of Pittsburgh Press.

Magnier, Mark. 2000. "Japanese Don't Pop the Pill." *Los Angeles Times.* September 14.

Mansbridge, Jane J. 1990. "The Rise and Fall of Self-Interest in the Explanation of Political Life." In *Beyond Self-Interest,* ed. Jane J. Mansbridge, 3–22. Chicago: University of Chicago Press.

March, James G. and Johan P. Olsen. 1989. *Rediscovering Institutions: The Organizational Basis of Politics.* New York: Free Press.

Marmor, Theodore R. 1973. *The Politics of Medicare.* Chicago: Aldine.

———. 2000. *The Politics of Medicare,* 2nd ed. New York: Aldine-De Gruyter.

Meunier Sophie. 2000. "The French Exception." *Foreign Affairs* 79 (4): 104–16.

Mitsunobu, Sugiyama. 1988. "Should Foreign Workers Be Welcomed?" *Japan Quarterly* 35: 260–65.

Mohr, James C. 1978. *Abortion in America: The Origins and Evolution of National Policy, 1800–1900.* New York: Oxford University Press.

Moon, Marilyn. 1993. *Medicare Now and in the Future.* Washington, DC: Urban Institute Press.

Murray, Charles. 1994. *Losing Ground: American Social Policy, 1950–1980.* New York: Basic.

New York Times. 2002. "1 in 3 Hospitals Say They Divert Ambulances." April 9: A23.

Nordlund, Anders and Richard M. Coughlin. 1998. "Who Hates the Welfare State? Evidence From Sweden." Paper presented at the annual meeting of the Western Political Science Association, Los Angeles, March 21.

Nozick, Robert. 1974. *Anarchy, State, and Utopia.* New York: Basic.

O'Connor, Karen. 1996. *No Neutral Ground: Abortion Politics in an Age of Absolutes.* Boulder, CO: Westview.

Okin, Susan Moller. 1989. *Justice, Gender and the Family.* New York: Basic.

Olsen, Gregg M. 1996. "Re-Modeling Sweden: The Rise and Demise of the Compromise in a Global Economy." *Social Problems* 42: 1–20.

Organisation for Economic Co-operation and Development. 1985. *Social Expenditure, 1960–1990: Problems of Growth and Control.* Paris: Organisation for Economic Co-operation and Development.

———. 1994. *OECD in Figures: Statistics on the Member Countries.* Paris: Organisation for Economic Co-operation and Development.

———. 1995. *National Accounts: Volume II, Detailed Tables.* Paris: Organisation for Economic Co-operation and Development.

————. 1997. OECD *in Figures: Statistics on the Member Countries.* Paris: Organisation for Economic Co-operation and Development.

————. 1999. OECD *in Figures: Statistics on the Member Countries.* Paris: Organisation for Economic Co-operation and Development.

Pallon, Paul. 1993. "Serving Elderly Patients: The Benefits of Integrated Long Term Care in British Columbia." In *Looking North for Health: What We Can Learn From Canada's Health Care System,* eds. Arnold Bennett and Orvill Adams, 102–12. San Francisco: Jossey-Bass Publishers.

Patel, Kant and Mark E. Rushefsky. 1993. *Health Care Politics and Policy in America,* 2nd ed. Armonk, NY: M. E. Sharpe.

Pechman, Joseph A. 1985. *Who Paid the Taxes, 1966–85?* Washington, DC: Brookings.

————. 1987. "Introduction." In *Comparative Tax Systems: Europe, Canada, and Japan,* ed. Joseph A. Pechman, 3–32. Arlington, VA: Tax Analysts.

Pedersen, Jean Elisabeth. 1996. "Regulating Abortion and Birth Control: Gender, Medicine, and Republican Politics in France, 1870–1920." *French Historical Studies* 19: 673–98.

Pempel, T. J. 1982. *Policy and Politics in Japan: Creative Conservatism.* Philadelphia: Temple University Press.

————. 1989. "Prerequisites for Democracy: Political and Social Institutions." In *Democracy in Japan,* eds. Takeshi Ishida and Ellis S. Krauss, 17–37. Pittsburgh: University of Pittsburgh Press.

Pempel, T. J. and Keiichi Tsunekawa. 1979. "Corporatism Without Labor? The Japanese Anomaly." In *Trends Toward Corporatist Intermediation,* eds. Philippe C. Schmitter and Gerhard Lehmbruch, 231–70. Beverly Hills, CA: Sage.

Peters, B. Guy. 1996. *The Future of Governing: Four Emerging Models.* Lawrence: University Press of Kansas.

Petersson, Olof. 1994. *The Government and Politics of the Nordic Countries.* Stockholm: Fritzes.

Pollack, Ron. 1993. "Eleven Lessons From Canada's Health Care System." In *Looking North for Health: What We Can Learn From Canada's Health Care System,* eds. Arnold Bennett and Orvill Adams, 142–76. San Francisco: Jossey-Bass Publishers.

Putnam, Robert D., with Robert Leonardi and Raffaella Y. Nanetti. 1993. *Making Democracy Work: Civic Traditions in Modern Italy.* Princeton, NJ: Princeton University Press.

Pye, Lucian W. 1988. *The Mandarin and the Cadre: Aspects of Chinese Political Culture.* Ann Arbor: Center for Chinese Studies, University of Michigan.

Rawls, John. 1971. *A Theory of Justice.* Cambridge, MA: Harvard University Press.

Reynolds, Sian. 2000. "How the French Present Is Shaped by the Past: The Last Hundred Years in Historical Perspective." In *Contemporary French Cultural Studies,* eds. William Kidd and Sian Reynolds, 23–37. New York: Oxford University Press.

Richardson, Bradley M. 1974. *The Political Culture of Japan.* Berkeley: University of California Press.

Roemer, Milton I. 1996. "Lessons From Other Countries." In *Changing the U.S. Health Care System: Key Issues in Health Services, Policy, and Management,* eds. Ronald M. Andersen, Thomas H. Rice and Gerald F. Kominski, 340–351. San Francisco: Jossey-Bass Publishers.

Rohrschneider, Robert. 1994. "Report From the Laboratory: The Influence of Institutions on Political Elites' Democratic Values in Germany." *American Political Science Review* 88: 927–41.

Rosenblatt, Roger. 1992. *Life Itself: Abortion in the American Mind.* New York: Random House.

Ross, Marc Howard. 1997. "Culture and Identity in Comparative Political Analysis." In *Comparative Politics: Rationality, Culture, and Structure,* eds. Mark Irving Lichbach and Alan S. Zuckerman, 42–80. New York: Cambridge University Press.

Sandel, Michael J. 1982. *Liberalism and the Limits of Justice.* New York: Cambridge University Press.

Savage, Grant T., Mark L. Hoelscher and Elizabeth W. Walker. 1999. "International Health Care: A Comparison of the United States, Canada, and Western Europe." In *Health Care Administration: Planning, Implementing, and Managing Organized Delivery Systems,* 3rd ed., ed. Lawrence F. Wolper, 3–52. Gaithersburg, MD: Aspen Publishers.

Schieber, George J., Jean-Pierre Poullier and Leslie M. Greenwald. 1993. "Health Spending, Delivery, and Outcomes in OECD Countries." *Health Affairs* 12(2): 120–29.

Schlesinger, Arthur M., Jr. 1986. "The Cycles of American Politics." In *The Cycles of American History,* 23–48. Boston: Houghton Mifflin.

Schuck, Peter H. 1998. "The Legal Rights of Citizens and Aliens in the United States." In *Temporary Workers or Future Citizens? Japanese and U.S. Migration Policies,* eds. Myron Weiner and Tadashi Hanami, 238–91. New York: New York University Press.

Schumacher, E. F. 1973. *Small Is Beautiful: Economics As If People Mattered.* New York: Harper and Row.

Schumpeter, Joseph. 1950. *Capitalism, Socialism and Democracy,* 3rd ed. New York: Harper and Row.

Schwarz, Michiel and Michael Thompson. 1990. *Divided We Stand: Redefining Politics, Technology, and Social Choice.* Philadelphia: University of Pennsylvania Press.

Science Council of Canada. 1972. "Innovation in a Cold Climate: Impediments to Innovation." In *The Canadian Challenge,* eds. Abraham Rothstein and Gary Lax. Toronto: Committee for an Independent Canada.

Sen, Amartya K. 1977. "Rational Fools: A Critique of the Behavioral Foundations of Economic Theory." *Philosophy and Public Affairs* 6: 317–44.

Shafer, Byron E., ed. 1994. *Is America Different? A New Look at American Exceptionalism.* New York: Oxford University Press.

Sheeran, Patrick J. 1987. *Women, Society, the State, and Abortion: A Structuralist Analysis.* New York: Praeger.

Shinkawa, Toshimitsu and T. J. Pempel. 1996. "Occupational Welfare and the Japanese Experience." In *The Privatization of Social Policy? Occupational Welfare and the Welfare State in America, Scandinavia and Japan,* ed. Michael Shalev, 280–326. London: Macmillan.

Skocpol, Theda. 1987. "America's Incomplete Welfare State: The Limits of New Deal Reforms and the Origins of the Present Crisis." In *Stagnation and Renewal in Social Policy: The Rise and Fall of Policy Regimes,* eds. Martin Rein, Gøsta Esping-Anderson and Lee Rainwater, 35–58. Armonk, NY: M.E. Sharpe.

———. 1992. *Protecting Soldiers and Mothers: The Political Origins of Social Policy in the United States.* Cambridge, MA: Harvard University Press.

Skowronek, Steven. 1982. *Building a New American State: The Expansion of National Administrative Capacities, 1877–1920.* New York: Cambridge University Press.

Smith, Tom W. 1987. "The Welfare State in Cross-National Perspective." *Public Opinion Quarterly* 51: 404–21.

Sniderman, Paul, Joseph F. Fletcher, Peter Russell and Philip E. Tetlock. 1988. "Liberty, Authority, and Community: Civil Liberties and the Canadian Political Culture." Centre for Criminology, University of Toronto and Survey Research Center, University of California, Berkeley.

Starfield, Barbara. 1991. "Primary Care and Health: A Cross-National Comparison." *Journal of the American Medical Association* 26: 2268–71.

Starr, Paul. 1982. *The Social Transformation of American Medicine: The Rise of a Sovereign Profession and the Making of a Vast Industry.* New York: Basic.

Steinmo, Sven. 1993. *Taxation and Democracy: Swedish, British and American Approaches to Financing the Modern State.* New Haven, CT: Yale University Press.

———. 1994. "American Exceptionalism Reconsidered: Culture or Institutions?" In *Dynamics in American Politics,* eds. Lawrence Dodd and Calvin Jillson, 106–31 Boulder, CO: Westview.

———. 1995. "Why Is Government So Small in America?" *Governance: An International Journal of Policy and Administration* 8: 303–34.

Steinmo, Sven, Kathleen Thelen and Frank Longstreth, eds. 1992. *Structuring Politics: Historical Institutionalism in Comparative Analysis.* New York: Cambridge University Press.

Steinmo, Sven and Jon Watts. 1995. "It's the Institutions, Stupid! Why the United States Can't Pass Comprehensive Health Care Reform." *Journal of Health Politics, Policy, and Law* 20: 329–72.

Stephens, John D. 1996. "The Scandinavian Welfare States: Achievements, Crisis, and Prospects." In *Welfare States in Transition: National Adaptations in Global Economies,* ed. Gøsta Esping-Andersen, 32–65. Sage: London.

Stetson, Dorothy M. 1986. "Abortion Law Reform in France." *Journal of Comparative Family Studies* 17: 277–90.

Steven, Rob. 1983. *Classes in Contemporary Japan.* New York: Cambridge University Press.

Stith, Richard. 1987. "Constitutional and Penal Perspectives on Spanish Abortion Law." *American Journal of Comparative Law* 35: 513–58.

Strathern, Andrew. 1971. *The Rope of Moka: Big-Men and Ceremonial Exchange in Mount Hagen, New Guinea.* Cambridge: Cambridge University Press.

Sunstein, Cass R. 1997. *Free Markets and Social Justice.* New York: Oxford University Press.

Takeda, Isami. 1998. "Japan's Responses to Refugees and Political Asylum Seekers." In *Temporary Workers or Future Citizens? Japanese and U.S. Migration Policies,* eds. Myron Weiner and Tadashi Hanami, 431–51. New York: New York University Press.

Thompson, Michael. 1982. "The Problem of the Center: An Autonomous Cosmology." In *Essays in the Sociology of Perception,* ed. Mary Douglas, 302–27. London: Routledge and Kegan Paul.

Thompson, Michael, Richard Ellis and Aaron Wildavsky. 1990. *Cultural Theory.* Boulder, CO: Westview.

Toronto Star. 2000. "Family-Values Group Plans to Form Network Within Canadian Alliance." August 16.

———. 2001. "Pro-Choicers Fear Complacency Endangers Women's Right to Abortion." May 8.

Toulmin, Stephen E. 1961. *Foresight and Understanding: An Enquiry Into the Aims of Science.* Bloomington: Indiana University Press.

Tribe, Laurence H. 1992. *Abortion: The Clash of Absolutes.* New York: Norton.

Tsurumi, Kazuko. 1970. *Social Change and the Individual: Japan Before and After Defeat in World War II.* Princeton, NJ: Princeton University Press.

Tuohy, Carolyn Hughes. 1999. *Accidental Logics: The Dynamics of Change in the Health Care Arena in the United States, Britain, and Canada.* New York: Oxford University Press.

Turnbull, Colin. 1972. *The Mountain People.* New York: Simon and Schuster.

Turner, Christena. 1989. "Democratic Consciousness in Japanese Unions." In *Democracy in Japan,* eds. Takeshi Ishida and Ellis S. Krauss, 299–323. Pittsburgh: University of Pittsburgh Press.

Turner, Frederick Jackson. 1962. *The Frontier in American History.* New York: Holt, Rinehart and Winston.

Uchendu, Victor C. 1965. *The Ibgo of Southeast Nigeria.* New York: Holt, Rinehart and Winston.

United Nations. 1966. International Covenant on Economic, Social and Cultural Rights and International Covenant on Civil and Political Rights. United Nations General Assembly Resolution 2200 (XXI), A/6316, December 16.

Van Wolferen, Karel. 1990. *The Enigma of Japanese Power: People and Politics in a Stateless Nation.* New York: Random House.

Verba, Sidney, Steven Kelman, Gary R. Orren, Ichiro Miyake, Joji Watanuki, Ikuo Kabashima and G. Donald Ferree, Jr. 1987. *Elites and the Idea of Equality: A Comparison of Japan, Sweden, and the United States.* Cambridge, MA: Harvard University Press.

Walzer, Michael. 1983. *Spheres of Justice: A Defense of Pluralism and Equality.* New York: Basic.

Warren, Samuel and Louis Brandeis. 1890. "The Right to Privacy." *Harvard Law Review* 4 (5): 193–220.

Weber, Max. 1946. "The Social Psychology of the World Religions." In *From Max Weber: Essays in Sociology*, eds. H. H. Gerth and C. Wright Mills, 267–301. New York: Oxford University Press. [Weber's essay was initially published in 1915.]

Weil, Patrick. 1991. *La France et ses Etrangers: L'aventure d'une Politique de L'immigration de 1938 a nos Jours*. Paris: Calmann-Levy.

Weil, Patrick and John Crowley. 1994. "Integration in Theory and Practice: A Comparison of France and Britain." *West European Politics* 17: 110–26.

Weiner, Myron. 1998. "Opposing Visions: Migration and Citizenship Policies in Japan and the United States." In *Temporary Workers or Future Citizens? Japanese and U.S. Migration Policies*, eds. Myron Weiner and Tadashi Hanami, 3–27. New York: New York University Press.

Weiner, Myron and Tadashi Hanami, eds., 1998. *Temporary Workers or Future Citizens? Japanese and U.S. Migration Policies*. New York: New York University Press.

Weissert, Carol S. and William G. Weissert. 1996. *Governing Health: The Politics of Health Policy*. Baltimore, MD: Johns Hopkins University Press.

White, Joseph. 1995. *Competing Solutions: American Health Care Proposals and International Experience*. Washington, DC: Brookings.

Wildavsky, Aaron. 1991. *The Rise of Radical Egalitarianism*. Washington, DC: American University Press.

———. 1994. "Why Self-Interest Means Less Outside of a Social Context: Cultural Contributions to a Theory of Rational Choices." *Journal of Theoretical Politics* 6: 131–59.

Wilensky, Harold L. 1975. *The Welfare State and Equality: The Structural and Ideological Roots of Public Expenditures*. Berkeley: University of California Press.

Wills, Gary. 1987. *Reagan's America: Innocents at Home*. Garden City, NY: Doubleday.

Wilson, Graham K. 1998. *Only in America? The Politics of the United States in Comparative Perspective*. Chatham House, NJ: Chatham House.

Wilson, Richard W. 1997. "American Political Culture in Comparative Perspective." *Political Psychology* 18: 483–502.

Wilson, Woodrow. 1885. *Congressional Government: A Study in American Politics*. Boston: Houghton Mifflin.

Witte, John F. 1985. *The Politics and Development of the Federal Income Tax*. Madison: University of Wisconsin Press.

Wolfe, Alan. 1993. *The Human Difference*. Berkeley: University of California Press.

Wood, Gordon S. 1992. *The Radicalism of the American Revolution*. New York: Knopf.

Yamanaka, Keiko. 1993. "New Immigration Policy and Unskilled Foreign Workers in Japan." *Pacific Affairs* 66: 72–90.

Zisk, Betty. 1992. *The Politics of Transformation: Local Activism in the Peace and Environmental Movements*. New York: Praeger.

Notes

1. Germany was not an innocent victim in this scenario. In forging modern Germany, the Prussians had used warfare, among other tools, to unite both previously independent Germanic regions as well as territories wrested from several neighboring societies.
2. Instances of severe social dislocation do not always arise from conditions beyond social control. Political elites sometimes launch their societies on massive mobilization programs of national development (e.g., the Meiji restoration beginning during the 1860s in Japan or Stalin's industrialization drive of the 1930s in the Soviet Union) which create extensive social dislocation.
3. Across the territory into which it progressively expanded, the United States periodically confronted Native Americans with distinctly inferior military technologies.
4. Numerous scholars have used institutional peculiarities to explain various aspects of American exceptionalism. With respect to the relative absence of socialism, for instance, Lipset (1977) contends that the early introduction of universal white manhood suffrage meant that American workers did not organize simultaneously politically and economically as European workers frequently had to do. Skowronek (1982) and Shafer (1994) argue that, since—in contrast to Europe—American political parties developed prior to public bureaucracies, workers' organizations were more concerned with patronage positions than with ideology.
5. While these principles are implicit in aspects of the Revolution and the 1787 Constitution, they are more clearly, if ideally, framed in Thomas Jefferson's Declaration of Independence and the *Federalist Papers,* especially those by James Madison.
6. This experience need not be firsthand. Persons learn by precept as in the stories and advice they receive from others. Further, while later experience likely has more capacity for overcoming early experience than some political culture theorists contend (Eckstein 1988), early experience

prints on a relatively more open mental slate and is likely more difficult to displace.

7. While this claim is controversial, it is less limiting than the widely accepted notion that only two ways of life—hierarchy and individualism—are socially viable; see Lindblom (1977). Further, Fiske (1993), Lichbach (1995) and Peters (1996) have derived similar typologies. Also, a fair amount of empirical analysis supports this claim; see Evans-Pritchard (1940), Dumont (1980), Strathern (1971) and Uchendu (1965). Finally, grid-group theory includes a fifth, non–socially interactive way of life—the hermit's—that I do not apply in this study; see Thompson (1982).

8. There are a few exceptions to fatalists' general reticence. See *Ecclesiastes* 9:11 and Schopenhauer's *The World as Will and Representation*.

9. The relatively low levels of extra-familial social interaction sustained by fatalists lead me to reduce the attention accorded them from here on in this study. Briefly, fatalists perceive context as random, and humans, fittingly, as capricious. Accordingly, they attempt to stay out of harm's way by minimizing their interaction with unpredictable, uncontrollable social forces. Fatalists are integral to the analysis in chapter 4, and we encounter them again there.

CHAPTER 2

1. Wilson's (1885) effort in this regard remains an anomaly.

2. Several studies have acquired grid-group theory survey data on the United States (Dake and Wildavsky 1990; Jenkins-Smith and Smith 1994; Ellis and Thompson 1997; Coughlin and Lockhart, 1998). All affirm grid-group theory's capacities for explaining a broad range of public attitudes, but unfortunately none to date has been done in a fashion that affords estimates of the proportions of the American population adhering to the rival cultures. In order to estimate these proportions it is necessary to use indices for grid and group, rather than the cultures themselves, and then assign respondents to cultures on the basis of their grid and group positions. This approach is necessary because the orientations of grid-group theory's rival cultures all hold some face validity since each accurately portrays certain swaths of human experience. Thus when indices for the cultures themselves are employed in surveys, ordinary citizens are prone to load themselves onto the indices of more than one culture. Political activists and elites generally avoid this tendency and appear much more culturally pure (Ellis and Thompson 1997). For examples of indices for grid and group, see Grendstad (1999) and Lockhart et al. (1998).

3. The letters stand for individualistic (I), egalitarian (E) and hierarchical (H). The first position identifies the leading partner in the coalition, so the Federalist coalition was dominated by individualists who allied them-

selves with hierarchists. This coalition emphasized values that adherents of these two cultures share (e.g., social order, the protection of private property).

4. These townsmen were owners of significant property. Universal manhood suffrage, and thus the representation of workers, was introduced only in 1907. Women were enfranchised in 1921.

5. I discuss some alternatives to this causal sequence in the final section of this chapter.

6. That is, great wealth is apt to be due to exceptional genetic endowment, highly favorable social environments for personal development or a combination of the two. Further, the persons who enjoy these advantages are not, strictly speaking, responsible for their fortunate circumstances.

7. This represents a shift from the practices of egalitarians such as Rousseau, Paine and Jefferson. Egalitarians' general objectives have—as they must—remained constant: selectively reducing existing differences in circumstances among persons. But over the last 150 years, their choice of means for achieving these objectives has increasingly entailed an active (frequently welfare) state rather than the limited-state means popular among most earlier egalitarians. The primary reason for this shift is the tremendous concentration of private capital (and the state's vulnerability to its influence) that occurred across the nineteenth century. In the face of the incredible material differentiation that resulted from the (generally individualistic) public influence of great capital, most egalitarians came to believe that they had little recourse but to organize their numbers so as to influence democratic states to support more egalitarian public objectives.

8. However, even into the present, a faction of Japanese hierarchists that I have elsewhere labeled "traditional" (Lockhart 2001b) or "bureaucratic" (Lockhart 2001c) remains adverse to democracy. These hierarchists appear among central state executives (particularly officials in the Ministry of Finance or Ministry of International Trade and Industry) who, as the persons responsible for economic development in a "late developer" society, perpetuate a tradition of near-obsession with maximizing the pace of development. Consequently, these officials prefer to keep as large a proportion of material resources as possible in the private sphere where corporate executives—frequently guided by central state officials—can apply these resources to achieve optimal national economic development. These officials, then, seek to help weak and vulnerable citizens through an ambitious industrial policy (i.e., providing jobs in sufficient numbers and of appropriate types so that households can provide for themselves through the work of their members) rather than extensive social programs. Indeed as a result of this orientation the Japanese welfare state developed slowly and, for a time, selectively. These traditional Japanese central state executives remain fearful of excessive public (i.e.,

the citizens or their parliament) influence on social policy questions which they associate with what they call the "English disease": that is, societal economic evisceration as a consequence of a government beholden to the unrealistic welfare state expectations of a short-sighted and self-centered citizenry (Campbell 1992).

9. Roughly, this distribution has what economists refer to as a "light-bulb" shape. That is, imagine the right-hand half of an ordinary incandescent light bulb, stem up. The middle will bulge furthest out to the right (the predominant middle classes), the bottom will narrow from this, but will still have considerable width (the relative poor), and the top (the stem) will be both longer and narrower (relatively smaller numbers of high-income citizens stretching up the income scale).

10. Calculating "tax burdens" as a percentage of measures of "national income" is a complex enterprise requiring numerous complicated judgments. The somewhat different results of varying authors reflect, not only variations among statistical sources, but different judgments as to how to treat a variety of perplexing matters. See Pechman (1985, 17–19).

11. Iceland is an exception. Its public revenues are more modest (36.3 percent) in spite of its being—similarly to Sweden—a "high-group" society. Iceland has unusual characteristics that help to explain this anomaly. First, its population is sharply smaller than those of the other societies in either table 2.1 or table 2.2. Second, its population lives in a remarkably compact area. Third, its population is highly homogeneous. Fourth, this small, compact and homogeneous population is highly isolated. Under these circumstances—in which a high proportion of Icelanders have family ties to a large segment of the population—Iceland appears to achieve objectives through private means that other high-group societies turn to public policy to accomplish.

12. American states vary in their tax practices. In this and the next two paragraphs I emphasize the practices of the United States national government.

13. For instance, these two advantages are extended to two homes per family, and the portion of the population able to take advantage of this largess is relatively high income. In contrast, renters who predominate among low-income persons derive no benefit from these tax-law provisions.

14. While the vehemence of their views varies, a majority of citizens in all societies would like to see their own taxes reduced (Smith 1987, 409, 419–20). Yet the willingness of Swedish voters to repeatedly elect representatives who they know favor prevailing and relatively high tax rates is clearly far greater than that of their American counterparts. Such cross-societal variation likely rests in part on differences in citizens' perceptions about the quantity and quality of the goods and services that their taxes provide.

15. Similarly, as I indicated at the end of chapter 1, culture also complements rational choice explanations. Persons' persistent efforts to realize certain

interests (e.g., an active as opposed to a limited state through extensive as opposed to modest taxes) cannot explain why they have these particular interests rather than others. The explanation of disparate interests is exogenous to an instrumental (preference implementation) conception of rationality. Yet the distinctive beliefs and value priorities held by the adherents of rival cultures can explain why various persons conceive of their interests differently. See Lockhart (2001b, ch. 1).

16. Actions routinely have unanticipated consequences. The world works in sufficiently complex and ambiguous ways so that "social engineering" is a demanding endeavor. As Jervis contends, political actors can "never do merely one thing" (1997, 10). For instance, while doing away with the upper chamber reduced a significant constraint on the responsiveness of Swedish public policy to popular majorities, it added a new constraint by reducing the incentives for compromise in Swedish politics and thus making any party's legislative program more difficult to realize. The Liberal Party does not appear to have foreseen or at least intended this outcome.

CHAPTER 3

1. Indeed since the 1993 Canadian national election, the Liberals may reasonably claim to have been the only truly national contemporary party. The Conservative loss in that election prompted a splintering of conservatives into multiple parties, each with a distinct regional base.

2. Lipset draws, in turn, on Atwood (1972, 171) for this observation.

3. Bismarck pioneered the introduction of public social programs, beginning with medical-care insurance for industrial workers in 1883. See Dawson (1973).

4. I prefer the term "medical-care insurance" to the conventional "health insurance." Public programs assuring citizens financial access to medical care cannot assure health which is jeopardized by genetic endowment, environmental hazards in the home and workplace as well as lifestyle choices (e.g., smoking, excessive alcohol consumption, poor diets and inadequate exercise). Assuring financial access to largely therapeutic medical care can neither prevent nor completely repair many of the heath difficulties arising from these sources.

5. This was actually the last gasp of the second major American effort to achieve national health insurance. The first effort had been initiated by the American Association for Labor Legislation (AALL) during the Progressive era. This effort received a boost when Theodore Roosevelt ran for president on the Progressive Party ticket in 1912, but the effort met resistance from physicians and was eventually overwhelmed by American hostility to anything with German origins (the AALL plan was modeled on Bismarck's pioneering social programs) after the initiation of the First

World War. Other authors subdivide efforts that I have organized into broad assaults and thus identify a larger number of more specific efforts (Patel and Rushefsky 1993, 262).

6. Nixon's interest in national health insurance was derailed by Watergate (Kronenfeld 1993, 136).

7. My calculation of the proportions of the American population in various categories with respect to medical-care financing in this and the next two paragraphs is based on Brown and Wyn (1996, 42), Roemer (1996, 345–46), and Beauregard, Drilea and Vistnes (1997, 1998).

8. All insurance schemes have weaknesses. When American physicians were in charge of their patients' care and earned fees for various services, boosting physician income by prescribing unnecessary services was a common practice. Now that insurers are in the saddle and have an economic incentive to maximize profits by cutting care, refusals to pay for physician-recommended care have become a frequent problem. In a less market-based setting such as the British National Health Service (NHS), physicians have little incentive to add to their workload and may under-prescribe patient services. There is no perfect system, but the ills of some specific institutional designs may be worse than others.

9. A final note on the current situation seems warranted. In the past two decades several states—most notably Hawaii, Oregon and Minnesota—have improved the financial access of some or all of their citizens to medical care on their own initiative. Hawaii and Oregon provide the most ambitious examples. Hawaii has assured the vast majority of its population financial access to medical care for a broad range of health problems by mandating that employers provide coverage meeting certain minimum criteria. So financial access to medical care varies across the states and is better in a few states than the general situation that I have portrayed in this section.

10. While I believe that this statement is accurate, I agree that assessments of medical-care quality are complex and difficult. For instance, the breadth of providers offering various sophisticated treatments (e.g., heart transplants, laser eye surgery, mammograms) in the United States is generally offered as an index of the quality of care. Patients can regularly have these services performed in "their own back yards." Yet as Evans (1992) points out, providers who engage in a large number of these procedures generally make fewer blunders. So although Canadians, for instance, may have to travel farther from home to receive services such as these, they may suffer fewer mishaps in the course of being treated by more centralized providers who are more accustomed to delivering the service in question.

11. More by tradition than by actual specification in the British North America Act of 1867, most health responsibilities in Canada have fallen to provincial governments rather than being a federal activity (Hatcher, Hatcher and Hatcher 1984).

12. In this list "accessibility" refers to the distribution and mobility of services across a geographic region so as to assure that all citizens can reach medical care (or vice-versa) within a limited period of time. Throughout this chapter I have used the term "(financial) accessibility" as a rough synonym for the criterion of "universality" in this list. That is, medical care becomes universal because receiving it is no longer contingent on one's personal financial resources. Canada's large geographic area and extensive regions of low population density highlight a sense of access that is generally less problematic in the United States.

13. There are some, generally marginal, exceptions. In some provinces self-referral to a specialist may incur patient charges. Patients pay for elective cosmetic surgery. Also, while provinces have insurance plans for out-patient prescription drugs and dental expenses, these insurance programs, similarly to their United States counterparts, are generally neither universal nor comprehensive. Further, long-term care involves patient copayments.

14. The Canadians refer to their national health insurance plan as Medicare, the same term Americans use for social insurance medical coverage for the elderly. In order to avoid confusion, I have used this term only with respect to the United States.

15. Analysts frequently argue that Canada's well-recognized slowness in technological innovation (vis-à-vis the United States) has no noticeable deleterious consequences for the population as a whole—i.e., no reduced life expectancy (Armstrong, Armstrong and Fegan 1998. 133; Fooks 1999, 163–64). Nonetheless, relatively slow innovation may deny specific Canadian patients treatments that are available to similarly afflicted Americans with excellent insurance. And this disparity alarms individualists who believe that persons ought to be generally free to acquire whatever goods and services they have the resources to purchase.

16. For more detailed health status comparisons across a broader range of societies, see Blendon et al. (1995), Schieber, Poullier and Greenwald (1993) and Starfield (1991). Canada's edge over the United States seems more secure under closer inspection.

17. This causal sequence is extremely difficult to test in terms of the causal models employed by mainstream statistical analysis since the dependent variables in this causal flow influence, as we see below, the sequence's independent variables through another causal flow (Brady and Collier 2003). This feature, known technically as endogeneity, is better dealt with through the process tracing approach of George and McKeown (1985).

CHAPTER 4

1. Center-right is in quotes because, although Americans cluster near the center of the American range of opinion, the entire American ideological

spectrum is skewed to the Right in comparison to the range of most other advanced industrial societies, which includes numerous socialists.

2. RPR and UDF are the current titles for the parties historically associated with Charles de Gaulle and Valéry Giscard d'Estaing, respectively. French political parties, particularly those on the Right, change their names frequently in response to the rise and fall of particular personalities or issues. In order to avoid the confusion of identifying what is essentially the same political party with multiple names, I use generic labels—e.g., social conservatives or clerical Right (RPR), economic conservatives or secular Right (UDF)—as much as possible.

3. The counterpart for "natural rights" today is likely "human rights." But human rights come in a variety of forms: civil, political, social, economic, developmental and cultural (Center for the Study of Human Rights 1994; United Nations 1966). Characteristically, individualists are supportive of only the first two types—civil and political (or civil-political) rights.

4. It would be fair to ask how, in what I have portrayed as a highly individualistic society, policies toward abortion similar to those I have associated with hierarchy predominated for lengthy periods. Okin (1989) provides the answer. Until fairly recently women lived beyond the boundaries of liberal individualism—which prevailed to considerable degree in the public domain—in a private realm dominated by gender hierarchy. So individualistic ideas of human equality and pervasive individual rights simply did not extend to women.

5. State practices frequently vary from what I have just suggested is national policy. A state may introduce new restrictions on abortions and practice accordingly unless the new practices are subsequently rejected by the courts. Abortion issues have such a high profile in the United States and the right to an abortion is so zealously guarded by abortion advocates that significant restrictions which might be disallowed by the courts rarely continue for extended periods. Some states are also more supportive of women's efforts to acquire abortions than federal standards require. For instance, 19 states pick up the full cost (their own and the federal government's portion) of abortions for poor women through the Medicaid program.

6. Post-1920s penalties have not always been modest. During a portion of the Vichy regime (created after France's early defeat in the Second World War), abortion was a capital offense, and an abortionist was guillotined (Stetson 1986, 178).

7. In contemporary terms these parties were the Gaullist RPR and Giscard-d'Estaing's UDF, respectively. But precursors of these contemporary parties included the Union of Democrats for the Republic and the Independent Republicans, respectively. Since the changing names of these French political parties are ancillary to the focus of this chapter, I

have used the generic clerical Right and secular Right from Lijphart's (1984) triangular model instead.

8. For background on Anglo-American rights to privacy see Warren and Brandeis (1890).

9. Allowing abortions in these three instances is universal among advanced industrial societies. See Glendon (1987, 14).

CHAPTER 5

1. Flanagan does, however, caution (1982, 409) that this label as well as the "traditional" label for the more hierarchical respondents are "not optimal" and "merely shorthand for the four defining subdimensions" (i.e., frugality, piety, conformity and deference—each opposed to its opposite). Indeed, neither Flanagan nor anyone else finds much evidence of "libertarians" in the Western, minimal, noninterventionary state sense in Japan.

2. The initial post - Second World War Japanese prime minister, Yoshida Shigeru, offers a fine example of such a bifocal cultural bias. See Dower (1988).

3. Gurowitz points out that "Japan's ratification rate for international agreements on human rights is significantly lower than that of almost all other OECD countries" (1999, 422–23). Since hierarchy is the culture most hesitant with respect to human rights (Lockhart 2003), this low rate of ratification serves as yet another index of hierarchical influence in Japan.

4. I am using "nativist" in a broad sense, to indicate a general disinclination toward immigrants. Schuck (1998) distinguishes between nativism, principled restrictionism and pragmatic restrictionism (1998, 242–245). My use of nativist is broad enough to cover the first two of these categories, but Schuck's pragmatic restrictionism (i.e., a preference for restricting immigration based on its perceived negative consequences when the perceptions are open to changing evidence and are reversible) is a highly flexible category. Nearly anyone might acquire pragmatic restrictionist views under sufficiently distressing conditions (e.g., preferring not to admit numerous immigrants to a society currently experiencing a severe depression).

5. Koshiro points out two early "waves" of immigrants, Korean intellectuals in the eighth century and some aristocratic Chinese Ming dynasty asylum seekers in the 1640s (1998, 151). But both of these earlier "waves" were fairly modest in size relative to the Japanese population.

6. Cornelius (1994, 377) argues that Japan shifted from being a society of emigration to a society of immigration at some point in the mid-1960s. But, he contends, this shift was not really noticeable until the heavy immigration of unskilled workers in the latter 1980s.

7. Only in 1985 was a law passed allowing Japanese citizens who marry foreigners to take their spouse's foreign name. Gurowitz argues that this represents a significant change: "being Japanese is no longer absolutely equated with having a Japanese name" (1999, 430).

8. According to Weiner (1998, 14), across the four decades from 1952 to 1992, only 221,000 foreigners have been accepted for Japanese citizenship. Additionally, children born to foreigners residing in Japan are not considered Japanese citizens.

9. Students are permitted to work part-time in order to help finance their studies; trainees are permitted to work in conjunction with their training, but technically they cannot be paid for the work. They generally receive a stipend for their training programs instead (Yamanaka 1993).

10. Or, rendered in Japanese, these are: *kitani, kiken* and *kitsui.*

11. Technically, foreign workers who are in Japan legally are generally eligible for a reasonable range of public social program benefits. But they generally cannot or at least have not yet remained long enough to earn expensive public pensions. Further, persons who have overstayed visas issued for various other purposes, and who are thus working in Japan illegally, are not eligible for most benefits (Hanami 1998, 225–26).

12. Indeed the tortured interpretations (e.g., Kajita, 143; Hanami, 228) that some of the Japanese academic contributors to Weiner and Hanami (1998) develop serve as clear indices of the hesitancy of Japanese elites to accept a more diverse society.

13. The five-year period need not be continuous, but it would still be extremely difficult for persons to legally accumulate this stretch of time through a series of student, tourist or trainee visas. Japanese law does allow foreigners to remain in Japan legally if they are married to a Japanese citizen. Across the last two decades, this "loophole" has helped to foster a market in "mail-order" brides (Kajita 1998, 142; French 2002b). After three years of marriage and a year's residence in Japan, the spouse of a Japanese citizen may seek Japanese citizenship.

14. Across this period there were, nonetheless, frequent bitter conflicts over distribution and sometimes societal direction between Japanese socialists and more influential social conservatives as well as narrower conflicts among factions of the elite about specific objectives and the most appropriate policies for realizing them.

15. Unfortunately, persons of color have often had a more difficult time acquiring informal social and sometimes formal legal acceptance. The problems that have faced African Americans represent the most poignant example. To a considerable degree, these difficulties arise as a consequence of the failure of previous immigrants to completely adopt the values of the American creed, particularly equality of opportunity.

1. Australia also shares this characteristic. It has an even higher proportion of foreign-born persons among its population. (See table 5.1—p. 138.) Indeed, Australia rivals the United States on other indices of individualism. (See table 2.2—p. 42.) These three large (all in terms of area, only the United States in terms of population), initially Anglo-émigré societies appear to share a greater degree of openness to outsiders than most other large societies (Freeman and Birrell 2001).

2. See chapter 2, note 8 and chapter 5, p 129.

3. Placing abortion decisions in the hands of experts does not necessarily mean that access to abortion will be restricted. The experts may favor a relatively permissive stance toward abortion. The hallmark of hierarchy on this issue is that ordinary persons will not have ultimate decision-making authority but must act through state-sanctioned experts.

4. This proximity of the culture and policy formulation steps in the sequence is explicit in my versions of the model. In institutionalists' versions culture is sometimes implicit owing to the importance they place on the policy constraints posed by the developmental paths of broad political institutions. Among institutionalists, Steinmo (1995, 327–28) offers a relatively explicit statement of a cultural step.

5. Adding cultural variables to historical and institutional factors also fails to produce a determinate model. Adherents of a particular culture, for instance, have different personality characteristics that produce different responses to comparable stimuli. The argument for stopping with culture rather than including personality rests largely on parsimony. At least in terms of grid-group theory, there are limited categories of culture, and thus considerable explanatory power to cultural differences. In contrast, personalities are arguably unique to individuals and thus afford less explanatory power. Personalities could, of course, be grouped (Franzwa and Lockhart 1998). For thoughts on how to distinguish these groups of personalities from culture, see Greenstein (1992).

6. Fatalists reveal yet another distinct, culturally constrained rationality. Briefly, persons are driven to fatalism by experience with human environments, both natural and social, which they perceive as essentially random and thus as beyond their control. Their perception that the world works randomly prompts a conception of their fellow humans as essentially capricious. These beliefs place a high priority on trying to stay out of harm's way—particularly by reducing to a minimum unpredictable encounters with other persons, especially those with significant power. Another prominent value for fatalists is good luck. Fatalists' aversion to regular social interaction (beyond the confines of the family, which is necessary for procreation and survival) means that they do not strive to construct particular macrosocietal institutions. They characteristically

live in societies dominated and largely constructed by other cultures. They likely prefer hierarchically dominated societies because of the straightforwardness of the rules which sometimes, but not always, govern their social interactions. When fatalism becomes the dominant or even a prominent culture in society, chaos or minimally societal near-incapacity to respond to problems is apt to ensue. See Turnbull (1972) and Banfield (1958) or Putnam with Leonardi and Nanetti (1993), respectively.

Index